A Pilot at Wimbledon

The Memoirs of
Air Chief Marshal Sir Brian Burnett
GCB, DFC, AFC

With best wishes
Brian Burnett
June '09

A Pilot at Wimbledon

The Memoirs of
Air Chief Marshal Sir Brian Burnett
GCB, DFC, AFC

Blenheim Press Limited
Codicote

Published in 2009
by
Blenheim Press Ltd
Codicote Innovation Centre
St Albans Road
Codicote
Herts SG4 8WH

ISBN 978-1-906302-13-9

Typeset by TW Typesetting, Plymouth, Devon

Printed and bound in Great Britain by
CPI Antony Rowe, Chippenham and Eastbourne

ACKNOWLEDGEMENTS

During the writing of my memoirs frequent reference has been made to my diaries and photograph albums, and to the Wimbledon Programmes for the years 1961 to 1983.

I am greatly indebted too to my daughter-in-law Chryssie Burnett who did all the initial typing, for reading my writing!

CONTENTS

INTRODUCTION

To my great surprise at the age of ninety-two, I found that my grandchildren, Ben particularly, seemed to be interested in the life and fairly successful career of their grandfather, so I have been encouraged to try and record some of the details for them.

I have certainly been incredibly lucky all my life. Lucky to be very fit with no major ailments or injuries; lucky to have a marvellous mother and an elder brother with similar sporting interests; lucky in nearly all my RAF appointments including taking part in the World Non-Stop Long Distance Flight in 1938 and lucky enough to survive my tour on Operations in Bomber Command in 1941 and then have two years commanding a Navigation Training Station in Canada during the War; lucky then to marry a lovely wife, Val, who was such a wonderful support throughout my career; and lucky with our two sons and daughters-in-law and our four grandchildren. I was lucky, too, to reach the highest ranks in the RAF and to end up at the top of the Air Chief Marshal's list in the 1971 RAF List before retiring. And finally, I was lucky to start a very enjoyable second career in the Lawn Tennis world when I was elected Chairman of the All England Lawn Tennis Club in 1974.

People often say that you make your own luck but I don't think this is altogether true, and the most important thing is to make the most of it if and when a 'little bit of luck' happens to come one's way. I certainly enjoyed more than my fair share and have had a most interesting, exciting and marvellous life. How lucky can you be!

Part I

Early Years (1913–34)

1

THE EARLY YEARS AND EDUCATION

INDIA (1913–18)

I was born on 10 March 1913 in Hyderabad, India where my father Kenneth Burnett was a teacher at the Nizam's College. After leaving Keble College, Oxford he had joined the Hyderabad Education Service and, in due course, married my mother Anita Evans and had two sons – my elder brother Douglas in 1911 and myself two years later.

My memories of India are few, as I was only five years old when we left, but I remember we lived in a fairly large white house, open-plan with fans in the ceilings, with a large garden for us to play in. There were a few trees which Douglas and I enjoyed climbing and there was one particular incident which I recall vividly. After running about in the garden one morning, Douglas and I sat down to rest in the sun on the steps leading into the house. After a short while our father came round the corner of the house and saw, to his horror, a large cobra only a few yards away, stationary but looking towards us. He nipped quickly into the house to fetch a gun with which he returned in a few seconds and shot the cobra. Well done, Dad! As was normal out there in those days we had an *ayah*, an Indian nursemaid, to look after us boys, as well as other staff help. We did not have a car – and in fact neither my father nor my mother ever learnt to drive! – but we had a nice little pony and trap, and there were horses on which we were taken riding, with me initially in a basket-saddle. There were often two great-aunts there with us – one who was also a school teacher out there and the other a doctor who actually brought me into this world, and kept a car out there which we often found very useful.

So we lived there happily until 1915 when World War I had started and my father joined up to serve in France in the Army, leaving us behind in Hyderabad. Fortunately my father survived the war in the horrific land battles around Ypres and the River Somme. When it was all over in 1918 my mother then brought Douglas aged seven and me aged five back to go to school in England. Unfortunately my father had to return to his job in Hyderabad so we only saw him when he was able to come home on leave for three months every three years (1922, 1925, 1928 and when he finally retired in 1932). When my brother and I were in boarding school my mother consequently spent a lot of time travelling to and from Hyderabad which in those days by sea took approximately three weeks.

PREP SCHOOLS IN ENGLAND (1919–26)

In 1918 Douglas and I spent a year as day boys at the Dragon School in Oxford before going for a short while to another school in Horsham, Surrey. At that time we had no house or home in England and we relied on rented rooms until we moved on to Fernden School, Haslemere as boarders at the comparatively young ages of nine and seven. My mother then settled in a bed-sitting room in a small country cottage tea-shop at Newchapel, just off the London–Brighton road, next to a nice common and only about three miles from my father's younger sister who had a small chicken farm. We also had a bedroom upstairs there for Douglas and me for when we came on holidays, and this to all intents and purposes became our temporary home for a number of years. My mother's bed-sitting room was small but very nice and with an open fireplace. In those days we had no central heating, of course, and no TV or even radio, so one had to develop one's own interests and we usually read a lot or played card games or chess. We were able to play football and cricket on the common, and in the winter to skate on the pond there whenever it was frozen, which seemed to happen quite a lot in those days. We had no basins or taps with running water in our rooms, and for washing and so on water had to be brought in, heated in the kitchen and carried upstairs to a portable basin or a small rubber bath. There was also no 'loo' as such, but an outside 'thunder-box'. It is surprising how one seemed to get used to this sort of existence! To visit us at school once a term, at half-term, my mother used to bicycle over some forty miles and stay a night in a room locally. For shopping or anything we all used to bicycle in the four miles to East Grinstead, the nearest town.

Incidentally, when young, my mother had been to Art School in England and enjoyed painting when she had the time, and when we were at boarding school she put this to good use by selling quite a lot of her

Mum outside at Newchapel

paintings to help pay for our school fees. She also did some private coaching and in fact coached one small boy (later Sir Henry Mance) who had lost a leg and had to miss school, into getting a scholarship to Charterhouse, one of the top Public Schools at the time.

In the school holidays she often took us abroad, as it was in many ways cheaper, and we spent several holidays in Brittany and Paris. We went more frequently to Alassio on the Italian Riviera, where there was an excellent tennis club and swimming, at Easter, and to Le Zoute in Belgium in the summer for tennis, golf and bathing in the sea there. Douglas and I played a lot of tennis together including one or two Under 16 and Under 18 tournaments. One I particularly remember was in a lovely place called Karersee in the Italian Dolomites in 1927 when we both got to the final and he beat me. I also remember a famous victory I had in an 18 and Under tournament at Alassio when only twelve years old against a six-foot tall Italian aged 18 called Villiani. My racket was broken and I couldn't afford a new one so I was playing with an old warped racket which had been left behind in our hotel and, after losing, my opponent complained to the referee that it wasn't fair as he couldn't tell which way the ball was going to go!

My first tournament win. A giant killer!

We especially enjoyed Alassio as there were a number of English home-owners there whose young usually came out in the holidays, and whom we got to know well. My mother often agreed to escort some of them to and fro on the long overnight train journey from England. This helped towards our own rail fares and on one occasion there were as many as fourteen of us for her to look after – passports, tickets and all. Quite a responsibility!

On several occasions also we were taken on motor tours abroad by an adopted godfather, Lt. Col. V. F. Jackson (whom we called 'Cap' but later 'Vee'). He had served in the Indian Cavalry but retired very early after World War I. He had a small house near Felbridge, East Grinstead which he called 'Stonewall' after the American Civil War General Stonewall Jackson. Many years later he bought the two-acre plot of land adjoining Traddles, which we had bought in 1932, and shared the enlarged garden with us in exchange for living in the house with us. He was not married, except to his cars, of which he had a series of Rolls-Royces which he enjoyed driving abroad. In 1924 we did a very interesting tour with him of World War I battlefields in France and Belgium around Amiens, the River Somme, Arras and Béthune where I believe tanks were used for the first time, and Ypres. Surprisingly we were still able to pick up a few bits of military equipment such as helmets and bayonets lying in the fields. We kept a bayonet for a number of years that we used as a poker in the fire!

The next summer we did Brittany and the châteaux of the Loire and in the winter holidays Belgium, including Bruges, Bruxelles and the fields of Wellington's famous Battle of Waterloo, before going on to Volendam on the Zuider Zee in Holland. In the summer of 1927 we did a wonderful tour to Switzerland, Austria and northern Italy to Karersee in the Dolomites before returning via France to Le Zoute in Belgium for two weeks tennis before going back to school at Charterhouse. That was, I think, the best of all our many tours abroad.

My father came home on leave for a month or two every three years and always arranged it during our school holidays so that he could join us. It was always good to see him then, and I remember particularly holidays with him in 1922 at Instow near Barnstaple in Devon, at Swanage in Dorset and Le Zoute in Belgium in 1926 and at Alassio in 1928. Sadly it was not until he retired in 1932 that we really got to know him properly.

Dad at La Zoute with Douglas and me

When staying at Newchapel, he used to take us bird-nesting on the common and in the nearby woods. He was very knowledgeable about all birds and in India had apparently discovered a 'white cuckoo' which was, I believe, to be named the 'Burnett cuckoo' after him.

At Fernden prep school, we both did quite well and played in the first XI at both cricket and football and I started a small tennis competition for the boys. We were near the top of the school in work, Douglas only just missing a scholarship to Charterhouse in 1924. He went on that year to Bodeites House there, and I followed two years later in September 1926.

CHARTERHOUSE SCHOOL (1926–30)

At Charterhouse, I'm afraid neither of us particularly distinguished ourselves though we played for our House, Bodeites, at most games, and at squash rackets we both became pretty good and represented the school for many years. Douglas played squash for Cambridge and the Army, whilst I represented Oxford and the RAF. At nearly all Public Schools in England at that time, team games took priority and at Charterhouse tennis was not encouraged at all. The few hard courts that were available were very poor and to get a decent game one or two of us joined a local tennis club down the road where we occasionally went on our bikes to play on Sundays. I was also invited a few times to play on a grass court at the house of the maths master, C. O. Tuckey, who was a regular and very useful tournament player during the school holidays. His wife had also been a Wimbledon player and twice winner of the Mixed Doubles in 1909 and 1913, and their son Raymond, who I did not know at Charterhouse because he was about four years older than me, was later Wimbledon Doubles Champion in 1936 and Davis Cup player with G. P. (Pat) Hughes. The Tuckeys' younger teenage daughter, Kay, used to come and do ball-girl for us, I remember, when we played on the grass court at their home. She too became very good and was a regular Wimbledon and Wightman Cup player around 1947–51. So the inspiration for Charterhouse tennis players was there but sadly not taken advantage of.

One important thing I did learn at Charterhouse, however, was the 'will to win' at games. I was being beaten every time by my friend Adam Hulton at squash rackets after a very close game, though I really thought I was just as good as him. One day I got angry with myself and decided I jolly well could beat him by exerting that little extra concentration, effort and determination at key points. I therefore taught myself to do this then and always tried to remember to do so later in life.

In 1929 Douglas joined the Army and went to the Royal Academy at Woolwich where he later passed out in the top three and was able to choose to join the Royal Engineers. He was then sent to Clare College, Cambridge University for two years to get his Honours Degree before his first proper Army appointment.

In 1930 I had intended to go into the Foreign Office but needed two languages so left Charterhouse early and went for a year to Heidelberg University in Germany as a *Hörer* to improve my German before going to Wadham College, Oxford University, to obtain my degree in Modern Languages (German and French). In the summer holidays before this, however, I had won the Surrey Junior Tennis Championships which was quite a feather in my cap in those days and helped towards my tennis at Oxford later.

HEIDELBERG UNIVERSITY (1930–31)

At Heidelberg in July 1930 I lived in the small Pension Cronmuller in the Anlage Strasse, which was run by a retired German cavalry

Surrey Junior Champion, with J. R. Fawcus

Oberstleutnant (Lt. Col.) and his wife. There were several other students also staying there, one from Japan, one from Holland, one from France and a girl from Sweden (Harriet Hagberg) and we all had meals together with the family at one large table. Only German was allowed to be spoken, which was good. Before joining the University lectures in Alt Heidelberg on Modern History, I organized some lessons locally and worked hard at my German so that I could understand them.

In my spare time I joined the riding school run by the Oberstleutnant and learnt how to ride the German military style – bumping up and down when trotting rather than rising in one's stirrups. He also made us practise riding without reins or stirrups, but I did not enjoy that much so gave up after a while. Needless to say I joined the tennis club and met up with the son of the lady who used to run it. He was a bank clerk called Willy Baudendistel, whom I got to know very well. He was very good at all sports and played for South Germany at both tennis and hockey so I was lucky to be able to play quite a lot with him. As there didn't seem to be any football for me in Heidelberg, Willy persuaded me to take up hockey and before long, I found myself playing in the Heidelberg Hockey side, not only with him but also, much to my amazement, alongside two German International inside forwards! It was rather embarrassing at times when I played badly but great fun, particularly on some of the away matches. In the summer there was also excellent swimming in the River Neckar and I had an old second-hand bicycle to get around everywhere.

The Dutch student, Peter Hierneiss, and I got on very well and in May of 1931 we went together on a bicycle tour from Heidelberg down to Baden-Baden with a one-night stop each way and two nights in a small hotel there. In Baden-Baden we rather rashly went to the Casino but fortunately we both won initially so had a good time before finally losing again nearly all our winnings.

During the university holidays, I travelled quite a bit on the hard wooden-seated railway carriages and went to places like Köln, Bonn, Darmstadt, Frankfurt and Karlsruhe, and I played in a tennis tournament at Heilbronn not far from Heidelberg which I won.

I did not see a lot of the regular German students at the University who were mostly wrapped up in their *Verbindungen* and I didn't really enjoy their heavy beer drinking sessions in the evenings. They seemed to drink only to get drunk, and later in the evening could often be seen in line astern with their walking sticks in the tramlines going down the main street in order to find their way home!

Heidelberg Schloss and Alte Brücke over River Neckar

Duelling was not permitted at the time in Heidelberg so the students used to go very early in the mornings to a special *Gasthaus* in Neckargemund the other side of the river where it seemed to be allowed. I did go with some of them to watch it early one morning but I thought it was a barbaric sport, fought with unsheathed swords, and a duel was only over when one of the contestants had his cheek slashed badly, needing stitches and leaving an ugly scar for life. This was regarded, I think, as a sign of bravery and something to be proud of and, surprisingly, was greatly admired by all the girls.

It was an interesting time to be in Germany with Hitler on the rise and gaining in popularity. He used to come to Heidelberg to harangue the students and march through the town with his SA and SS followers. On one occasion I came out of my Pension Cronmuller to go on my bike to the tennis club only to find Hitler and his gang marching down the Anlage. Suddenly from the other side of the railway line opposite there was a shout from two young men, '*Heil Moscow, Heil Moscow*!' Hitler was clearly furious and quickly detailed four of his men, saying, 'Go get them.' His men rushed across the level crossing nearby and they did – beating them to death and leaving them both dead on the railway line. I was a bit shaken and was about to go over to see if there was anything I could do to help, but there were a number of other Germans there and I decided that it would be wiser for the young English student not to get involved, so I went inside and waited a while before going on my peaceful way to the tennis club.

There were two other particularly interesting matters which I discovered while I was at Heidelberg. One was the way in the Modern History lectures that they tried to convince themselves that it was not Germany who started World War I but France and Great Britain. This was quite different to what I had always been led to believe and I used to have some quite heated arguments with them about it. The other more serious matter for the future, I thought, was the way German society was being turned upside down. Many of my friends who were well educated and training to be doctors, lawyers or solicitors were being made to attend SA or SS Parades certain evenings every week. This they were reluctant to do and often did not go, with the result that they were not promoted and got left amongst the lower ranks while all the butchers and bakers and tough guys who attended regularly, clicking their heels at the right time, took over the higher and more important ranks in the SA and SS. What influence this may have had on the future conduct of Germany I do not know, but it must have had some.

By the end of my year at Heidelberg, which I had thoroughly enjoyed, I was sorry in many ways to leave; in due course though I received my *Hörer* Certificate and went back happily to England, looking forward to my time at Wadham College.

OXFORD UNIVERSITY (1931–34)

Later in 1931 I fortunately passed the Entrance Exam for Wadham College, despite having to take Latin again after a long gap, and I was delighted to join the College that September. I had a room in College my first two years but in the third year had to move out into digs, which I shared with three other good friends, which was great. My German and French tutors lived about a mile up the road and I used to go on my bike to see them for my tutorial once a week. As I was fairly fluent in both German and French I had expected it all to be quite easy but had not realized that speaking the language was taken for granted and that the major part of the degree was based on the literature of the country concerned, and one might as well be reading English. I mostly worked on my own with books though I was pretty idle, I'm afraid, and did not attend half the lectures I should have done, but I thoroughly enjoyed myself playing all games for the College – football, hockey, cricket, tennis and squash rackets; including squash in 1932 and 1933 and lawn tennis in 1933 for the University for which I was awarded 'Blues'. I also played hockey for the 'Occasionals' but failed to get my 'Blue' for that, although I played in a number of matches for the University who had three international players in the side, and considered myself unlucky! In the University squash match in 1932 Douglas, playing for Cambridge, and I were in opposing teams but did not actually play each other, though in tennis in 1933 we did. This was unusual to say the least and fortunately, I'm glad to say the younger brother managed to win, though our Dad didn't think this was quite right! Altogether that year I managed to win four out of my five matches (in the doubles my partner was Brian Hone, the Oxford Cricket Captain) and I was lucky enough to be chosen to play for the combined Oxford and Cambridge Prentice Cup Team to play Harvard and Yale, and spend some six weeks in July and August in the USA. In those days, of course, there were no Atlantic flights and we had four or five very enjoyable days on RMS *Aquitania* to New York. Our team was headed by Jimmy Nuthall, with Peter Young and Douglas Freshwater of Cambridge and Grady Frank, Bill Moss and myself of Oxford. It was a wonderful tour and a marvellous experience and we made many life-long friends such as Uppy Moorhead, the Yale captain, and the Jonklaas family.

Incidentally Ernest Jonklaas who was in charge of our team in the USA had played in the match eight years earlier and when playing against the Rockaway Hunt Club he suddenly stopped at 5-all in the final set of his singles match and, pointing at a pretty girl watching at the side of the court, said, 'That is the girl I am going to marry!' He then proceeded to win the next two games and went and proposed to the girl, Alice Cox. She was already engaged to someone else but Ernest persuaded her to change her mind and marry him. Ernest then got himself a good job in New York, never returned to England and lived happily on Long Island ever after. Interestingly, later in 1947 when we were posted to New York, Alice Jonklaas became one of our younger son Bob's godmothers.

In our match against the Club we won the Prince of Wales Cup, which was presented by the late Duke of Windsor when visiting in 1924, and a very nice small silver miniature of it was presented to each of us. I still have it decorating my dining room table with a rose usually in it. We also later won the Prentice Cup by 12 matches to 9 at Newport, Rhode

Oxford and Cambridge Tennis Teams 1933

Back row: D. I. Burnett, B. K. Burnett, H. Benavitch, B. W. Hone, D. G. Freshwater, W. F. Moss, R. N. A. Leyton
Front row: D. W. Jones, C. L. Burwell, J. W. Nuthall, G. C. Frank, P. S. Young, F. C. de Sarem

Island. We were based primarily at the Rockaway Hunt Club, Cedarhurst, Long Island, which could not have been better. We played in a number of tournaments at some of their other lovely clubs, including Seabright, Philadelphia, and the American Men's Doubles Championships in Boston, Massachusetts. On one occasion at the Newport tournament I was drawn against Frank Shields, the 1931 runner-up at Wimbledon and number 1 seed at Newport. At the party the night before Fred Perry came up to me and said, 'Bad luck, Brian, I see you have drawn Frank but I will take the base line in your match and tell you how to beat him.' He did the next day but needless to say I didn't! I thought that was pretty good from our top Davis Cup player and future Wimbledon and US Champion to a young undergraduate. It wouldn't happen today.

Following this tour and our return on RMS *Berengaria*, I was happily made a member of the International Lawn Tennis Club of GB, so that I could in the future, put back something into the game which had given me so much.

When my father was due to retire in 1932 the Nizam of Hyderabad asked him to escort the two princes, AJ aged I think twenty-two, and MJ twenty, on a three-month tour round Europe. They were accompanied by quite a large retinue of people but my father was in charge of their full programme, all the financial and other arrangements. In London they all stayed at the Savoy Hotel and my father was provided with an Army Captain (later Major General Sir Julian Gascoigne) as a kind of ADC, to show the princes round the night clubs and so on and arrange introductions to some of the more glamorous and well known actresses of the day including Gertrude Lawrence who MJ rather fancied. The princes certainly enjoyed their London nightlife.

They then went on to Dublin where they proceeded to buy, amongst other things, several polo ponies to send back to India. From there to Berlin, where I also joined them for a few days in the famous and luxurious Adlon Hotel in Unter den Linden, which was later occupied during World War II by the Gestapo with special reserved suites for the prominent Nazis. From there they proceeded to Paris and later to Cannes in the south of France where I also joined them in the Carlton Hotel. These visits of mine were a good insight as to how the rich lived and were fun while they lasted. Both princes were extremely extravagant, as can be imagined as the sons of the reputed richest man in the world, and at the drop of a hat (or a kiss more likely!) would give many of the girls they met all sorts of expensive jewellery, pearls and diamonds which even they could not afford as the Nizam (a well-known miser) kept them on a tight rein. My father also had a relatively limited budget from the Nizam for the whole tour and frequently had the difficult job of going round the next day to ask for some of the jewellery back!

While they were in Paris, the Nizam sent my father a telegram saying, 'Before the princes return to India please arrange for them both to get married.' This caused quite a stir and my mother and father got going to invite many eligible princesses in Europe to a large party and ball in Paris. They discovered quite a number – about fifteen or so, I seem to remember – with several very attractive Turkish princesses. At the ball the princes selected about six whom they took down to Cannes with them for further consideration. The younger Prince (MJ) was very good looking with an amusing and attractive personality and all the princesses fell for him, and my mother persuaded him to choose Nilüfar, one of the most attractive Turkish princesses who was her favourite. The elder Prince (AJ) was less of an extrovert and more serious but he eventually chose another tall and beautiful princess from the Turkish royal house. Both the marriages took place in November in Nice and seemed very happy. They lasted many years after they got back to India and the Nizam particularly approved of AJ's bride, Her Imperial Highness Princess Durruhsehvsar, who became the Princess of Berar and was the mother of the next Nizam.

Before I went up to Oxford my father had been a bit doubtful about affording to send me to university, but I was very keen to go and said I would get jobs in the long summer vacation to try and help pay for one of the three years. He had been impressed by this and finally agreed. Unfortunately my first job in July/August 1932 was not a great success, earning only 10*s*. 6*d*. a day for teaching some backward boy Latin! The next year the Oxford University Appointments Board could not offer anything better and I returned to Wadham rather depressed. However, on the lodge noticeboard was one saying, 'Join the Reserve of Air Force Officers and earn 21*s*. 6*d*. a day.' That's better, I thought, and learning to fly might come in useful one day, so the next day I went to the University Air Squadron (OUAS) where the CO (Wing Commander Keith Park later of 11 Group and Battle of Britain fame) enrolled me in the OUAS and arranged for me to join the RAFO.

Having finally retired as Principal of the Nizam's College my father returned to England in 1932 and he and my mother started looking for a house, preferably in the Henley-on-Thames area as he had been a keen rowing man at Oxford and enjoyed a boat on the river. In this they were successful and they bought a lovely old fifteenth century cottage called Traddles at Hurley village, half way between Henley and Maidenhead. It only had four small bedrooms and one bathroom but had recently been modernized with central heating and so on. Originally it had been two old cottages joined together, and in due course they were able to build on the equivalent of a third cottage in old brick to match. It had a small but nice lawn and garden, which suited them well, and it became our home in England for the next thirty years or so.

It was during that summer vacation from Oxford in July 1932 that I started to learn to fly in the RAFO at De Havilland's Flying Club at Hatfield, Hertfordshire – first of all on DH Gypsy Moths on which I completed a total of 30 hours, and then 10 hours on the DH9J (an old World War I bomber aircraft). My instructor was Eddie Fulford, a South African who had served in the Royal Flying Corps (RFC) during World War I, and he arranged for me to do all my daily flying in the mornings

Dad by the front door of Traddles

so that I could play tennis in the afternoon in the Cumberland Lawn Tennis Tournament, or with Ted Higgs, an old 1927–33 Wimbledon and Davis Cup player who lived near by. Incidentally, Eddie Fulford at that time at Hatfield was also taking it in turns to teach flying to Kay Stammers, the British Wightman Cup player and later Wimbledon Ladies Doubles Champion with Freda James in 1935 and 1936 and runner-up in the Singles Final against Alice Marble in 1939.

It was at this time I bought my first car, a Morris Minor, for £5, which I later swopped for a slightly larger Clyno worth £15!

When back at Oxford I continued to fly with the Oxford University Air Squadron whenever I could, in 1933 and 1934, on the Avro 504K and the Avro Tutor aircraft with which the OUAS was equipped at RAF Abingdon. This ended with a Central Flying School test and a two-week Practice Camp at RAF Eastchurch for intensive aerobatics and formation and low flying including practice forced landings and cross-country flying to various RAF stations. It was great fun. The only trouble was that the more I flew the more I loved it and later decided to give up the idea of the Foreign Office and join the Royal Air Force in 1934. This was not very popular with my parents as flying was then considered dangerous and the RAF unlikely, they thought, to provide a very stable career. Understandably, this was the normal reaction of parents at that

DH9

time. My father also felt, I think, that I had wasted all his efforts to send me to University, but they were very good about it and accepted my decision.

All this and my sports activities were in the end rather disastrous for my degree in 1934 and I only got a miserable 4th Class Honours Degree made up, I believe, from a 2nd in German and only just a 'Pass' in French Literature. Both my German and French tutors had said they were confident I should get a 2nd in both, but I am afraid I didn't help this by going on a three-week College Cricket Tour before the Viva part of the exams, instead of revising as I should have done!

However, a 4th Class Honours Degree was acceptable in those days for the RAF as I had by then completed the necessary 100 hours flying, and I was finally awarded a permanent commission as an Acting Pilot Officer in the GD Branch of the RAF in September 1934.

Part II

Life in the RAF 1934–72
(Pilot Officer to Air Chief Marshal)

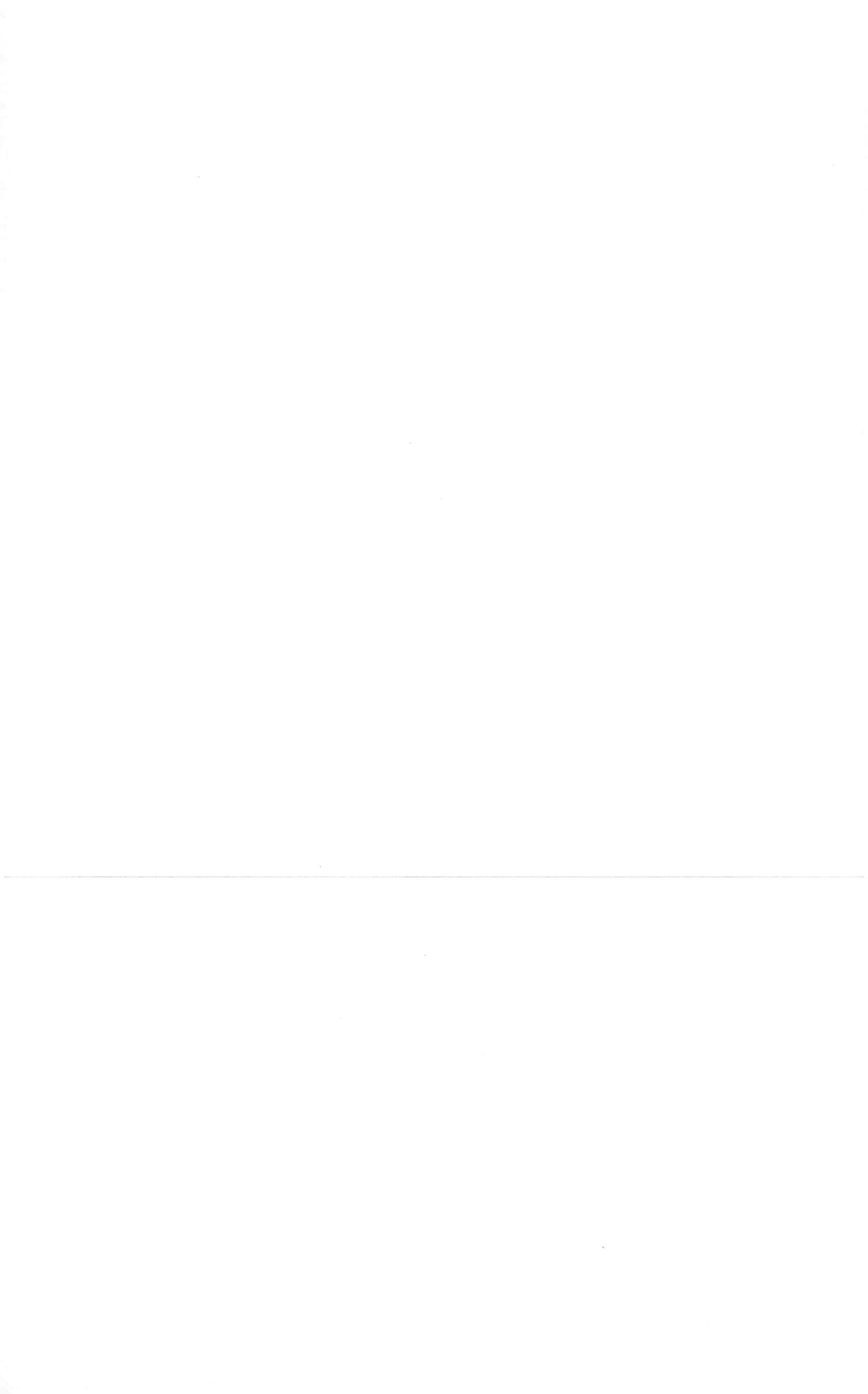

2

PRE-WAR RAF (1934–39)

RAF CADET COLLEGE, CRANWELL

My entry was the first of the University Entrant courses at RAF Cranwell in Lincolnshire and consisted of just seven of us, three from Oxford, three from Cambridge and one from Dublin. It was a six-month course primarily to advance our flying experience, including Instrument Flying, and to bring us up to RAF Squadron standards, but it included various technical subjects such as engines, armaments and signals and also there were fitness and drill parades for which we joined in with the cadets – otherwise we were separated from the Cranwell cadets and as Acting Pilot Officers, lived in the Officers' Mess, not the Cadet College. We flew mainly Hawker Harts but also the Avro Tutor for instrument flying.

Earlier in 1934 I had joined both the Escorts Squash Club and the Jesters Club and played a number of squash matches at weekends with them. This helped to keep me fit and in good practice and the matches were great fun as they were often organised by people with their own private court and one met many keen squash playing friends. At Cranwell I played a certain amount of squash but unfortunately was not allowed time off my Cranwell course to play in the RAF Squash Championships that year, which I had hoped to win. Based on my previous record, however, I was automatically selected to play No. 3 for the RAF in the two-day only Inter-Services matches that winter, which was fair enough. During the Christmas break I had also reached the semi-final of the South of England Squash Championships but was not able to extend my leave and unfortunately had to scratch and return to duty at Cranwell.

As March 1935 came around, we had to pass all the usual flying tests including, of course, aerobatics and cross-country, and also the fairly elementary engine, armaments and signals tests before being passed out fit to join our various squadrons. We were then confirmed in rank as

No. 1 University Course, RAF Cranwell, with me in front on the left. Group photo in 'Best Blue' which in those days meant breeches and puttees

Hawker Hart of 18 Squadron at RAF Upper Heyford

Pilot Officers, with six months ante-date as University entrants, and I was pleased to be posted to No. 18 Day Bomber Squadron on Hawker Hart aircraft at RAF Upper Heyford, not far from Oxford, on 16 March.

NO. 18 SQUADRON

It was a great life in the RAF in those days for a young pilot officer. We were living and working alongside many like-minded young friends looking forward to our new exciting career, and we lived very comfortably, usually in one of the new Officers' Messes with a room of our own and a batman to help. The food was usually very good and, unless one's bar bill was unnecessarily high, the mess bill was usually only about half one's monthly pay (16*s*. 6*d*. a day or 82 ½p in today's currency) – leaving enough for most other needs including running a car and holidays. Leave was a month a year with weekends and Wednesday afternoons reserved primarily for sport. Sport was greatly encouraged and, if not actually playing, you were expected to stay on the station to watch your squadron or other teams. This helped to build up the squadron spirit and camaraderie, and being good at sport certainly seemed to be in a young officer's favour. Military discipline was far more relaxed than in the Army or Navy and, apart from a few colour-hoisting parades and taking one's turn at overseeing airmen's pay and clothing parades, Station Orderly Officer duties and occasionally helping in the Air Traffic Control Tower, there was little to distract one from the main task of flying training. This, of course, continued under the supervision of our Squadron and Flight Commander with plenty of formation flying, practice 'dog-fighting', air gunnery including firing on towed aerial drogues with live ammunition, and bombing with practice bombs on the nearby bombing range. Frequent cross-country flights practising map-reading and dead-reckoning (DR) were carried out, and surprisingly, one was often free to fly the aircraft away to another RAF station and have lunch with a friend before returning. This made a nice break and, to make it more worth while, a practice forced-landing in a field was often made en route. We were also able to take the aircraft away for the weekend and return on Monday morning, and this all counted as navigation/flying training! I often did this to a small airfield at Sutton Bridge in Lincolnshire to stay with my friends George and Dulcie Thompson at Holbeach Hurn, where they had their own squash and tennis courts.

The Under Secretary of State for Air around that time was Sir Philip Sassoon, who was keen on lawn tennis himself and used to take a great interest in the RAF team. I was in the team by then and he used to invite several of us at weekends to play with him at Trent Park, his estate in north London, where he also had an indoor covered court. There were usually other guests, including one day Sir Anthony Eden and his first wife, and after lunch we played tennis with them and then enjoyed the outdoor heated swimming pool. Sir Philip also invited some of us down to play at his country estate near Lympne in Kent and one weekend he sent his private Percival aircraft to pick me up from Upper Heyford and fly me down to RAF Hawkinge for the day. Lunch with him at Lympne was always interesting with several Government Ministers present, including Winston Churchill on one occasion.

Early in July 1935 it was King George V's Silver Jubilee and No. 18 Squadron flew to RAF Mildenhall for the Royal Review of the Air Force which took place there. It was remarkable in that, apart from King George V, two future Kings (Edward VIII and George VI) also took part in the Review and inspection of the several lines of squadron aircraft and their crews. Unfortunately I was given the less glamorous job of escorting and looking after the 18 Squadron ground crews who went there. It was, however, an historical event and interesting to be in attendance.

Later in July and August that year 18 Squadron was sent to RAF Catfoss in Yorkshire for about six weeks' Practice Camp to carry out live

King George V in front car and two future kings (Edward VIII and George VI) review the Air Force at RAF Mildenhall

bombing and gunnery at the range near there. This involved fairly intensive flying and was always great fun, apart from giving one confidence in operating the aircraft properly. There followed in September four days taking part in various Army manoeuvres, during which we

Fairey's airfield, now Heathrow!

camped in tents on Woodley airfield and Fairey's airfield, which is now Heathrow airport but which was then just a grass airfield with only one hangar!

After that I took a few days' leave to play in the RAF Lawn Tennis Championships (then held at the Chiswick Park Club) where I lost in the final of the singles but won the doubles with F/Lt R. G. (Dick) Shaw.

Later that year (1935) I found myself attached to RAF Andover for the Short Navigation Course during which, apart from the lectures and exercises, we took our turn at DR navigation in the Prefect and the large amphibious Saro Cloud, which was interesting.

After getting back to 18 Squadron at Upper Heyford in January 1936, another move followed when the squadron was moved to RAF Bircham Newton, an old World War I station in Norfolk, and I became Flight Commander of 'B' Flight, re-equipped with Hawker Hinds. Flying training carried on much as before and the squadron had a good Practice Camp at RAF North Coates Fitties and Theddlethorpe Range in April. I was then posted in November 1936 as the Navigation instructor to No. 11 Flying Training School (FTS) at RAF Wittering, where I continued flying Harts and Audaxes with my pupils, teaching them basic map reading and DR navigation.

RAF WITTERING

By 1935, it had become apparent from re-arming reports from Germany and their withdrawal from the League of Nations, that war might come sooner than had been thought likely, so the expansion of the RAF was greatly speeded up. Orders for the Hurricane and Spitfire aircraft, recruiting of pilots and the building of many new air stations were put in hand. This meant about a five-fold increase in the size of the RAF and promotion came fairly rapidly. With my six-months University ante-date on entry, I had soon become a Flying Officer and was now promoted to Flight Lieutenant.

Earlier in 1935 at RAF Andover I had unfortunately put the cartilage out in my left knee whilst playing hockey and was unable again to play in the RAF Squash Championships that year. The knee continued to give me a lot of trouble so I went to RAF Uxbridge Hospital to have the cartilage removed. However, after X-raying it, the RAF Group Captain surgeon said he could not guarantee more than a 2 per cent chance of a successful operation as the cartilage was split into many small bits. (Unfortunately keyhole surgery was not available in those days.) In fact,

My 'B' Flight of Hawker Hinds at RAF Bircham Newton

he said he would not operate and told me to go away, give up playing sports for the rest of my life and take up some other hobbies. This news at my age, then only twenty-two, was pretty shattering but fortunately it didn't affect my flying or navigation instructing though it made it difficult climbing in and getting out of the Hart or Audax. I decided, however, to do what the Group Captain recommended and take up my German again by applying for the three month language leave in Germany before taking the RAF Interpretership Exam. This would give me a specialist qualification 'I' against my name which could be helpful later in the promotion stakes.

Approval for this came through later, so in the summer of 1936 I set forth in my new little Ford 10 – which cost £110 new in those days! – to drive down to Heidelberg to meet up with some old friends there and work on my more technical German. The interpreter exam involved the use of many aircraft and aviation technical terms and, as there was no such thing as a military dictionary in those days, I used to buy up all the aircraft and glider magazines to get to know the technical terms that way. I also applied through our Air Attaché in Berlin to do a glider course at Darmstadt in Germany as that would be better still and lots of fun as well.

In Heidelberg I was soon at home with many old friends and after a while met up with an attractive English girl, Yvonne Rolph, who invited me to play tennis. I explained that I couldn't because of my knee but said that I would come and watch her. This I did for a bit, but she was so bad I felt I could play walking about and not attempting to run. The extraordinary thing was that this gradually and miraculously made my knee better and taught me never to underestimate the powers of a pretty woman! The knee has fortunately held out remarkably well for the next seventy-eight years despite severe testing with all my squash, tennis, golf and skiing activities, though I have had to be careful and rest it from time to time. Later that summer I did manage to play in the RAF tennis again but was beaten in the semi-finals of the singles, though my partner (F/Lt R. G. Shaw) and I retained our doubles title.

Whilst in Germany I also travelled quite a lot in my car, heading further south to Stuttgart and Munich, and then on for a few days to a lovely place called Bad Schachen near Lindau, on the Boden See. There I met some old friends from Bonn and played in the tennis tournament and enjoyed the swimming. On my way back to Heidelberg I passed through Friedrichshaven, the home of the German Zeppelin industry, but I did not get close enough to see anything of interest.

On return to Heidelberg I received my instructions from our Berlin Air Attaché to report to Darmstadt for the gliding course. On arrival I met various members of the previous course who said I was going to be lucky as there were fewer of us on this one and more gliders to fly. However the next morning I was informed 'the course was full' and I could not stay. There were many apologies and, on contacting Berlin, it was agreed to arrange another gliding course for me later on the island of Sylt in Schleswig-Holstein, Northern Germany. This was done and on the way up north I arranged to stay a couple of days in Bremen where my friend Willy Baudendistel had moved. One afternoon there I set off to play tennis with him but suddenly realized I had left my rackets behind, so returned to collect them from my hotel room. There I found two Gestapo men searching through all my luggage. They were reasonably polite but said they were under instructions and soon left saying there was no problem but leaving me with everything all over the floor! As I was a Flight Lieutenant in the RAF and obviously keen to do glider training over two particular areas of Germany (the Rhine and the Heligoland Bight) where much military activity and re-arming was going on, they must have thought I might be spying. This probably accounts for the fact that Darmstadt turned me away, as the Germans were re-arming the Rhine, and the same thing happened when I got to Sylt where I also was told 'the course was full'. On referring again to Berlin, another course was arranged in East Germany but I decided not to go. It was a great pity as I would have loved the opportunity to fly gliders. Anyway, that was that, and not long afterwards my three months were up and I returned to England where in due course I passed the Interpreter exam and received the £100 gratuity for doing so. To me, however, the great thing was that my knee was so much better and I could take part in sports again.

Back at RAF Wittering for a few months I continued with the navigation instructing, but it was not long before I arranged to join my brother skiing for two weeks at St Anton in Austria in January 1937. My girl friend Yvonne, who was a very good skier, was also there with her sister. This was the first of my many annual skiing holidays in Austria, Switzerland, France, Italy, Spain, Canada and the United States, and a source of much enjoyment throughout the rest of my life until the age of nearly eighty. It was also a great joy to be able personally to introduce later both my sons to this wonderful sport at which they have both become such keen and excellent skiers. At St Anton in those days there were no main lifts and, apart from practising on the nursery slopes, the best plan was to catch the bus to the top of the Arlberg Pass and then climb carrying one's skis – and the girlfriend's! – to the top at Galzig before the good long run down. In the afternoons this usually ended at the Post Hotel for the tea dance in our ski boots which was always great fun. I have always remembered since then the favourite tunes: 'There's a small hotel, with a wishing well' and 'Dancing cheek to cheek'.

SPEC 'N' COURSE, RAF MANSTON

I remained at RAF Wittering until June 1937 but was then posted on to the six month Specialist Navigation Course at RAF Manston. As a permanently commissioned GD officer one was expected after four or five years to specialise and I had selected Navigation, rather than Armament, Engineering or Signals, so this move was expected and I transferred down to Manston in Kent for this fascinating course which included Astro-navigation, then new to me. There were only twelve of us on the course and we took our turn at navigating the Avro Ansons all round England as well as out over the sea where one relied on drift sights by day and the stars by night.

On the whole we were kept pretty busy but I had managed to get away to win the RAF Tennis Championships for the first time in August, and to play in the Inter Services matches. Earlier in June I had tried to qualify for Wimbledon but was beaten in the last round. I also played quite a bit of squash rackets in the Manston court to keep fit, and ended the year by winning the RAF Squash Championships though I lost to my brother Douglas, the Army Champion, in the Inter-Services match.

Around then, having passed the Spec 'N' exams, I was sent for by the Officer in charge of Postings at the Air Ministry and, to my surprise, was told that I had been selected to go as a pilot/navigator on the new Long Range Development Unit (LRDU) at RAF Upper Heyford which was being equipped with the Vickers Wellesley bomber aircraft. He explained what was involved, including a crack at the World Long Distance Record as well as the inevitable extra risks of flying long distances over water in the single-engined aircraft, and asked me if I would like the job. I had to be under twenty-five, very fit, unmarried and in my case a Spec 'N' navigator as well as a pilot, so I fitted the bill. It was, of course, a wonderful opportunity and I naturally accepted there and then without hesitation. Incidentally, when I told the family about my new appoint-

Inter Services Tennis Teams 1937. Seated from left. Capt. Horn, G/C Saul, G/C Hunter, BKB, Cdr. Muspratt, Col. Jameson, Cmdr. Glover, F/Lt Shaw. My brother Douglas is in the very back row on the right

ment my mother was slightly worried and said, 'Isn't it a bit dangerous with only one engine?' I replied, 'Well, there's only one engine to go wrong,' which seemed to satisfy her for the time being!

Later I was told that our Secretary of State for Air, Sir Kingsley-Wood, had been concerned about Hitler's warlike intentions and was keen, as at least some small deterrent, to show the Germans that although the RAF was still very small it was very efficient and capable of giving a good account of itself. At the end of 1937 he had, therefore, issued a decree that by the end of the next year (1938) the RAF was to have achieved the World Height record, the Speed record and the Long Distance Flight record. These were in fact all achieved but I'm afraid had no noticeable affect on Hitler!

My new posting to the LRDU was then a very satisfactory end to the year 1937. We had done quite well in the sporting field too, and my brother and I were ranked No. 3 and No. 5 respectively at Squash Rackets in England; Douglas also got to the Final of the Amateur Championships where unfortunately he lost to K. C. Gandar-Dower. I did also then manage to fit in another skiing holiday with Yvonne at Davos Dorf over Christmas before reporting to RAF Upper Heyford – now my favourite RAF station!

LRDU Group Photo

LONG RANGE DEVELOPMENT UNIT 1938

Two other members of my Spec 'N' course, George Musson and 'Scruffy' Sanders, were also selected for the LRDU and I already knew several of the other officers posted to the Unit which made it rather nice. We all reported to RAF Upper Heyford at the beginning of January 1938 together with some thirty Airmen Ground Crew under F/Sgt Hearnden.

The CO of the Unit was Wing Commander Oswald Gayford who had previously held the Long Distance Flight record in 1933 when he flew in the Fairey Monoplane with Flight Lieutentant Nicholetts from RAF Cranwell to Walvis Bay in South West Africa – a distance of 5,300 miles. He would not be taking part as one of the LRDU crews but as the 'non-playing captain' his experience would be invaluable to us all.

The Flight Commander was a Squadron Leader Richard Kellett and the aircrews were as follows:

Aircraft No	*Captain/1st Pilot*	*Navigator/2nd Pilot*	*W/Operator/3rd Pilot*
L2638	S/Ldr Richard Kellett	F/Lt Nick Gething	P/O Larry Gaine
L2639	F/Lt Harry (Rupert) Hogan	F/O George Musson	F/Sgt Dixon

My crew, Andrew Combe, self and Sgt Gray

L2680	F/Lt Andrew Combe	F/Lt Brian Burnett	Sgt Gray
?	F/Lt Gardner	F/O Thompson	?
?	F/Lt Paddy Dunn	F/Lt Sanders	Sgt Houghton

All the aircrew were pilots and took their share of flying the aircraft, and each crew was allotted a particular aircraft which was very helpful as we were then able to carry out all the tests ourselves on our own aircraft. The Wellesley had been designed by Barnes Wallis (well known later as the designer of the so-called bouncing bomb and Dam Busters fame) and was very strong with its geodetic construction. There were already two squadrons of them in RAF service but the LRDU aircraft were specially modified. The engine was different and was a 1010HP Rotary Bristol Pegasus XXII. It had a Rotol constant speed airscrew, used 100 octane fuel and was fitted with special long range tanks in the wings to hold 1,290 imperial gallons. The aircraft was also fitted with an automatic pilot. We did a lot of flying to get to know the aircraft and test the

LRDU Wellesleys in formation near Oxford

various items of new equipment, as well as to find out the best speeds to fly at to get the most economical fuel consumption. The fuselage was pretty narrow and congested, with the navigator and w/operator positions in line behind the pilot so, to change pilots, the first pilot had to have his seat let down from behind and climb out backwards while the 2nd pilot squeezed by to grab the flying controls and climb in for the seat to be pushed up behind him! If the automatic pilot was working this was not too bad, but it wasn't always! And one had to move fairly smartly.

On the record flight it was not intended to carry oxygen so the flight was planned for 10,000 feet but we were provided with special warm flying kit. Parachutes were also discarded because the extra weight was required for additional fuel. Also for the same reason we did not carry a dinghy, although about 60 per cent of the Egypt-Australia route was over the sea. This route was selected to enable a Great Circle course to be flown chiefly over British Commonwealth or diplomatically friendly territories. If forced to ditch in the sea the plan was to jettison all the fuel and hope that, as anticipated with the large wing span, the aircraft would remain afloat for quite a while. As an additional safety precaution, arrangements were also made to have three naval vessels (HMS *Deptford*, HMIS *Investigator* and HMAS *Swan*) stationed and in wireless communication in the Arabian Sea, the Bay of Bengal and the Timor Sea. Fortunately none of this was needed but it was comforting to know!

Roller map of our planned route for the record flight. S/Ldr Kellett, F/Lt Gething, F/Lt Musson, P/O Gaine, Sgt Dixon, F/Lt Hogan, Sgt Gray, Sgt Houghton, BKB, W/Cdr Gayford, F/Lt Sanders, F/Lt Dunn, F/Lt Combe

The lengths of our practice flights in England were gradually increased to 5–8 hours all round the British Isles. This was in itself unusual for a single-engined aircraft in those days but was essential to develop our long-range capability and our aircraft fuel consumption. In March we each did a longer 11-hour flight, including night flying of course, and in May all the crews were involved in a 12-hour duration flight. This was completed successfully by all the others but in L2680, my aircraft, we had engine trouble with a broken oil pipe and had to force-land at RAF Eastchurch after only 8.5 hours. This was particularly disturbing as we had earlier lost F/Lt Gardner and F/O Thomson and their aircraft on one of the long night flights over the North Sea. We were also due to do a 32-hour non-stop flight in only a few weeks' time to Ismailia via Alexandria in Egypt to the Persian Gulf, down to Basrah and back non-stop to land at Ismailia. The betting amongst the airmen on our crew in L2680 making it was not very high but fortunately all went well this time.

32-HOUR NON-STOP FLIGHT

At Cranwell it was foggy on take-off but we quickly climbed up through it and in due course, over France, we were rewarded with the amazing si-ght of the top of the Eiffel Tower sticking out above the fog or layer of low cloud. Otherwise the 32-hour flight on 7/8 July was uneventful and all four aircraft completed the long 4,300 mile trip successfully, at an average ground speed of 135 m.p.h. They then returned to Upper Heyford a week or so later in another non-stop flight of 16 hours.

Final preparations were then set in hand for a detailed inspection and service of the aircraft and engines prior to attempting the record flight from Egypt to Australia in October, which was thought to be the best month weatherwise.

However in August, the Prime Minister Neville Chamberlain returned from Munich and his negotiations with Hitler, believing that he had won 'peace in our time'. Everything, therefore, came to a halt with the LRDU and we went on leave. However, it was not long before we were all back again by the beginning of September, preparing for the record flight now postponed until early November. There was still much to do in checking fuel consumption figures following the thorough inspection and servicing of the engines. This was finally completed and all five aircraft flew out again to Ismailia, this time via Hal Far in Malta, on 24/25 October, and the Wing Commander also came out as an extra passenger in the fifth aircraft.

At Ismailia all the aircraft were ready to go on the record attempt but the Air Ministry insisted, despite an appeal by the W/Cdr, that the flight should be a formation of three aircraft only. This was a great pity and a grave disappointment to No. 4 (Paddy Dunn's) crew, and indeed to the rest of us who had been working so closely with them.

After the final preparations for an early start on 5 November, including weather briefing particularly concerning wind forecasts over the route, the aircrews went to bed early, while the three aircraft were rolled out on to the end of the specially lengthened runway and topped up fully with fuel. This was not done before owing to possible damage to the undercarriage with the take-off weight of 19,000 lbs, an overload of approximately 71 per cent.

3

THE RECORD 48-HOUR NON-STOP FLIGHT

ISMAILIA (EGYPT) TO DARWIN (AUSTRALIA) (5–7 NOVEMBER 1938)

The crews got up at 4.00 a.m., breakfasted at 4.45 a.m. and were down at the runway by 5.15 a.m. It was still quite dark but after bidding our farewells to the Wing Commander and the others it had become light enough to see the whole length of the runway, and the three aircraft took off satisfactorily. The No. 1 and No. 2 aircraft (LR1 and LR2) climbed to 10,000 feet and set off in formation at our planned speed of 180 m.p.h. In LR3, however, we were unable to raise the undercarriage so could not join them to start with. After struggling for about an hour we cut a hole in the port side of the fuselage and with the aid of the long arm of a fishing net (which I had conveniently brought to help pass things to the 1st Pilot and the Wireless Operator without getting up from my middle seat position) we managed to lever it up. Fortunately it stayed up and we were able to continue heading east and regain our proper track. It was with a big sigh of relief that we told LR1 and LR2, with whom we were in radio contact, that we were now on the way and would try to catch them up. Navigation over the Arabian Desert was mainly DR and track maintained by frequent drift readings and position lines from sun observations. For the latter and for Astro, the Mark VIII Sextant and Dreisenstok's Tables were used and, before the days of averaging sextants, it took a good twenty minutes to take and work out one sight to get a position line. The wireless operator was also able to get an occasional D/F bearing from Basrah north of our track, which gave us a check on our ground speed, and he regularly reported our position.

The weather cleared over the Persian Gulf with good visibility and we caught sight of LR2 for a few minutes before we reached Jask as the sun

Wireless Operator Sgt Gray inside our aircraft LR3

was setting on our first day. The first night was to be over India and we saw a bit of the west coast in the moonlight, but the mainland was completely covered by cloud and we had to rely entirely on celestial observations and a D/F bearing from Karachi. Dawn broke as we reached the east coast of India and we were able to pinpoint our position, about two or three miles north of track, to give us a good start across the Bay of Bengal where LR1 warned us that there were bad thunderclouds building up and suggested we try to avoid flying through them if possible. We soon ran into them and were in and out of thunderclouds and rain storms for the next four or five hours. I was flying myself part of this time and on one occasion banked very steeply to avoid a storm cloud and then found it really very difficult to get the aileron up and the aircraft level again, as I think the wing tank fuel must have moved across to weigh that wing down. It was rather alarming, as I seemed to be stuck for a while going round in circles, so I was rather more careful after that.

After my turn of piloting I returned to my navigating, and two successive sun sight position lines showed us that after all the cloud avoidance we had strayed quite a lot north of track, so course was altered to gradually close the gap by the time we were due to reach Malaya.

After that the weather improved a bit and we picked up the Malayan coast under good conditions and we were able to pinpoint our position. After crossing the Malay Peninsula, however, the storm clouds began to build up as night fell. We saw nothing of Borneo as we were in extremely heavy thunderstorms, rain and lightning for about six hours. We tried, unfortunately without success, to fly around some of this. Although the aircraft was bonded against lightning, it was very frightening to see it running along the leading edge of the wings (this is known as St Elmo's fire). After a while we decided to fly due south for thirty minutes or so and the weather was slightly better, so we altered course again to gradually close in on our original track and little by little the worst of the storms were left behind. We managed to get a D/F bearing from Singapore and a moon sight position line, which showed that we had deviated south of the track owing to the storms. On approaching Macassar Strait we got a sight of Banjermassin, and a further D/F bearing from Singapore and a moon position line confirmed that we were almost back on track again.

About an hour later we passed Macassar, and it was not long before we overtook the existing Russian record of 6,300 miles (from Moscow to San Francisco) which we celebrated with a nip from my brandy flask. The second night was nearly over, dawn was breaking with the worst of the weather left behind and we were reasonably confident then of making Darwin. It had been arranged with LR1 that the three aircraft should rendezvous over Lomblen Island before deciding on whether we had sufficient fuel left to get to Darwin across the 400-mile shark-infested Timor Sea. We had just done one circuit of Lomblen Island when we received information by R/T that LR1 had pushed on for Darwin a few minutes earlier and that LR2 was going to have to land at Koepang to refuel. After checking again very carefully our fuel position and our ground speed, ignoring a favourable tail wind forecast and assuming it to be a head wind, I was confident we could reach Darwin with about 13 gallons to spare, or about 45 minutes flying time – not a lot after almost two days in the air! We set off immediately for Darwin making frequent checks of drift and a D/F bearing from Darwin to ensure no possible error might creep in at the last minute. A rendezvous at Bathurst Island had been arranged with LR1 but this was unnecessary as LR1 was sighted ahead about three hours later. After making sure of ample fuel, we increased speed and joined up in formation with LR1 for the last 200 miles or so and landed together at Darwin airport at 0400 hours GMT

The two successful crews of LR1 & LR3 after landing at Darwin

(1300 hours local time) on 7 November after 48 hours, 5 minutes in the air. We had had an average head wind throughout of 10 m.p.h. instead of the slight tail wind forecast, and our average ground speed was 149 m.p.h. It had been tantalizing earlier to have to keep reducing our air speed as our weight went down in order to get the most economical fuel consumption. Towards the end we were supposed to be down to 115 m.p.h. only. In LR3 we were slightly concerned about the undercarriage, but it went down satisfactorily, and stood up all right on landing, thankfully.

The Aerodrome Control Officer at Darwin immediately inspected the fuel tank, engine, airframe and barograph seals of both the aircraft and took charge of the papers and barographs for forwarding to the Royal Aero Club, London to claim the World's Non-Stop Long Distance record for us of 7,162 nautical miles.

After landing at Darwin, LR1 still had a comfortable 44 gallons of petrol left and in LR3 we had 17 gallons which at our reduced weight and ground speed should have been enough for nearly another one hour flying time providing all went well. LR2 had been in a very unenviable position, so relatively close to its destination, but with even less fuel left the decision to land and refuel at Koepang was unquestionably right and they later flew straight on to Darwin and landed there about four hours later. They too had beaten the Russian record by some 350 miles.

In our aircraft, LR3, Andrew Combe did most of the piloting, about 24 hours; I did 13 hours as well as all the navigating and Sgt Gray did about 11 hours piloting and all the wireless operating. Sleep under the conditions inside the aircraft was hardly possible, particularly for the navigator who had to plan ahead before taking his turn at piloting and then catch up with the navigating immediately afterwards, but we were invigorated by successfully completing the flight and we had all managed to shave and wash and look smart before arrival, much to the surprise of the many people there to welcome us including Flight Sergeant Hearnden and some of our ground crew who had been flown out earlier on scheduled flights.

DARWIN (7–11 NOVEMBER)

After completing all the necessary formalities at the airport, the two Wellesley crews were taken down to a very welcome lunch at Government House or the Staff Corps Mess, before returning later to welcome the arrival of LR2 from Koepang. Later, after a bit of a rest, a shower and change we were all taken to a cocktail party, a Guest Night Dinner and a Victoria League Dance in the Town Hall, where the warmth of the Australian welcome was a sign of things to come!

The next day, after a late morning, official calls were made on the Resident, the Staff Corps Mess, the Naval District Officer and so on while the ground crew carried out inspections on the aircraft. We were also busy receiving and answering telegrams of congratulations and writing our official reports. Later F/Lt Paddy Heffernan of the Royal Australian Air Force, who was in charge of the RAAF Anson flight which was to fly some of our ground crew around, arrived; we all ended up at another cocktail party on HMAS *Swan* which had come in from the Timor Sea where it had been on patrol for us.

It was, of course, very hot in Darwin and particularly so for our ground crew working on our aircraft, which were picketed out in the open on the airfield, there being no hangar accommodation available. It was remarkable that only a few minor replacements were found necessary after such an exacting flight, including the broken spring in LR3's undercarriage which had caused us so much concern after taking off from Ismailia.

Unfortunately swimming in the sea was dangerous at that time of the year with nasty jellyfish, apart from possible sharks and crocodiles. Some

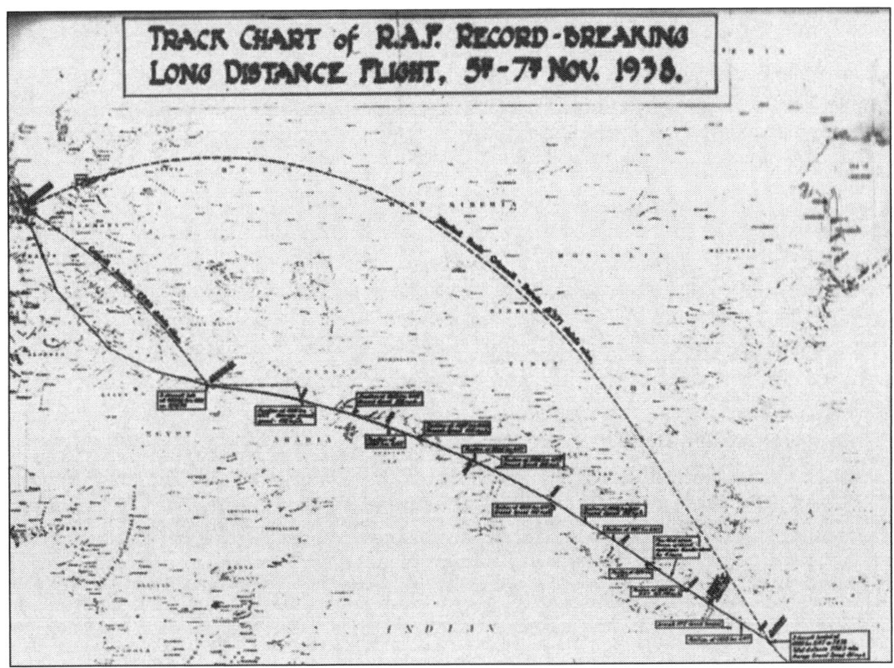

Record route, Egypt to Australia (compared with shortest route from England)

of the 'Poms' however, did go bathing but Nick Gething got stung by a jellyfish, though luckily not too badly. George Musson and I, more sensibly, played some tennis with the local champions, and we all had a very pleasant quiet evening round at Government House.

The following day was 11 November and we all attended the Armistice Day parade before checking the aircraft for our departure the next morning. The officer aircrew went for a pre-lunch drink at the Residency where we were persuaded to teach Dorothy Abbott, their daughter, the 'Lambeth Walk' and the 'Palais Glide', the latest London favourites. Incidentally, most of us had wanted to fly on south towards Brisbane straight away but Richard Kellett decided to stay on in Darwin for the five nights. We didn't discover until later that he was busy courting Dorothy Abbott who in due course he duly married! Anyway it enabled us to catch up with some of our report and letter writing in reply to the many telegrams and messages we received.

That afternoon George and I played golf but abandoned the ball if it went into the rough which was full of poisonous snakes! The so called 'greens', or rather 'browns' were interesting to putt on as snakes had often crawled over them and left their marks which had to be smoothed over first.

Our route round Australia

Another amusing party that evening with the 'Returned Soldiers League' in the Town Hall rounded off our interesting stay in Darwin and our first experience of the very warm hospitality extended to us throughout Australia.

CLONCURRY (12–13 NOVEMBER)

The next day we took off in formation to fly to Cloncurry and we got a good idea of the vast extent of the bush land and scrub in Northern Australia, with the dried up river beds and occasionally a few houses constituting a small town. There were millions of flies and a large crowd to greet us with the usual official speeches before we were driven to the Post Office Hotel where we were to stay. Later there was the inevitable beer drinking and the local cinema show.

Cloncurry is a relatively small town in the centre of the copper mining area in Queensland and the next day some of us were driven out to see some of the mines whilst others went out on a kangaroo, emu and wild turkey hunt which was very interesting. In the evening there was another very enjoyable 'Returned Soldiers' party with the usual speeches by everyone. One of the remarks overheard was: 'Good on the bastards; their blood's worth bottling!' Another was 'We diggers' wives are short of husbands tonight!'

BRISBANE (14–16 NOVEMBER)

The next day we took off early in formation for Brisbane and complied with a number of requests to fly round low over three or four airfields en route before landing at Archerfield at 1500 hours LT after a 7.5 hour flight. There was a colossal crowd there and a great reception organized with a welcome by the Governor of Queensland (Sir Leslie Wilson) and then speeches by the Premier and the Lord Mayor and others, to which Richard Kellett had to reply, before making further broadcasts on the record flight. The aircraft were wheeled into the large new hangar which Qantas Empire Airways had very kindly cleared out for us, and we were driven to the Bellevue Hotel where we were staying. Richard Kellett and three of the aircrew later dined with the Governor and the other three were welcomed to a wedding party and dance at the Bellevue.

The next morning was taken up with official calling, a Civic Reception in the Town Hall by the Lord Mayor with a very big crowd and lots of speeches and autographs, then lunch at the University Club. The ground crew, who had come on in the RAAF Ansons, were busy servicing and cleaning down the Wellesleys. In the afternoon there was golf at the Indooropilly Club or squash for some, and in the evening George and I were invited to a private dinner party and dance at the Bellevue.

Arrangements had been made by the Premier on the following day for the whole of the LRDU party, including the maintenance personnel, for a drive out to Southport beach for surf bathing. Schools had been given a holiday to line the route and they had a field day of flag waving and autograph hunting. For us it was a lovely day of relaxation and at 'Surfer's Paradise' we changed quickly into our bathers to enjoy the big surf. After lunch at Southport we were driven on to Coolangatta and Tweeds Head, where we saw a shark in the water and were given demonstrations of their efficient life-saving system.

Back in Brisbane, George and I were taken to the dance at the Bellevue again by some of the 'Brisbane beauties', and Wing Commander Gayford arrived from Egypt to join the LRDU for the rest of the tour.

After showing friends round the aircraft the next morning we were seen off by the Premier and, needless to say, a koala bear or two! As we took off for Sydney we were all very sorry to leave Brisbane where everyone was so hospitable.

SYDNEY (17–28 NOVEMBER)

The flight down the east coast in formation was very pleasant with a number of pauses to circle round towns as requested – Southport, Coolongatta, Casino, Grafton, Newcastle and others – before rendezvousing with the RAAF escort of Ansons and Demons over Narromina to fly over Sydney and land at Mascot (Kingsford-Smith) Aerodrome at 12.30 after about four hours. Here, there was a colossal crowd and reception by the New South Wales (NSW) Premier, Lord Mayor and other dignatories with a lunch party in the Club and the usual speeches and broadcasting.

During lunch and, despite the presence of RAAF guards, some of the public had somehow got into the Wellesleys to do a bit of souveniring and went off with three of the officers' Field Service Caps, including mine, which became embarrassing at some of the official functions later. Fortunately after comments in the local press they were returned to us after a few days.

The Wellesleys arriving over Kingsford-Smith Aerodrome

After further showing people around the aircraft, we took off again for the thirty-minute flight to RAAF Richmond where we were to be staying and were welcomed by the Station Commander, Group Captain De la Rue. There we were able to settle down in the Mess, unpack, write letters and answer invitations as well as catch up with the rest of our luggage and clothes which had been flown out for us from England.

Richmond was about forty miles out of Sydney so we were provided with three Wolseley 14 h.p. cars by General Motors, as well as free petrol by Shell. We drove ourselves in to Sydney in the morning to go to the bank and post office, and to make our official calls on the Premier (Mr Stevens) at Government House – also the Lord Mayor, Victoria Barracks and HMAS *Canberra*. Lunch was at the Imperial Services Club before returning to Richmond for a quiet evening.

From then on the hospitality and entertainment, both official and private, was relentless with lunches, cocktail parties, dinners and dances at Romanos almost every day – so much so that we decided to avoid a lot of the driving to and from Richmond and to move in to stay in town at one of the clubs – three of us at the Union and three at the Imperial Services Club. The highlight of the official welcome was probably the ticker-tape drive in open cars through the city with a colossal turnout of the crowds, finishing up at Parliament House for a Public Reception and State Lunch with the usual speeches by the Premier, the Deputy Leader of the Opposition and replies by the Wing Commander, and this time Rupert Hogan on the Record Flight (in the absence of Kellett who was ill in bed). There was lunch for four of us at Government House, the Lord Mayor's Reception when he was presented by Oswald Gayford with a silver memento of the visit by the LRDU; later the famous Australian aviator Sir Keith Smith's cocktail party was also special.

Other day time activities were, of course, surfing on Bondi and Manly beaches, sailing, golf, squash, watching the Inter-State Tennis (Victoria and NSW) and a drive up into the Blue Mountains to the Lapstone Hotel for a swim in their pool followed by a dinner and dance. At the weekends we tended to split up into twos or threes to join particular friends, and George and I had a lovely final Sunday with Jo and Pat Hughes out at Cronulla Beach where the surf was quite big and good fun. So, a wonderful time was had by all, except for poor Richard Kellett who had not been feeling well since Brisbane, and who seemed to be getting worse. He had stayed in bed over the weekend with a temperature and couldn't make it for the ticker-tape and official reception on the Monday.

Ticker-tape reception in Sydney

The doctors were very worried as they couldn't diagnose his illness though they thought he had got meningeal poisoning. I suspected it was something to do with a bad oyster. Richard loved them and it was the height of the oyster season. I don't like them myself so Richard always invited me to sit next to him so that he could have mine as well! Perhaps I was lucky there. He was, anyway, very seriously ill and some even feared for his life. He was moved into Tusculum Hospital where they decided to operate. After this he made satisfactory progress but it was going to be some time and it was unlikely for him to be able to join us for the rest of the tour.

At RAAF Richmond a forty-hour inspection and servicing of the Wellesleys was carried out by the ground crews and only minor repairs and changes, for example to a magneto showing unusual wear, were found to be necessary.

On Monday 28th, when final packing and preparations were being made for our departure from Sydney the next morning, engine and test flights were carried out when disaster struck LR1 which was being flown by Nick Gething (Richard Kellett still being in hospital). He was extremely unlucky for the engine to cut out just after taking off at about 500 feet and he did very well to get the Wellesley down as he did in a ploughed field, which was the only flat ground within range. No one was hurt luckily and, although the airframe was a write-off, it might have been very much worse.

That evening, our last in Sydney, the LRDU gave a large cocktail party for some 250 people in return for the great hospitality accorded us by everyone in Sydney, and some of us ended up in a dinner dance party at the Lapstone Hotel until the early hours.

We were again extremely sorry the next day to leave Sydney, where we had had a magnificent time, and still more sorry of course that we were having also to leave Richard Kellett and the LR1 crew behind, who would have to go back to England by boat.

CANBERRA (29–30 NOVEMBER)

LR2 and LR3 took off early for Canberra which was only a 1.5 hour flight. There was the usual reception at the airfield, though somewhat smaller, of course, than at Sydney or Brisbane. We were then taken for a drink at the Canberra Hotel, where the Federal Government were very kindly putting us up, and we then went for an hour's drive round the town and up Red Hill to look down on the famous circular layout of the capital. After a short visit to Parliament House, where there was a debate on the Estimates going on, and after introductions to some of the leading Ministers we returned to the Canberra hotel for lunch with the Premier (Mr Lyons) and his Ministers. Whilst there, Prime Minister Lyons in his speech stressed that the LRDU flight had shown that the range of modern aircraft was increasing rapidly and that Australia was now much closer to the outside world. The danger of aggression was probably greater but he emphasized the importance of even greater co-operation in Imperial Defence and, in particular, between Great Britain and Australia. There had, I was told, been some concern regarding Japanese intentions, particularly in the north-west of Australia, where they were involved in the pearl fishing off the Australian coast. In any case, the Australian public undoubtedly felt happier that our flights had shown that GB could come to their aid fairly quickly if need be, and this I think was probably the main reason for their great interest in the LRDU aircraft and their wonderful welcome and hospitality to us throughout our two-month tour.

After lunch we were driven to visit Duntroon Military College, and a party of the cadets then came to the aerodrome to be shown around the aircraft and given a short talk by Hogan and Musson on the record flight and the navigation involved. Andrew Combe and I were taken on a fifty-mile drive in the country to see a typical sheep station by a Mr and Mrs Eddison whose son had been one of my pupils at No. 11 FTS, RAF Wittering.

The next morning we had a swim in the hotel pool before breakfast and then called on the Governor General (Lord Gowrie) who came out after lunch to the airfield to say goodbye to us and see us take off for Melbourne.

MELBOURNE (30 NOVEMBER–4 DECEMBER)

Less than three hours later, after meeting up with the RAAF escort of Ansons and Demons, we landed at Essendon Aerodrome outside Melbourne. Surprisingly we had to fly through rain and snow storms en route, and it was very cold at Essendon so we were glad to get into our blue uniform again. There was the usual reception by a very large crowd, many speeches and a tea party, before showing people round the Wellesleys and taking off again for the RAAF station at Laverton where we flew low round the town before landing half an hour or so later. A few drinks were then had in the Mess before a shower and change into Mess kit for a Guest Night dinner.

This was another big visit and it started the next morning with an open car drive with police escort through the streets of Melbourne; a call on the Governor (Lord Huntingfield); a call on the Lord Mayor and a Civic Reception at the Town Hall and finally a call on the Premier at Parliament House followed by lunch with the State Government. After that we settled in at the Australia Club, where we had decided to stay, and got down to some letter writing and answering of the many invitations. Later there was a cocktail party given by Air Commodore Goble of the RAAF and we were all guests at the theatre for *I Married an Angel* when we visited the Angels at the back in the interval!

The next day there were further calls to be made and lunch with the Governor (Lord Huntingfield) while the ground crew were busy servicing the aircraft. Rupert Hogan and I also fitted in a game of squash at the Naval and Military Club. The Shell Company gave a cocktail party at the Menzies Hotel, where there was also a reception given by the Royal Society of St George with the High Commissioner for GB (Sir Geoffrey Whiskard) and the LRDU as the guests of honour with a little light musical entertainment. Later George Musson and I were taken to a dance party at the Palais de Danse. Our two wireless operators (Dixon and Gray) were also there and after much Australian champagne, all four of us had to get up and say a few words before the microphone.

The weekend was relatively quiet with some golf and bathing in the sea, and Hogan took Lord Huntingfield and his ADC up for a flight in LR2 as they had showed such great interest in the aircraft. On the Saturday evening we were guests of the Royal Aero Club at a dance at Essendon, with our own parties of friends, and it all ended up at the Embassy Night Club until dawn.

Sunday was a quiet morning and in the afternoon we went our different ways; Hogan and Combe to see friends at Geelong and George Musson and I for a long drive into the country to see some distant relations of George. We all returned for an early night at the Australia Club before an early take-off the next morning for Hobart in Tasmania.

HOBART, TASMANIA (5–7 DECEMBER)

It was about a three-hour flight to the Cambridge Airfield, the other side of the river from Hobart town and the Imperial Hotel where we were staying, and we were warmly welcomed by Mr Roche of the Royal Aero Club. Official calls were then made and the good news of Hogan's promotion to Squadron Leader came through. A proposed quiet evening then developed into a big one after champagne for dinner, drinks with the ground crew and a private house party.

The next morning we were all taken on a very pleasant cruise on the Premier's launch round Hobart harbour, with bathing for some and plenty of beer for everyone. This we followed with a drive up Mount Wellington and back a different way to see some of the lovely country. Later there was a cocktail party at the Naval and Military Club before a dinner given by the Royal Aero Club of Tasmania.

Inspections and checking of the aircraft the following morning were then carried out before George and I played golf at Kingston with Mr Nettlefold, who had also organized a fishing expedition for Hogie and Andrew Combe in the Great Lakes. The last two arrived back very late and very wet from heavy rain, but at least Andrew was happy having caught one fish!

We got the ferry across the harbour the next morning to drive out to Cambridge airfield and we took off for Adelaide after what had been a very pleasant and relaxing visit to Tasmania.

ADELAIDE (8–11 DECEMBER)

The flight to Adelaide took about six hours and we landed at Parafield airfield after circling low over the town. It was very warm there after Tasmania, and after the usual welcome reception and speeches we were driven into town to the Richmond Hotel, where we were to stay. It was then a quiet evening for all, though George and I were kindly dined first by Dr and Mrs Wunderly who seemed to be in charge of most of the excellent entertainment arrangements.

The following morning was spent answering invitations and official calls, with a reception by the Lord Mayor and lunch at Government House while the ground crew carried out a twenty-hour inspection of the aircraft. The next two days over the weekend there were several lunch parties, golf both days for George and me, and the races at Victoria Park for the others, as well as a motor trip to Victor Harbour arranged by members of the Royal Aero Club and Australian Flying Corps Association. Every evening ended up at the Wunderlys and on the Saturday they entertained us to one of the best parties of the trip at a dinner and dance at the South Australia Hotel, escorted by her four 'Wonders' and a visit to the Blue Grotto later for further dancing and bacon and eggs in the early hours. Mrs Wunderly was truly wonderful the way she looked after us all and we were sorry to leave her and Adelaide on the Monday morning.

PERTH (12–14 DECEMBER)

We took off from Parafield about 9.00 a.m. and, after a 9.25 hour flight, landed at RAAF Pearce where we were met by Wing Commander Brownell. There it was very warm and we were glad to be wearing khaki shorts and shirts only. Considering the airfield was some thirty miles outside Perth, there was quite a large crowd to welcome us, but there was apparently considerable disappointment that we had not flown over the town before landing, particularly as an escort of RAAF Ansons had been waiting for us there. We had had no information about this, so agreed to make up for it when departing. Not long after landing, we were driven into town to stay at the Perth Club.

The programme for the next day was the usual official calls ending up with a Civic Reception by the Lord Mayor, whilst the aircraft were inspected and refuelled by the ground crew at Pearce. After the lunch we were taken to Cottesloe beach for a bathe and then a cocktail party at the

Ready to set off from Perth. BKB, Smithers, Musson, Gayford, Pat Keenan, Hogan

Naval, Military and Air Force Club; after which we all ended up at the Oyster Beds for food, dance at Rosy Lee's and finally a midnight bathe at Cottesloe. Several future long-term friends, Pat and Mary Keenan, 'Smithers' and others were in the party and helped to make our stay in Perth most enjoyable. The following day we were taken for a drive up the coast to Yanchep for a bathe, State Luncheon and visit to caves. In the evening the Royal Aero Club gave a cocktail party at Maylands and we had a very enjoyable dinner with the Keenans.

Early the next morning we were driven out to RAAF Pearce where we showed round the aircraft to many friends before taking off and flying low over Perth and Fremantle and heading north to Port Hedland.

PORT HEDLAND, WA (15 DECEMBER)

It was another fairly long 7.5 hour flight to Port Hedland where there was a Civic Reception for us at the local pub (Pier Hotel). It was the most amazing, if not the best to date and, when the speeches were over, they all drank the Wing Commander's health and sang 'Why was he born so beautiful'! Amongst other priceless remarks Port Hedland was referred to as the 'Liverpool of Western Australia' and when the Wing Commander said to a small girl holding a little dog, 'I suppose that is a Port Hedland terrier?' she replied indignantly, 'No, it's a Marble Bar Pom!'

After some heavy beer drinking it was early to bed for all, and competition for the beds on the balcony was great as it was very hot and sticky. The temperature at Marble Bar (fifty miles away) was 117 degrees and was reputed to be the hottest place in WA. It was an early rise the next morning as we were due for another longish flight to Darwin and we took off at 0800 hours.

DERBY, WA (16–26 DECEMBER)

After about four hours Hogan's aircraft (L2639) with the Wing Commander also on board, developed a bad oil leak and was forced to land on what (from 10,000 feet) looked like quite a good open space half way between Derby and Wyndham. After landing, the crew jumped out to show that no one was hurt. In L2680 we circled overhead pinpointing the position accurately and dropping all available sandwiches and food, cigarettes, matches etc. (in a spare flying topee!) before flying back to Derby the nearest airfield (about one hour away) to organize a rescue party and more food. By then the RAAF Ansons with our ground crew were at Derby, as they had to refuel there anyway, and I went later that afternoon with one of them to drop a message on the Aboriginal Mission at Walcott Inlet asking them to send out a rescue party. It was the nearest habitation, and was thirty-three miles by air from the L2639 crash site (known in future as Rotol Reach where the Rotol Airscrew ceased to function). Unfortunately there was not time as well, before dark, to drop more food and other things for the crew of '39 who had to spend the night in the bush in or around the aircraft. Andrew Combe and I and the Anson RAAF officers were very kindly put up by Mr Rowell of Monger and Company on his house verandah and the others stayed at the small Port Hotel in Derby. The evening was spent trying to find some better local maps and discussing local landing grounds at Munja and Mt. House.

The next morning we took off early in L2680 to show one of the Ansons the way to Rotol Reach, to drop a cargo of food and anything else the '39 crew might need, as well as messages explaining the position about the rescue party. We then went to find Mt. House landing ground but it was too small for us and still under construction. We also had a good look again at Munja, the Walcott landing ground which, though also rather small and inclined to be boggy after rain, we hoped might be all right for our remaining Wellesley to take off from with a light load.

Forced landing of No. 2 aircraft at Rotol Reach

On landing at Rotol Reach on what proved to be the pretty rough ground of a dried up lake, '39 had badly damaged its undercarriage and tail unit, and the chances of getting repairs done and a proper runway cleared in the near future were nil, particularly as the rains had just started with heavy storms every night making the ground boggier every day. We decided, therefore, to concentrate on evacuating the crew of '39 first before recommending any decision on salvaging the aircraft. W/T communication with Wyndham W/T station had been set up, using '39's accumulator while it lasted out, and with that of '80's from Derby, as well as through the local post office; so progress reports were sent daily to the Air Ministry and the Melbourne Airboard.

There were no supplies of our special 100 octane petrol or oil for the Wellesley at Derby so we had to make do with the same as the Ansons, which were more suitable anyway for the supply dropping and consequently used more often, whilst '80 underwent further thorough inspections clearly needed after so many long flights. One night there was a particularly big storm over Derby which they called a 'Cockeye Bob' and which lasted much longer than usual. It started with a sudden gale filling the houses with sand and dust, and was followed not long after by a deluge of rain with almost continuous flashes of lightning. Luckily there was a guard out on the aerodrome and they were kept busy hammering in the pegs picketing the aircraft down. One of the Ansons was swung round in a circle but fortunately was well clear of the other aircraft so no damage was done.

The Ansons maintained a continuous patrol by day with either Andrew Combe or me on board, to drop food or messages for the '39 crew and also for the Walcott rescue party (one white man, Mr Burgin, and five Aboriginals) who had set out for Rotol Reach over the weekend and needed pointing in the right direction periodically. The rescue party made themselves easy to locate by lighting a bush fire as soon as they heard or saw us overhead. They finally arrived at the aircraft on the Monday afternoon of 17 December and were gladly welcomed by the '39 crew, but some of them were rather exhausted having moved very fast and covered the forty-five miles or so over very difficult rough terrain in only two days, so Mr Burgin decided not to start back with the '39 crew until the following morning. This they did, with the Ansons keeping an eye on them, and dropping further food including blocks of ice to keep it cool. The Aboriginals had not come across ice before and were rather frightened by it, being puzzled by the burning sensation when they first picked it up!

With several days of hard walking through the rough bush ahead of them, the '39 crew had difficulty, before abandoning the aircraft, in deciding which of all their valuables to take with them as very little apart from the food could be carried. Progress was necessarily fairly slow over the steep, stony and hilly country, and they had to have four night stops on the way, usually near a pool of water to wash in. The locals showed their skill in catching any alligators by shoving a big stick down their throats as soon as they opened their jaws, and then dragging them out and beating them to death. Unfortunately one of the men (Adcock) slipped up on one occasion and did get bitten. Luckily it was only his arm and, with the aid of the medical kit they had with them, they managed to stop the flow of blood with a tourniquet and put the arm in a sling. He was still in much pain, however, and on the last day was sent on ahead to Munja for further treatment. There he also helped by organising a chair party to be sent out the last few miles for Sgt Dixon, who had had an accident earlier and scalded a leg badly so that he could only hobble along fairly slowly and was holding up the others. George Musson incidentally kept a diary of their adventures during their enforced stay at Rotol Reach and their five-day trek back to Munja. This was published in the *RAF Quarterly* in October 1939 and makes interesting reading.

W/Cdr Gayford, Musson and Hogan returning through the bush with Aboriginal rescue party

When not involved in any way with the rescue, some of us at Derby went shooting in the bush and came back with several kangaroo skins – also a baby roo which we fed with goat's milk and kept on the Rowells' verandah, where it hopped about and kept us awake at night!

One of the days, also, Andrew and Sgt Gray did a dummy run to Munja landing ground in '80 to make sure it was OK and on Saturday 24 December he landed there again, ready to evacuate the crew of '39 who finally got there about 1.00 p.m. with Dixon carried back in state in the portable chair! After a warm welcome by Mr Reid (the CO at Walcott) and his wife, with iced drinks, beer and food, and many photos of the 'bushmen' who were looking the part with eight days' growth of beard, Andrew flew back George and Dixon to Derby. He then refuelled and set off again for Munja to collect the Wing Commander and Rupert Hogan whom he brought back to Derby before dark. Dixon had been admitted into hospital straight away so that his leg could have proper treatment, and the others were glad to have a good shower and change into borrowed clothes at the Rowells' house. After supper all felt rather weary and decided on an early night, although George and I were persuaded to put in an appearance at the Children's Party and the Bachelor's Dance but didn't stay long. Our ground crew, however, and

F/Lt Paddy Heffernan, in charge of our Australian escort, with baby roo

the Australian Anson group apparently kept the Christmas Eve party going until the small hours.

The next day, Sunday, was Christmas Day and we were glad to have the crew of '39 back again and little the worse for their adventure in the barren north-west Australian bush. Most of the morning was spent in washing clothes and finding some to lend to the '39 crew who had had to leave almost everything behind at Rotol Reach. A magnificent Christmas dinner had been prepared for us at the Port Hotel, with turkey and plum pudding and even crackers, and of course, large jugs of beer! It developed into quite a party with everybody's health being drunk in turn, including the owner of the Ice Bar and the cook who had difficulty not only in speaking but in standing up, as she had drunk all the brandy sauce for the pudding!

The Wing Commander had had plenty of time at Rotol Reach to discuss with Mr Burgin any possible plans for salvaging '39 and had reluctantly decided that it would have to be abandoned. A message had been sent accordingly to the Australian Board and Air Ministry. This was confirmed so, before leaving, the '39 crew packed all the instruments in the aircraft and clothes in their suitcases in the wing boxes; and they left in the aircraft cigarettes and native tobacco and, what the aboriginals liked even more, plenty of red and yellow striped message bags! This was to encourage the proposed return party later, with Mr Burgin and a pack of mules, to salvage the luggage and as much of the equipment and instruments as possible.

A signal was finally received on Christmas Eve from the Air Ministry to say that '80 was not to fly back alone and that all LRDU personnel were to return by boat, with '80 dismantled and shipped back to the Middle East. It was probably a wise decision as the Wellesleys with their single engine had undoubtedly taken quite a beating with all the long flights and without the possibility of any real major servicing. Nevertheless, we in '80 were extremely disappointed and it signalled a rather sad end to our wonderful tour of Australia. Arrangements for our return to UK by boat were put in hand straight away.

It had been an interesting enforced stay at Derby over Christmas with the temperature in the 90s, tremendous storms, enormous boab trees and the long tram ride down the pier to its tide of 36 feet – supposed to be the second largest in the world. In '80 we finally took off on 27 December for Perth again, taking the Wing Commander with us, seen off by most of Derby after we had thanked them all profusely for all their willing help over the last eleven days. We landed at RAAF Pearce in the early afternoon followed later by Paddy Heffernan and his Ansons, and although the station had virtually closed down over the Christmas period, we were all able to stay the night there. The aircraft '80 was put into a hangar ready for dismantling for shipment to the Middle East. We were sorry to leave it as it had done us so well for so many hours of flying.

Hogie, George and Dixon were collected from Derby a couple of days later by two RAAF Ansons from Pearce, as Paddy Heffernan and his escort party had left for Adelaide and Sydney having completed their job of escorting the Wellesleys round Australia – and very well too.

PERTH AGAIN (27 DECEMBER–2 JANUARY 1939)

The Wing Commander and four of us all moved into Perth and our headquarters were made at the Weld Club, when bookings were made for us on P&O SS *Strathnaver* due to leave Fremantle on 2 January. The Imprest Account and other business needed to be finalized and the '39 crew had to get busy buying a few clothes to wear on board ship as they had had to leave everything at Rotol Reach.

Our aircraft LR2680 at Perth

In the meantime, Pat and Mary Keenan and 'Smithers' had got busy organizing parties for us, including bathing at Cottesloe beach every day and an enormous New Year's Eve party at the Karryump Golf Club. New Year's Day was a late morning for all of us before two drinks parties before lunch to say goodbye and thanks to the many friends we had made in Perth. On our last day we had the best surfing so far at Scarborough, before sailing from Fremantle after a great party on board ship with all the many friends who had come to see us off.

RETURN TO UK ON SS *STRATHNAVER* (JANUARY 1939)

The journey home on SS *Strathnaver* was very pleasant, particularly the first part as Pat and Mary Keenan were also on board as far as Bombay in India where he was stationed in the Army. Later, I somehow got German measles and was banished to a cabin on my own in quarantine at the aft end of the ship, so was restricted primarily to reading. But it was a good rest lying in the sun and catching up with letter writing.

Richard Kellett had gradually got better in Sydney and with his other '38 crew members, Nick Gething and Larry Gaine, embarked on RMS *Orford* in Melbourne for their return to UK. Incidentally, one of the passengers on board was a Miss Mardi Gepp who got engaged to Nick

On Strathnaver

Gething and later married him in England. What with Kellett's marriage to Dorothy Abbott, the daughter of the Governor of Northern Australia, the LRDU had not done badly on the romantic front in bringing back two Australian girls to England!

After returning to UK the LRDU was dissolved and we all went to new appointments, but we got together on several particularly memorable occasions. Shell invited us to a reception including a film of various aspects of our Wellesley flights and made a very nice presentation to each of us – a silver cigarette case with the Ismailia to Darwin route for the Long Distance Flight marked out in morse code 'Per Ardua ad Austral(ia)'– the bit in brackets being the amount by which the 7,162 miles had beaten the previous Russian record.

Another big event we all attended on 24 February was an enormous luncheon at Leathersellers Hall given by the Lord Mayor of London and Sir Kingsley Wood, the Secretary of State for Air, to meet the LRDU crews and a representative party of our maintenance personnel. The Chief of the Air Staff (Air Chief Marshal Sir Cyril Newall) and the whole of the Air Council were present together with hundreds of other guests who had been associated in any way with the LRDU and the Record Flight. Many congratulatory speeches were made to which Wing Commander Gayford and Richard Kellett made replies.

The other big occasion for some of us lucky ones was, of course, the Investiture at Buckingham Palace. In the New Years Honours list the two crews who had successfully made it to Darwin were awarded the Air Force Cross (AFC), with the AFM for Sgt Gray. This was unfortunately badly spoilt for us as the crew of '39 who had landed first in Timor were most surprisingly, and most unfairly we all thought, not included in the awards, so much so that the six of us lucky ones tried to refuse our awards, but were not allowed to. They had after all been in on the long distance flying development work and had held the world record for a few hours before the two of us landed at Darwin. Regretfully all appeals, however, were in vain.

Another incidental worry I had that day was that the full dress uniform which I had hired from Moss Bros for the occasion arrived for me at the RAF Club on the morning of the Investiture without any RAF Wings on it. The King was known to be very strict over dress and, as the award was a flying one, I was sure he would notice the missing Wings and perhaps refuse to give me the AFC! I think he probably did notice but was kind enough not to embarrass me and spoil the day for me! It may seem strange that as a regular permanent commission officer I did not have my own full dress uniform and was having to hire one. To a new entry Pilot Officer on 16*s.* 6*d.* a day it was a very expensive item particularly bearing in mind that it was only worn normally for weddings or investitures. Consequently a tradition had grown up over the years with Burberry's, the main provider of RAF uniforms and clothing in the 1930s, that they would hire out our full dress uniforms with appropriate badges of rank free if an officer kept a debit account of more than £10. This was not difficult to arrange and had always worked extremely well in the past. However, the uniform earmarked for me on this occasion had been hired out for a wedding to an Equipment Officer who had handed it in a day or two late and it was sent to me in a hurry at the RAF Club only on the morning of our Investiture without it being checked properly. Needless to say I was not pleased and made sure it would not ever happen again – to me anyway!

I should have mentioned earlier that in 1934, when on my initial course at RAF Cranwell, I had been persuaded to join the RAF Club in London for half a day's pay which was of course exceptionally good value. I used it regularly for many years before the War to stay the night when I visited London and played squash for the Club in the Bath Club Cup. I have now been a member for seventy years and for free after fifty years!

4

SCHOOL OF AIR NAVIGATION, RAF MANSTON (1939)

My new appointment in the UK was as the Navigation Instructor on the Short 'N' Course at the School of Air Navigation at RAF Manston and I was soon back to normal RAF life, having been promoted to Squadron Leader on 1 April. This was good going at the age of just twenty-six, even with the rapid expansion of the RAF at that time. It was not long then before Rupert Hogan's wedding to Venetia took place, followed in May by Andrew Combe and Eileen. All the LRDU officers attended as Guards of Honour in full dress uniform. Great occasions, both of them, as we had known the brides-to-be for some time when we were at RAF Upper Heyford before we did the Australia flight. Richard Kellett and Nick Gething also got married around that time to their Australian girlfriends, who had come back to England on the boat with them.

In March I had been selected to play squash for England in the International match against Scotland. It was the same weekend as the England/Scotland rugger match which was fun as we were able to go and watch that too. I was not sure how I was going to get up to Edinburgh in time, but luckily a Fleet Air Arm pilot landed at RAF Manston and was staying over the weekend. I persuaded him to let me fly his Wallace aircraft up there to RAF Turnhouse and back early on the Monday morning. It seems today extraordinary that this was permitted, but in those days, when aircraft were relatively simple to fly, pilots often used to borrow, for short flights usually, any different types of aircraft that landed on their station. It was considered to be quite useful flying experience. Anyway, this opportunity was a great relief to me and, after collecting my squash kit and seeing the Wallace refuelled, I set off happily on my way up north landing en route at RAF Cottesmore to pick up another member of the English squash team, S/Ldr Hank More. It

Andrew Combe at his wedding with me as best man

only took about three and a half hours flying each way and we got to the match on time! In Edinburgh Hank and I were kindly put up by an old tennis friend of mine, Nancy Dickin (by then Lady MacPherson-Grant) who also lent us their Morris Minor to drive about in. Over the weekend we won the squash for England.

That summer at weekends I played in several RAF tennis matches, including one against the All England Club, Wimbledon. Unfortunately we were rained off but Gus Holden and I played bridge with two members of the Club Committee (Eric Peters and Ted Avory) which led in due course to them putting us up for membership of the Club. However with the war intervening this didn't happen until 1950! Most of August then I was on leave and I played in the RAF tennis and regained the Championship, beating on the way my old friend Gus who had won in my absence in Egypt the year before. I also won the Doubles, again with my partner Dick Shaw for the fourth time. My brother Douglas also played for the Army in the Inter-Services match, but we didn't actually play each other. That month, I also played in the Bournemouth and Phyllis Court tennis tournaments. For the latter I was able to stay conveniently at home at Hurley and look after my Sydney girlfriend, Josephine Hughes, who had looked after us so well out there and had come to visit England. She had got a good job as

Jo Hughes at Traddles with Mum, Dad and cousins Dorlas and Sukie

private secretary to a big company chairman (GEC I think) in London and was able to come and stay with me and my family at Hurley most weekends. Finally in the last week in August I went to stay with my great friends the Thompsons at Holbeach Hurn and played with them in the tennis tournament at Hunstanton. There, I was in all three semi-finals – singles, doubles with George and mixed with Dulcie Thompson – but at 2.00 a.m. on 30 August we were woken at the little Beach House where we were staying by a policeman, who said I was to report as soon as possible to RAF Abingdon ready to leave for France later that day with the Advanced Air Striking Force. That ended the tennis tournament for me and my holiday in Norfolk, and I immediately packed and left in the dark thirty minutes later to drive south to Manston to collect my uniform and everything before heading west to Abingdon in Berkshire. My route took me past our home at Hurley, so I called in to say goodbye to my parents and telephoned RAF Abingdon to say I was running a bit late but would be there within an hour. I was then told, 'Don't worry, old boy, tomorrow will be time enough!' So I stayed that night at home and drove up to Abingdon in a leisurely fashion the next morning.

The squadrons there were equipped with Fairey Battles and were busy test flying and preparing to fly to airfields in France around the Rheims area. There were also one or two pilots rushing off to get married before leaving! There was not much confidence, regrettably, in the low level day bomber Battle aircraft surviving for long when faced with the German ME109s.

5

WAR TIME

HQ ADVANCED AIR STRIKING FORCE FRANCE (1939)

My wartime appointment was as a Navigation Officer at the Chateau HQ of the AASF at Rheims in France, but we remained at Abingdon until war was declared on 3 September 1939, so I had a few days to get used to the black-out in England before going over to France by boat and train escorting a group of airmen.

It is interesting perhaps to note that as an officer, I was issued with a Colt pistol before going abroad but only ten rounds for it were available which shows the sort of state of readiness we were in at that time! On reaching Rheims I was billeted with other officers in a small hotel in the main street and only about fifteen minutes walk to the HQ Chateau which was quite convenient. The war had not really started of course at that time, and there was not a lot for me to do at the HQ so I booked the little Magister communications aircraft at Rheims Champagne Airfield most days to fly round to the different landing grounds to visit the Battle squadrons and discuss the very limited navigational facilities

Miles Magister aircraft

available to them. They were all very short flights of twenty to thirty minutes but it was good to get into the air and get a fine view of the countryside, as well as meet all the Squadron Commanders and Navigators.

There were eight different dispersal landing grounds which I used to visit: Auberive, Berry, Bethéniville, Challerange, Condé, Villeneuve, Mourmelon and Coulommiers. However, I felt I was really wasting my time there and after about a month, I applied to return to the UK and Bomber Command, where there was at least some action over Germany. This was approved and I got a flight back to RAF Hendon in a DH86 in early October and was posted to a newly forming No. 1 Group at RAF Benson. Here again I was the Group Navigation Officer and there was not a lot to do while the Group was building up. At least I was able to help Wing Commander 'Mouse' Fielden with the interesting job of re-equipping and testing the new Hudson aircraft with which The Queen's Flight was being provided at Benson. I also managed to keep up my flying by piloting an Anson of 52 Squadron on the station on various navigation exercises. Altogether the couple of months I had at Benson were very pleasant and it was very conveniently only about thirty minutes' drive from our home at Hurley, so I was able to see quite a lot of my parents there and also Josephine before she returned to Sydney.

It was at this time that my mother, who had always worried about my flying, gave me a gold signet ring with the family crest and motto '*Virescit Vulnere Virtus*' engraved on it. She said it was to help with identification in case I was shot down on operations! Needless to say I have treasured it all my life and it has done me well for over sixty-five years.

HQ NO. 4 GROUP, BOMBER COMMAND (1940–41)

In December I was posted to HQ No. 4 Group at RAF Linton-on-Ouse, York to take over – again as Group Navigation Officer – from one of the well-known Waghorn brothers (David, the younger brother of the Schneider Trophy pilot). The Group was equipped with the Armstrong Whitley V twin-engined bomber, which was carrying out night bombing raids over Germany on their main marshalling yards, communication and military centres. Although the HQ offices were based at Linton, the officers had to be billeted out in York for accommodation so I found myself driving to and fro every day by car. This gave me an extra petrol allowance which was useful. Later that summer of 1940 the 4 Group HQ

Whitley Mk. I on early test flight

moved to a lovely old house called Heslington Hall just outside York and I too moved from my hotel in York into a one-room flat in another large house at Escrick Park which had recently been converted.

When I first reported to the HQ at Linton, it was a very cold day with quite a lot of snow on the ground but there was no sign of David Waghorn in his office. I was told that he was busy up at the airfield and when I went up there, sure enough he was there and, as befitted an ace skier, was enjoying himself being towed around on his skis by someone in a light aircraft, showing people how to do various turns such as the Telemark!

Unfortunately this was not included in my new job! which I nevertheless found very enjoyable and interesting, being so closely connected with one of the few ways that at that time British Forces were able to strike back at Germany, even if only in a small and not yet very effective way. I used to fly round to all the four Group stations in Yorkshire to talk to all the navigators and aircrew but found it increasingly difficult to analyse the navigators' logs and criticize, not having done any operations myself. In April 1940 I had an interesting attachment for a week to RAF Kinloss to support No. 77 Squadron from Driffield, which was sent to bomb German shipping in Trondheim harbour in the north-west of Norway. I was there as the HQ 4 Group representative to help with the briefing and debriefing of the aircrews and the routing, as the Whitleys were operating at their very maximum range. In June, also for the same reason, I was sent with the 4 Group detachment of Whitleys to Guernsey for the bombing of military targets in Milan and Turin on Italy's entry into the war. Other interesting work was in developing the use of the Astrograph and the new automatic sextant, and other possible navigation aids for use in the Whitleys, to try to improve the accuracy in finding the targets in Germany as well as our bases on return in bad weather and often foggy conditions. But I felt it was time I got operational experience myself and eventually the AOC Air Vice-Marshal (Maori) Coningham agreed – despite objections from the Spec 'N' Branch – to let me go to the Whitley OTU for conversion on to the Whitley V with a view to taking over one of his squadrons in due course. I was therefore glad in March 1941 to spend a couple of weeks at No. 10 OTU at RAF Abingdon getting a bit of flying practice on the old Whitley. Nevertheless, I had still done only three hours' night flying on the aircraft before being passed out and posted to command 'B' Flight, 102 Squadron at RAF Topcliffe.

NO. 102 SQUADRON, RAF TOPCLIFFE, YORKSHIRE (APRIL–MAY 1941)

I took over on 10 April and started in quickly with three ops the first week, on Bordeaux docks, Kiel and Berlin. On these trips I went as second pilot to get used to the usual procedure. This was also useful in view of my relatively little flying at night on the Whitley, particularly under black-out conditions, and during the next couple of weeks I found time to do some more night flying practice to gain confidence. Later I was on Kiel harbour again twice and Hamburg, and Brest to attack the *Scharnhorst* and *Gneisenau* which the Germans had in the docks there. As they were being repaired in dry docks we couldn't sink them and only caused further damage to keep them under repair a bit longer.

After three weeks with 102 Squadron at RAF Topcliffe I had only done 7 operations, and the Spec 'N' Branch at Air Ministry tried to get me back to the navigation world, but on protesting to my AOC he fully supported me and said he wanted me anyway in the first week of May to take over command of No. 51 Squadron at RAF Dishforth with the acting rank of Wing Commander, so that was fine and I moved smartly down the road to Dishforth and the new challenge of commanding a Whitley night bomber squadron, which was still one of the few ways we could take the fight back to Germany in those early days of the war.

Group photo of 51 Squadron at RAF Dishforth with Station Commander G/C Ward and myself and my two Flight Commanders, S/Ldr Putt and S/Ldr Mavor, in the centre

NO. 51 SQUADRON, RAF DISHFORTH, YORKSHIRE (MAY–DECEMBER 1941)

The job of a Squadron Commander was great, though much more demanding than I had thought. One was, of course, responsible for all the squadron aircrew, bringing on new crews, scheduling their operational flights, etc. but the ground crew and maintenance of the aircraft were equally important. Maximum serviceability was expected and a minimum number of aircraft made available each day to Group HQ for the next night's operations. Air tests were carried out every morning by the aircrews concerned before the aircraft were bombed up and any final servicing or adjustments carried out. The main briefing, with the Station Commander invariably present and all the specialists (Intelligence, Armament, Navigation, Weather etc.) was carried out later as there were often late changes or cancellations from Group or Bomber Command HQ. If not on the op oneself one always went to see the aircraft take-off and then much later, after a bit of a 'kip' in an armchair, return to the Operations Room to see how things were going, welcome the crews back and listen in to some of the debriefing. Unfortunately there was often one (sometimes more) of the squadron's ten or twelve aircraft on the raid missing on return which, of course, caused much sadness and grief though one always hoped the members of the crew had been able to bale

Whitley arming up at RAF Dishforth

out and survive. In any case everyone had to harden their hearts and not make too much of it, realizing that it could be their turn next time.

After debriefing then the luckier ones went for their well-earned customary bacon and eggs in the Mess, before retiring at dawn to catch up with some sleep, and hopefully look forward to an evening or two when they could enjoy a visit to the local pub with friends.

The Squadron Commander then had the unenviable job of informing the next-of-kin of any missing aircrew. This was particularly stressful if there were wives involved living on or near the RAF Station whom one had to visit, and I used to try to get particular friends or the local Padre to help out on these occasions. There was also correspondence and other work to catch up with in the squadron office, while the whole procedure started up again with the air testing ready for the following night.

There was some talk inevitably about LMF (Lack of Moral Fibre) when a crew member wanted to opt out, but I was fortunate in 51 Squadron not to have anyone that a couple of days off didn't sort out and get back to normal. I felt that it was my job as Squadron Commander to prevent my crews, if possible, from reaching breaking point. On one occasion, I particularly remember, one of my F/Sgt Captains came to see me earlier in the afternoon and said he really couldn't take it and go on that evening's raid. He was a good man and a good pilot and, as I was not down to go on that op myself, I said, 'OK, go and have a good rest and I will take your crew in your place this evening.' He was obviously under great stress and was clearly most grateful that I should take it that way and not accuse him of LMF. The interesting thing was that about three hours later he came to see me again to thank me and say he was now all right and felt quite ready to take his crew himself. This he did successfully, I am glad to say. This was one of the advantages, incidentally, of my usual plan of flying with different crews, so as to get to know most of them better, rather than with my own special crew as many squadron commanders preferred to do.

One of the most anxious times before an op, I always found myself, was when leaving my room, conceivably for the last time, after emptying pockets and valuables and any items which might help identification in case of being shot down. There was often a last letter also to my parents and Yorkshire girlfriend of the time (Margot) – just in case! However, once I had gone down to the aircraft preparatory to take off, there were many other things to think about, and as soon as airborne one had to concentrate on flying and ceased to worry much about anything except the weather and finding the target and how to deal with the German flak and night fighters. For the sake of morale of the crew, I always felt it was important also for the captain at least to appear completely confident, both on the ground immediately before take-off when there was usually an opportunity for a bit of a chat and banter before climbing on board the aircraft, and when speaking on the inter-com in the air, particularly on approaching enemy territory and in the target area.

In those early days of 1941 finding the target was usually very difficult unless it was a clear moonlight night, as one had to rely almost entirely on DR and the met. wind forecasts. I used to take my sextant with me to help the navigator with an occasional star sight, taken out of the side window or even through the windscreen, but I think this was very unusual for the aircraft captain to do. Sometimes inevitably one had to circle round in the target area looking for a gap in the clouds, but this was not very pleasant depending on the flak reception. On other occasions, when there were a large number of aircraft on the target, its position was given away by the searchlights and fires from bombs already dropped by earlier aircraft but one had to be careful not to be taken in by the German dummies. The steady straight and level run-in on the bombing run was the most dangerous time from the flak but I always felt it was rather like at rugger: if you hung around outside the scrum you usually got hurt but if you went in boldly and flat out you usually got away with it. The other bad time was if you were caught in the searchlights, when you were completely disorientated. It was very difficult to get out of them once coned and you were a sitting duck for a number of gun crews who then concentrated their flak on you. Whilst one hated to see some poor devil coned in the searchlights in that way, it was often sensible to take advantage of it oneself as it was a good time to nip in quickly to do one's bombing run, while the defences were concentrating on someone else. It was always a relief to start on the homeward flight, and it was often advisable to divert from the main route as it was there that the German night fighters tended to concentrate on what they expected to be the main bomber stream. Back at base there was always a warm welcome from the ground crew, who were glad to see their aircraft back in one piece, as well as from the Station Commander and Operations Room staff who had been anxiously waiting so long and were obviously glad to see one safely back.

I was very lucky in not suffering too much damage to the aircraft on my various ops, except after a very hot reception over Hamburg when I was clamped by searchlights and left with several chunks of jagged flak in the cockpit – fortunately nothing worse. Also on my fourth visit to Kiel, which was a good easy target to find but where there was always very heavy flak, the undercarriage was hit and starboard tyre flattened but worse still a rudder cable was damaged so that it was not possible to turn except very slowly with very wide banked turns. This left us very vulnerable to night fighters but we luckily managed to get back to base all right in the end and I successfully belly-landed on the grass airfield at Dishforth without anyone getting hurt.

Incidentally when I called base to explain our damage and to ask for the fire tender, ambulance and so on to stand by, the Station Commander suggested I should bale out the crew near the coast and leave the aircraft heading out over the sea after switching off the engines. I told the crew and said personally I was going to have a go at belly landing on the airfield, but gave them the option to bale out if they wished. However, I was glad that they all decided to stay with me and we all got back safely together. On another occasion after bombing Düsseldorf we were attacked by a ME110 night fighter over Holland on the way back, so I had to take fairly hectic evasive action and fortunately the tail gunner succeeded in frightening him off.

Most of our raids were about seven or seven and a half hours though my last two on Mannheim and Warnemunde, near Rostock, were around nine hours. For a week in August I had got myself attached to RAF Driffield to do a Lorenz Blind Landing Course which I found invaluable and it gave me great confidence looking ahead to the next autumn and winter weather when having to land back at base in foggy conditions. In September I was able to get away for my ten days' holiday at home with my parents at Hurley, which was a great rest and enabled me to come back to the job well refreshed. There were times of course after bombing some of the places, particularly those where I had known people before the war, when one looked back at the fires raging and couldn't help thinking about the civilian casualties including inevitably women and children; but there was nothing one could do about it except harden one's heart and remember that it was they and their government who started it all and bear in mind what they had done to places like Rotterdam, Coventry, Southampton and others, as well of course as the 'blitz' on London. The sooner we could win the war and defeat Germany the better it would be for everyone.

After I returned from leave there seemed to be a bit of a lull in the frequency of operations, whether this was due to the increasing loss rate at that time or just bad weather in October and November, I don't know, but I had three late cancellations myself after all preparations including briefing had been completed. This probably couldn't be avoided but it did cause unnecessary worry for the crews involved at the time of most anxiety.

By then the Spec 'N' Branch were after me again and I received another posting, which I could not get out of this time, to command No. 33 Air Navigation School (ANS) at Mount Hope, Hamilton, Ontario in Canada.

I was sorry to leave my No. 51 Squadron and the crews I had got to know so well, but I have to admit that it was in many ways a relief to have a rest from operations after about nine months. I had not done my full tour and only completed fourteen successful missions over Germany, but had commanded my squadron for seven months during a difficult time. This was recognized by my award in January 1942 of the Distinguished Flying Cross (DFC) which was most gratifying. Incidentally, it was a very nice coincidence when at the same time my brother Douglas was awarded the MBE for his good services with a Field Survey Company in the Middle East.

6

CANADA

NO. 33 AIR NAVIGATION SCHOOL, RAF MOUNT HOPE, HAMILTON (JANUARY 1942–JANUARY 1944)

In December, after a few more days leave at home, I left Liverpool in a small tramp ship on a rather hairy Atlantic crossing, zig-zagging about to avoid threatening U-Boats. There were only four of us passengers on the cargo ship and after a pretty miserable Christmas on board we eventually arrived at Halifax and jumped on the train to Montreal. There I stayed a night before meeting up with Group Captain Barnes (the Deputy Director of Navigation at Air Ministry) and flying round several days with him visiting Navigation Training Schools in Quebec, New Brunswick and Charlottetown on Prince Edward Island. After returning to Montreal, I then went on by train to Toronto and Hamilton where I was greeted by my old friend Nick Gething from the LRDU, who was the present CO of RAF Mount Hope and ready to hand over the Station to me the next day, when I also bought his very nice Dodge coupé car.

Mount Hope was a small station and hutted camp, with a pleasant little Officers' Mess, and a busy schedule of courses training navigators for the RAF and using Avro Ansons for flying. It was an uninterrupted period of change and expansion so there was much to look forward to in improving the facilities on the Station for the even larger number of students passing through. Amongst other things we managed to get the funds to build a new cinder running track and an outdoor swimming pool to help the students to keep fit in the summer months, and we had a large indoor drill hall which was frequently in use for various sports. There was, of course, much snow there in winter but by keeping the snow ploughs going all night, if necessary, it was my proud boast that unlike many other airfields in Canada our runways were never out of action. Mount Hope was only two or three miles outside Hamilton, whose people were

Avro Ansons at RAF Mount Hope in winter

very friendly and hospitable, and we invited many of them up to the Station from time to time for various functions and to look over the aircraft. We made many lifelong friends and, apart from enjoying the security of a life behind the lines with no black-out or wartime rationing, it was a very pleasant appointment. It was also a joy to be able to send food parcels home for my parents in England to help eke out their rations. I also got quite a lot of flying in the Ansons and, as the Station Commander, I had a small Stinson 105 single engine aircraft for local flying and communications. I joined the well-known Thistle Club in Hamilton with its indoor tennis court where I played fairly regularly with a particular friend, Bill Pigott of the Pigott Construction Company, who had before the war represented Canada in the Davis Cup. We always had quite a close game which was very enjoyable although he invariably beat me. I also played quite a bit of squash there and golf in the summer at the Ancaster Golf Club. In March I had a week's leave and went skiing at St Adele in the Laurentian Mountains above Montreal which was good fun though rather basic skiing and only rope tows.

It was, indeed, a great life at Mount Hope and hard to believe there was a major war on, but I was glad to have at least been on operations first as otherwise one would have felt rather guilty. We were very busy on the Station, expanding and turning out increasing numbers of

CO RAF Mount Hope as Group Captain

navigators to the extent that we doubled our output, and the ANS was up-graded to a Group Captain Station. This meant promotion to Acting Group Captain for me on 1 August which was not bad at the age of only twenty-nine. I had two excellent Chief Instructors at the ANS (first Squadron Leader Voyce and then Charles Simpson) who I am glad to say both went up in rank to Acting Wing Commander at that time.

Apart from piloting an occasional navigator training flight, I needed to fly round to some of the other Training Schools such as No. 31 ANS at Port Albert, the Gunnery School at RAF Picton (to present the Wings at their Passing Out parades) as well as to Ottawa to visit our UK Air Liaison Mission (UKALM) and Royal Canadian Air Force HQ (AHQ). I also used on several occasions to lead a formation of five Ansons flying low over Hamilton to drop leaflets, to help with Army week and also in aid of the Red Cross and the Victory Loan Campaigns. Sightseeing flights over nearby Niagara Falls were also in demand from VIP visitors from England, including the Deputy CAS (Air Marshal Colyer) who had inspected the Station and taken one of our Wings Parades in the Drill Hall because of bad weather in October. I always enjoyed taking these sightseeing flights myself.

Nearly all our trainee navigators were from England and the RAF, including a first cousin of mine (John Luard), but during the summer we had two unusual and interesting courses of twenty Polish officers for whose Passing Out Parade the Polish Inspector General in Canada (Group Captain Snzuk) came down and surprisingly presented me with my Polish Wings.

In July I had a week's leave up at Bigwin Inn, Lake of Bays, Ontario which was a lovely place and where the Northern Ontario Tennis Championships were being held, which much to my surprise I won. There was also golf there in the mornings, then swimming in the lake before tennis in the afternoons. A bit hectic but very nice people there and I was young then! Whilst in Canada I used to get hay-fever very badly in the summer so apart from the holiday it was a double relief to go up north amongst the Lakes.

As winter came round again and Christmas beckoned, I arranged to join Gige Frost and her two sons skiing at Mt. Tremblant in the Laurentians above Montreal. At the time it was the best skiing there in the east of Canada and it was good fun and the Mt. Tremblant Inn very comfortable. On one occasion I had the pleasure by chance of joining Princess Juliana of the Netherlands on the 'T' bar lift, though we were not very well balanced for weight! I did a couple of runs with her and on her very short skis she did very well and coped with all the steepest

Skiing at Mt. Tremblant with Gige Frost, Alan and Harry

slopes. My Mt. Tremblant holiday was a great success and I went again by myself several weekends during the rest of the winter, by catching the evening train from Hamilton on a Friday night – as a bachelor Group Captain I could afford a sleeper! – arriving in Montreal early in the morning, so that I was skiing at Mt. Tremblant by midday Saturday and all day Sunday until about 5.00 p.m., before eventually catching the night train back to Hamilton and getting back to my office at Mt. Hope by about 9.00 a.m. on the Monday morning after a super weekend.

I had been invited the following July to join my old LRDU friend, now Group Captain Harry (Rupert) Hogan, on a twelve-day tour of the Training Schools in the USA where we had RAF trainees. He had commanded a Hurricane squadron very successfully during the Battle of Britain and was to lecture on Fighter operations and I was wanted to do the same on Bomber operations. Rupert was based in Washington and we were loaned a C45 Beechcraft twin engined communications aircraft to fly ourselves round. The plan was to cover two (sometimes three) airfields each day across the USA, meeting all the RAF trainees and each giving an hour's talk at each Station before flying on to the next airfield. We ended up in Los Angeles where we were to pick up the Director of Training from Air Ministry (Air Commodore Carnegie) and then carry on visiting RAF trainees on the way back to Washington.

Needless to say I jumped at this opportunity to see so much of the USA flying visually at low level across most of the country. It was to be

C45 Beechcraft at El Paso, one of the training bases

a fairly hectic tour but extremely interesting and I flew down in one of our Ansons to join Rupert in Washington to start from there.

TOUR OF TRAINING STATIONS IN USA (JULY 1943)

Altogether we covered fourteen Training Stations on the way to Los Angeles, including Ellington, Randolph and Mesa airfields (Phoenix, Arizona), and nine others on the way back with Air Commodore Carnegie, including El Paso on the Mexican border, Fort Worth, Maxwell Field and Pensacola on the Gulf of Mexico before Clewiston (near Miami, Florida). We had got rather late by the end of my talk at Clewiston and, rather than wait another hour or so for Rupert on fighter operations, Paul Riddle, the civilian director of the Training School, suggested I should take his little single-engined Stinson Reliant aircraft and fly myself to the small Chapman Field near his home on the Florida coast, where he had kindly invited us all to stay the night. This I enjoyed doing and had a swim in the sea before the others arrived in our Beechcraft aircraft. The next day we all flew up to Savannah and Bollingfield, Washington DC, where I had to leave the others to return to Mt. Hope having received a message to say that the RCAF Inspector General had decided to inspect my Station the following day! Rather annoying without any notice, but I think he felt he would inspect the Station as it normally operated, without all the special spit and polish preparations usually made on these occasions.

BACK AT RAF MOUNT HOPE (AUGUST 1943–JANUARY 1944)

Fortunately I was able to get one of my Ansons from Mt. Hope to pick me up from Washington and get me back just in time to welcome the IG and we had a very successful visit when he also took a Passing Out Parade. He took the unusual step of telling the whole parade to break ranks and gather round while he addressed them. This rather alarmed me as I thought it would result in a bit of a shambles, but when he finished he told everyone to march back quietly to take their places where they were before on the parade ground, and much to my surprise they did, before being marched past properly for the salute.

By August the Station had reached the final stage of the expansion, as had the number of courses, so it was a busy time with Passing Out Parades every week. There was much use made of the new Athletics

Canadian IG after inspecting Passing Out Parade

Track and a Station Sports Day was held. There was also an Open House Day for the public to be shown around in aid of the Victory Loan. I played in the Hamilton Tennis Club tournament in September and was surprised but pleased for once to beat my friend Bill Pigott in the final. One evening in October I took part in some exhibition squash matches at the Hamilton Squash Club, when I beat two of the best Canadian players of the day, Jack Leibel and Bill Noyes, in quick succession which pleased me. In November I flew down to New York for a weekend and spent a day visiting Philadelphia to see a Mt. Tremblant skiing friend called Carol.

In December I flew in one of our Ansons to Winnipeg on an interesting visit to some of the Training Schools in that area, including Rivers and Carberry where there were more RAF personnel being trained under the Empire Air Training Scheme in Canada.

Soon after that my posting back to UK came through but I managed to fit in one more very enjoyable weekend skiing at Mt. Tremblant over the New Year, before getting ready to hand over Mt. Hope to my successor, another old Spec 'N' friend, Group Captain Paul Wood. There were, of course, many friends in and around Hamilton to say goodbye to, so there were lots of farewell parties including a dance in the

Officers' Mess at Mt. Hope to which we invited them. There was also the usual Dining Out evening for me at which the officers kindly presented me with a large and suitably engraved silver salver.

It had been a wonderful two-year command appointment for me and I was so lucky to have such a marvellous opportunity to see so much of Canada and also the USA while I was over there.

Finally, on 15 January 1944, I had a sad send-off by my particular great friends Bill and Hope Pigott and Gige Frost, who saw me on to the train to Montreal, where I reported to Dorval airfield. I was hoping to be allocated a Mitchell B25 for delivery across the Atlantic to the UK. Unfortunately there were none available at that time, so I was put on the next aircraft in the bomb bay of a Liberator, with a couple of other passengers! On the 19th we landed at Gander airfield in Newfoundland after four hours, to refuel before flying to Prestwick, Scotland in a further 7 hours and 40 minutes, which was only five minutes longer apparently than the quickest Atlantic crossing so far. I was glad it wasn't longer, as it was pretty cold and uncomfortable in the Liberator bomb bay, but it felt good in many ways to be back in the UK and to share again all the hardships of rationing and blackout after two such marvellous years in Canada.

From Prestwick I got a lift down to RAF Lyneham in an old Dakota DC3 and went home to Hurley for a few days' leave until I was due to report for my next appointment as Senior Air Staff Officer (SASO) of No. 25 Group, Training Command at Buntingsdale Hall, RAF Market Drayton in Shropshire.

BACK IN UK

HQ NO. 25 GROUP, BUNTINGSDALE HALL, RAF MARKET DRAYTON (FEBRUARY–SEPTEMBER 1944)

The AOC of 25 Group was Air Vice-Marshal 'Dizzy' Davis, well known in the RAF as an armament expert, and the Group which was in Training Command had seven Stations under command dealing with Bombing, Navigation and Air Gunnery Schools based all over the west and north-west of the country from Westmorland and Anglesey down to South Wales. For me this involved quite a lot of flying around visiting at least once or twice a week, either in an Anson or in a small single-engined Percival Proctor, to deal with their various problems. At the HQ I had a very nice large office overlooking the gardens but I was billeted out for bed and breakfast with a charming local family in Market

Valerie St Ludger

Drayton. There was also HQ No. 23 Group of Technical Training Command at Buntingsdale Hall, and we had a joint Officers' Mess and dining room.

The best thing of all for me was when I first went into the Mess and saw a lovely blonde Section Officer WAAF of 23 Group, sitting by the window, with whom I fell in love on first sight. I soon got myself introduced to her and her name was Valerie St Ludger. Luckily she felt the same way and we saw quite a lot of each other, including a weekend or two with both our parents who seemed to approve. In fact Val told her mother that if I didn't ask her to marry me she would go into a nunnery! So we couldn't have that! Anyway, as the war was getting nearer the end and I was unlikely at that stage to go back on ops, we soon decided to get engaged and to get married later in the year.

In May incidentally I had had a very pleasant interlude when I flew down to RAF Hendon in the Proctor for a couple of nights at the RAF Club in London to attend the Investiture at Buckingham Palace by the King for my DFC, and I didn't have any problems over my wings this time!

RAF STAFF COLLEGE COURSE (SEPTEMBER–DECEMBER 1944)

In September I was sent on the RAF Staff College course. It was at Gerrards Cross and had been reduced to only three months in war time. There I met up again with many old friends on the course including my very old tennis and squash friend Gus Holden whom I invited to be my best man at our wedding.

WEDDING (4 NOVEMBER 1944)

Our wedding had been arranged for 4 November in London at the Holy Trinity Church, Brompton. We, and both our families, stayed at the Rembrandt Hotel not far from the church and the reception afterwards was also held there. Luckily it was a lovely sunny day and a surprising number of relations and friends managed to come to join us, including of course Joan Horne, Val's best friend, who was our chief bridesmaid. Being wartime, our only honeymoon was a couple of weekends at the Savoy Hotel in London, so after an excellent reception with all the usual speeches Val and I departed for the Savoy and the theatre where we saw a very good variety show. All went marvellously but then it was sadly back to work on the Monday.

The next weekend Val and I met up again at the Savoy for the second half of our wartime honeymoon. On this occasion, however, while changing to go down to dinner and dance in the hotel we had a very nasty 'near miss'! There was an enormous explosion when a German V2 rocket landed in the Thames opposite blowing in all the south facing windows in the hotel and causing colossal damage all around. I ended up with the loo window in my lap and no harm, but Val who was in the main room near the big window got the worst of it including unfortunately some splinters of glass in her foot. That was the end of our dinner dance and, not surprisingly, being on honeymoon, we decided the best thing to do was to go to bed! We really were so very lucky the V2 had landed in the mud bank of the river at low tide, otherwise it would have been far far worse. Needless to say Val, as an ex-FANY driving heavy vehicles and ambulances during the Blitz in London before joining the WAAF, took it all in her stride; though we decided to leave the rest of our honeymoon until after the War.

After all this excitement my Staff College course ended quite successfully but instead of taking up my recommended new appointment

Wedding group photo Joseph St Ludger, Gus Holden, Mum, Me and Val, Joan Horne, Mrs St Ludger, Dad

of SASO 2 Group, which had been involved in the Arnheim and other operations in Germany and which I was looking forward to, I found myself being sent back as SASO, 25 Group as the AOC insisted he had only released me earlier for the Staff College on condition that I returned after the course, and he had been without a proper relief SASO for the three months I was away. After much argument with the Air Ministry, the AOC won the day and back I went to Market Drayton. There I found digs in a small cottage for Val and me to stay and it was lovely to be together properly at last.

7

POST WAR

RAF STAFF COLLEGE DS (MARCH 1945–DECEMBER 1946)

However, after only a couple of months, I was posted away again as an Instructor at the Staff College – so I must have done quite well on the course! – and this time the AOC had to give way and I was back at Bulstrode Park, Gerrards Cross by March 1945 as an Instructor on the next course. No accommodation was available and I had to be billeted out, but fortunately I was able to live at home at Hurley and commute daily to the Staff College. That was lovely and Val, who was P2b (in charge of WAAF postings) at 23 Group, soon managed to post herself down to 22 Group, within commuting distance also from Hurley, so that we could both live at home! Luckily, I think my parents seemed to quite enjoy us being there despite the inevitable extra work for my mother.

In the third week of March, I see from my log book, I flew in a Percival Proctor round to one or two of the Bomber Command stations including Coningsby, where the Staff Course students were visiting, and incidentally on my way back I picked up Section Officer Valerie Burnett from RAF Halton for a flight with me for the first time on the way to Woodley aerodrome near Reading for the weekend at Traddles.

By the end of the month, however, the whole RAF Staff College had to evacuate the large house and hutted camp at Bulstrode Park and move into another large building, which had been a block of flats, at Bracknell in Surrey. It was a great rush to get it ready in time for the next course and a completely new lecture hall had to be constructed and accommodation rearranged for the students. There were no sporting facilities at all except two not very good tennis courts, and some of us on the DS (Directing Staff) went round successfully to a few of the golf courses in the neighbourhood to try to arrange special facilities, and we were able to get the use of a private squash court near Ascot which was very useful.

The Staff Course was also extended again to six months and there were many relatively senior, highly decorated, officers on it with wide experience of the various Commands – bomber, fighter, coastal etc. – so it was a very interesting time, and we got many senior wartime commanders like Admiral Mountbatten to come and lecture. There were also a number of old friends of mine on the course which made it very enjoyable.

On 5 May when the war in Europe was finally over Val and I were tempted to go up to London for the VE Day celebrations, but it was such a lovely sunny day in the country we opted to stay at Traddles in Hurley and lounge about on the lawn and take the family punt on the river.

Not long after that Val became pregnant and applied for her discharge from the WAAF which was soon approved. We then decided to rent a small house called East Lodge at Ascot, near the far side of the racecourse, from where I could commute easily to the Bracknell Staff College on Val's autobike leaving her the car.

In June I went on a notable low level flight with fifteen of the Staff College students in a Dakota over Germany to see all the bomb damage caused over the Ruhr: Essen, Munster, Hamburg, Bremen, and Osnabruck, and back via Arnheim, Brussels and Calais. The devastation was fantastic and in the Ruhr we could see how the German people were coming out into the streets from the cellars below, where they were having to live. In July there was a gap between courses and Val and I had a quiet holiday for a couple of weeks down at Weymouth and at Swanage in Dorset.

Throughout the rest of the year, the DS were pretty busy writing exercises for the students on the new six-month course, marking and assessing their written work and chairing various discussion groups. Apart from the Air Vice-Marshal Commandant and Air Commodore Assistant Commandant, there were three Group Directors. The rest of the DS and all the students were divided into three Groups and I was put in charge of Group 'A'. There was plenty to keep us busy though I started playing a bit of tennis, squash and golf again locally. We actually had quite a good squash team with another RAF player, then Group Captain 'Digger' Kyle, and we won the RAF Inter-Unit Competition that winter. At tennis, I enjoyed playing singles with Margot (Lumb) Gordon who was a British Wightman Cup player, as well as the squash champion, and who lived not far away. In October, playing with Dan Maskell, our leading British professional who was still serving in the RAF at the end of the war, he and I won the RAF Inter-Command Tennis. In December 1945 I played in the RAF Squash Championships again, but was beaten in the final by Jim Dear, the professional champion of GB before the war who was also still serving in the RAF after the end of the war.

In the meantime, Val was getting on well and due for our first child so we booked her in to the Maidenhead Nursing Home for around Christmastime. At the same time, Elizabeth Wheeler, wife of Wing Commander 'Nebby' Wheeler also on the Staff College DS, was also expecting and she and Val later went in to the nursing home together which was nice for them. They both had their babies in quick succession, as planned, soon after Christmas on 27 December 1945 – Caroline Wheeler and our son, Bruce. I was at home at Hurley, only four miles away, for Christmas so was able to get over to see them easily every day.

All went well and we were soon back happily at East Lodge and the Staff College, where all went on as usual with another fairly high-powered experienced course. In February 1946 I went in a Dakota with ten of the students to Malta, El Adem in Tripoli, and Cairo for a visit to Middle East HQ. While in Cairo I met up with brother Douglas who was stationed there and he lent Nebby Wheeler and me his car for us to visit the Pyramids one day. Nebby and I stayed on with our new Staff College Commandant, Air Vice-Marshal (one-armed) Sanders, for his lecture and visit to the Staff College at Haifa, and we then returned together via Jerusalem, Damascus, Beyrouth, Athens and Italy. In March, there was another interesting visit with students to Rome, Naples and Caserta where the German forces in Italy had surrendered to the Allied Command earlier in 1945. During this period I hardly did any flying myself except a little in a Proctor to keep my hand in, from White Waltham near Maidenhead.

In April 1946 we had a big party at Traddles with both families and godparents for Bruce's christening in Hurley Church. He was christened Bruce St Ludger Burnett, the middle name being that of Val's father, and his godparents were Bill Kerr, George Thompson and Joan Horne, now Bearder, all very old friends of ours. Soon after that we got the chance to move house from our rather ordinary little East Lodge to a charming one named Brook Place Cottage at Cobham, with a lovely walled-in garden and a few fruit trees, which was much nicer for Val and Bruce, and still near enough for me to commute to the Staff College on Val's autobike. There too we had a nannie, Nora, who lived in to help Val with Bruce.

Bruce's christening party at Traddles

In June I started playing a bit more tennis and, by doing much of my Staff College paperwork in the evenings, I was able to get away in the afternoons and played in the St George's Hill tournament, reaching the semi-final. I was also accepted for Wimbledon in both singles and doubles with Peter Young who was on the Prentice Cup with me in the USA before the War. We both played in the pre-Wimbledon Queen's Tournament to practise a bit together. At Wimbledon I was unlucky in the Singles 1st Round to draw Geoff Brown, the Australian No. 3 seed and eventual finalist, who beat me very easily but it was rather fun to be the first match on Court 1 after the War, as we were, and it was a privilege to play there in the Championships at all. Geoff Brown, I remember, hit the ball tremendously hard and was ambidextrous to the extent that he served right-handed but smashed overhead with either hand: very disconcerting. In the doubles we also drew the No. 3 seeds (Mitic and Pallada of Yugoslavia) so didn't get very far there either!

In July we went for a week's holiday to Frinton-on-Sea where I enjoyed looking after Bruce on the beach in the mornings and playing in the tennis tournament in the afternoons where I won the singles event. Later that month came the RAF Championships at Wimbledon where I was beaten (7-9, 6-0, 8-6) in the final by Howard Walton, one of our Davis Cup players who was an airman (A/C) in the RAF at that time. The *Daily Mirror* headline the next day was 'Erk thrashes Group Captain!' which was a bit hard considering the score! Neil Cox, who was still on release leave from the RAF after a very successful war flying Spitfires in defence of Malta, won the doubles with me. He was the nephew of my friends the Thompsons and the brother of an old girlfriend of mine, Joy Cox, so we got on well together.

On August Bank Holiday we played the Inter-Services Tennis at Wimbledon when the Army beat the RAF by 9 matches to 8 although I won three out of my four matches. I then had the nice surprise in September of being selected by the LTA to play for an England team in Germany as the guest of the British Army of the Rhine. Our team was led by Hedley Baxter and Geoff Paish, our Davis Cup players, and we played matches in Hamburg and against the Combined Services at Bad Eilsen. It was all good fun and I enjoyed meeting again a very old friend, Col. Roderick Fyler, from Charterhouse and Alassio days.

The Staff College went on as usual but towards the end of the year I was due for a posting and surprisingly was asked to say what I would like to do. Everyone with Acting Rank was also due to revert to their Basic Rank, i.e. drop one or two ranks now that the war was over, and this influenced my ideas. Someone suggested and I thought it was a good idea to go if possible to the USA and the United Nations Military Staff Committee in New York. I felt reverting to Wing Commander after three and a half years as a Group Captain would be less noticeable for me perhaps over there in the States. There the overseas allowances were pleasantly high and would offset to some extent my loss of pay as a Wing Commander. I was also very interested in the UN Military Staff Committee task, as a five-power delegation with the Americans, Russians, French, Chinese and ourselves, in forming a UN Military Task Force to help maintain peace around the world. The Air Ministry managed to arrange this for me and I was posted in December to New York where I sailed from Southampton in SS *Samaria* after quickly re-gaining the RAF Squash Championships and settling Val and Bruce back with her parents at Bromsgrove. Unfortunately houses to let were in short supply around New York and Long Island at that time, so we Brits were not allowed to take our wives and families with us until we had found a house. I managed to do this more quickly than most, and had Val and Bruce (aged one) and a new young eighteen-year-old nannie, Pat, booked on HMS *Aquitania*, whose Captain conveniently happened to be Val's Uncle Jack, on 1 February 1947. We were, therefore, only apart temporarily for about three weeks and they were well looked after.

UNITED NATIONS MILITARY STAFF COMMITTEE, NEW YORK (JANUARY 1947–MARCH 1950)

I stayed in a hotel in New York those first few weeks as our British HQ was on the 62nd floor of the Empire State Building, but the house I rented was out at Douglaston on the north shore of Long Island, not far from the old Gyro factory at Lake Success, which was the United Nations HQ at first until the new building in New York was ready a couple of years later. I bought myself a super new Ford V8 car which, with UN discount, cost only what I had sold my old Ford 10 for (£199) before I left England, so I was able to get about well after taking my New York driving test. I joined the Rockaway Hunt Club at Cedarhurst Long Island, where I had stayed in 1933, for tennis, squash and golf. In New York I played squash regularly at lunch time at one of the Clubs, usually with Colonel Oscar Jameson, the British Army Champion, who was also on the UN Military Staff Committee. So I got plenty of exercise, and it seemed incredible to have no food or petrol rationing, and I couldn't wait to get Val and Bruce over there.

The other Brits on the Military Staff Committee were Air Chief Marshal Sir Guy Garrod (my boss), General Sir Edwin Morris and Rear Admiral W. R. Slater as the top team, with a second team at Colonel/Group Captain level, Col. Oscar Jameson, G/C Harry Eeles and Capt. Blair RN, and a third team at Lt. Col./Wing Commander level, Lt. Col. Cosmo Nevill, myself and Commander George Pound. There were also three others in the Military Staff Committee Secretariat (Captain Coleridge RN, Major White and W/Cmdr Ford). We all got on famously with each other and with our American, French and Chinese opposite numbers and were usually able to agree most of our requirements for a UN Military Force with them – but not I'm afraid with the Russians, who although quite friendly socially, tended all the time to hold up progress and at the end of each month refused to agree the otherwise unanimous report which we had to submit to the UN.

To get to our offices on the 62nd floor of the Empire State Building we used to get the elevator non-stop to the 60th floor and then walk up the next two. I shared a very nice large office with my Army and Navy colleagues, and we had a lovely view looking out over the Hudson River where we could see the big ships like the *Queen Mary* when they were coming in to New York harbour. The only frightening thing was when men came outside and leant back to clean the windows but fortunately they were well strapped in!

At the beginning of February 1947 I flew up to Hamilton, Ontario for a weekend with my friends Bill and Hope Pigott, before going on for a week's refresher flying in a Beechcraft C45 at RCAF Uplands near Ottawa, which the Air Ministry had arranged for us with the RCAF. I was then just in time to go and meet Val, Bruce and Pat in Montreal and bring them down to the house on Long Island.

They were thrilled to get there and soon enjoyed meeting everyone, and luckily our young teenage nannie got on very well with the similar young English nannie that the Pound family had. This worked excellently and the families got together when either of us wanted to go away anywhere. There was much social activity and entertainment between us all on Long Island with the relaxed post-war amenities and facilities, and Val and I thoroughly enjoyed the many new musical shows which were on in New York at the time – *Annie Get Your Gun*, *Oklahoma*, *South Pacific*, *Lorna Doone* and others.

When living on Long Island, I usually used to commute to work at our Military Staff Committee offices at the Empire State Building on the Long Island Railroad. However, sometimes I took it in turns to go by car with George Pound or one of the others via the Grand Central Parkway and Triborough or Queensborough Bridge, as we were very conveniently provided with a United Nations car sticker which allowed us to park near the offices in 32nd Street.

Occasionally we used to attend with the British delegation some of the UN Assembly or Security Council meetings at Lake Sucess, if any military matters were being discussed. These were invariably interesting, and enabled us to get to know some of the delegates of the other countries and to hear our British representatives, including sometimes our Minister of State for Foreign Affairs or Sir Alexander Cadogan, the Permanent Secretary, putting over our case to the UN.

Weekends were spent mostly at the Rockaway Hunt Club for golf or squash including doubles squash, which was new to me in the larger size court. We met up there with some of the members I had known in 1933, including particularly the Jonklaas and Cox families. I had managed to win the squash rackets singles at the Club and was invited to play in the

National Squash Championships in Detroit where Val and I went by air towards the end of February, but I didn't do very well there. The American game of squash was, incidentally, slightly different from ours with the court (I think) 10 inches shorter, the play line on the front wall a couple of inches lower, the ball much faster and the scoring per game up to 15 points instead of 9, with a point for every rally whether or not you were serving. This made quite a difference and the game consisted mainly of hard hitting to a length down both side walls with the minimum of errors and with little use of angles and drop shots which were my main speciality. It also made concentrating on every single point more vital than ever. I also found their custom of playing their Championships over the weekend difficult to get used to with the first round on the Friday afternoon or evening with a draw of 32 players, the next two rounds on the Saturday morning and afternoon, and the semi-finals Sunday morning after a late party the night before! The finals were played on Sunday afternoon. All very exhausting. I played in several of the Squash Championships over there including Boston and Baltimore, but only once succeeded in getting further at this top level than the semi-final on the Sunday morning, when I managed to win the Luckenback Trophy when the weather was so cold I was able to do my drop shots fairly successfully!

Towards the end of March we drove up to Manchester, Vermont – only about four hours – for a week's holiday where there was some fairly basic skiing but good fun. Interestingly we found there Val's old ski instructor from Andermatt in Switzerland who had emigrated out there on the outbreak of World War II.

In May the owner of our house in Douglaston wanted it back and our short lease was up so we had to move to another, 62 Webster Avenue, Manhasset, not far away. There we had a small garden with a lawn, where we could put Bruce's playpen out under a tree for shade, and we bought a small portable pool for him to paddle and lie down in when it got hot.

At the end of the month there was the Rockaway Hunt Club invitation tennis doubles tournament which was very interesting as many of the top American players came. On a minor note Peter Young, my old Oxford and Cambridge Prentice Cup and Wimbledon partner who was now based in Montreal, also came down to stay and play with me. We were lucky in the draw and got through two rounds before being beaten by Billy Talbert and J. Gilbert Hall, who went on to play the winners of Frank Shields and Guz Ganzenmuller v Sidney B. Wood and Earl

Cochell in the final. It was a great weekend with some excellent, relaxed and enjoyable tennis on the club grass courts.

In June I was due for another week's refresher flying course at RCAF Rockcliffe near Ottawa so with the addition of another ten days' leave, the family all set off on a leisurely trip by car heading north to Niagara Falls and four days with the Pigotts in Hamilton for some golf and to meet other friends who had not met Val before. We then drove on along the north shore of Lake Ontario, stopping for the night at Gananoque Inn at the 1000 Islands before going on to the Seigniory Club where we enjoyed the luxury of staying five days, and Val and I played more golf. We then drove on up to Ottawa where I had booked rooms for Val, Bruce and Pat from 15 to 21 June at the Mountain Lodge, Kingsmere, about twelve miles north in the Laurentians while I did my week's flying at RCAF Rockcliffe. Apart from one day on the Beechcraft C45 again, I was learning to fly the Grumman Goose 383 float plane, practising taking off and landing in the river. The latter was quite tricky with the numerous large logs floating down the river and was an interesting new experience for me. I am glad to say the family had also enjoyed their peaceful stay in the cool of the mountains, before we moved on to Montreal to stay for a week with Peter Young and his mother from 21 to 27 June. Peter and I enjoyed playing in the Quebec Provincial Tennis Championships but didn't do very well. We finally got back to Long Island by 1 July after a very enjoyable three weeks away from the noise and bustle of New York.

During the summer, work in the Military Staff Committee carried on as usual to try and form a UN Peace Keeping Force and, despite the very slow progress, maintained our interest as we could not believe that in the end the Russians would not go along with our sensible compromise proposals. Weekends were mostly spent at the Lawrence Beach Club for bathing with Bruce, as well as the Rockaway Hunt Club for tennis and golf. At both clubs, as usual in America, there were excellent restaurant facilities which made life very nice and easy. I won the Rockaway Tennis Championships and as Oscar Jameson, our Army champion, had now joined the club and the team, some Americans were surprised to find two Brits representing their club in matches!

In August my boss ACM Sir Guy Garrod had arranged to be flown out by Col. Ken Skaer on the US Military Staff Committee in a Mitchell B25 to visit his daughter in Seattle, and I was invited to accompany them. It was an interesting trip from Mitchell Field on Long Island and stopping off at Scott Field Illinois, Offutt Field Omaha, Hill Field near Salt Lake City, to McChord Field Tacooma near Seattle. It was planned to return via San Francisco and Los Angeles, where we stayed a night with Ken Skaer's parents in San Marino before heading back via Colorado Springs. We stayed a night there too and Ken picked up half a cow which he had kept for some time in a freezer there, and put it in the Mitchell bomb bay to take back to New York for dinner! After that there was only one more stop at Scott Field St Louis before landing back at Mitchell Field on Long Island. It was excellent flying practice for Ken to help keep up his annual flying hours, and a useful and enjoyable experience for me to visit so many USAF Bases. However, it was good to get back to the family after ten days away on the move.

Soon after that, in September, Val's mother (Dosh) came to stay with us for six weeks and enjoy her grandson Bruce, and it was lovely for Val to have her there and to drive her around Long Island to meet the Jonklaas family and some of our other friends. The US National Championships was on then at Forest Hills and I remember taking her one day to the semi-finals and watching Frankie Parker of the US beating John Bromwich of Australia in a marvellous five-set match on the grass centre court they were then playing on there. I think it was also around this time when at Forest Hills, in a Davis Cup match I saw Ted Schroeder (US) beat Sidwell of Australia in five remarkably good sets. It was very wet and drizzling most of the time but in those days players just carried on with spikes, if allowed, or socks over their shoes. In this case, I remember Schroeder took his socks off too in the final set and went on to win playing barefooted! This sort of thing all changed when open tennis and big money came into the game and players could no longer risk slipping and injuring themselves.

Another interesting team match took place in September 1947 at the Rockaway Hunt Club between the International Club of the US and a number of other IC Visitors, which the IC of the US won by 8½ to 7½ matches. Amongst those representing the US were Jack Kramer, Frank Shields, Bob Falkenburg, Dick Savitt, Vic Seixas, and Pancho Segura, with Jack Crawford, Enrique Morea, Bernard Destremau, B. Abdesselam, Manuel Alonso, Geoffrey Paish, Tony Mottram, John Oliff, and Derek Barton amongst the visitors. There were two other matches in which the well-known veterans Watson Washburn and Arthur MacPherson of the US split one set all with J. B. Wilkinson and Ted Avory, and the two Brians (Finnigan and myself) defeated James Van Allen and Larry Baker of the US. It was good fun and must have been a fairly unique collection of enthusiastic tennis players of just before and after World War II.

Val in the meantime was getting on well with producing our second child and in due course had to go into the nursing home at Glen Cove, where young Bob arrived on schedule on 29 November 1947. Val was allowed out after five days, which was considered very quick in those days, and we got a rather older more experienced nurse to live in for a couple of weeks at Manhasset to help with the new born babe. Earlier I had bought a new ciné camera so was able to take a lot of good pictures, including colour, of the family and Bruce from the age of twelve months. Incidentally, I continued to do this until he and Bob were twenty-one, so it is a nice record to have and I have since had these films converted on to a video so they are much easier to watch and are fun to show the grandchildren.

There was a lot of snow that winter but it didn't seem to stop us carrying on as before and towards the end of February 1948, Val and I went for a long weekend to Boston for the National Squash Championships where unfortunately again I did not do very well. This was

Bruce and Bob in garden at Manhasset

disappointing as earlier that month I had done well in the Apawamis Tournament at Rye NY, getting through to the semi-final by beating one of the American top players, Richard Cooley, and then Don Strachan, a previous US Champion, in 5 games. To make up for it we went for ten days' skiing early in March to the 'Hob Nob' at Stowe in Vermont. There was wonderful snow there then and excellent skiing down the trails on Mount Mansfield, but there was one day when it had rained overnight and the trails had frozen over and become a sheet of ice. There were few who even tried to ski, but there was an Australian girl staying at our Hob Nob Inn, who was ranked No. 4 in Australia, I believe, and who hired a ski instructor to show her how to ski under control on ice. Sure enough I was tempted to go up too and try to follow them down – usually on my backside! But it was interesting.

Spring followed shortly and in April we were able to have a delicious barbeque lunch out of doors with the Jonklaas family out on Long Island and Alice then agreed to be one of Bob's godmothers at his christening at the local Manhasset church. Peter Young was one of his godfathers and Bill Kerr, another. In May we had a lovely weekend at Cobble Court, Greenwich, Connecticut, the delightful home of Kay Valentine who had been so wonderful during the War in looking after, and having to stay, dozens of British sailors (mostly) who found themselves in New York on R&R (Rest and Recreation) for a few days. In May there was also a big and very enjoyable lunch party given by the USAF General Stratemayer at the USAF Base at Mitchell Field for my boss, ACM Sir Guy Garrod, who was heading back to UK on retirement and whom everyone was extremely sorry to see leave. As G/C Harry Eeles was also leaving about the same time, it was left to me to introduce Sir Guy's successor Air Vice Marshal (Gobbo) Gibbs to the interesting but unusual aspects of our job with the UN Military Staff Committee.

The next thing that happened that summer was the arrival of the Oxford and Cambridge Prentice Cup Tennis team at the Rockaway Hunt Club, where they were based as we had been in 1933. They were headed by Guy Jackson, the Irish Davis Cup player, and Tim Miles of Oxford and Linton Highett and Geoff Chandler of Cambridge, a smaller team than usual as funds were short after the War. The two-day match against the Club for the Prince of Wales Cup, which I mentioned earlier, ended in a 6-6 tie. It was extraordinary that two of the Club players, myself and Oscar Jameson, had formerly played for the visiting team against the club before the war. I started well on this occasion against Guy Jackson and led 4-0 but he went on as expected to win our single comfortably.

Later in November that year, 1948, Val and I decided to make up for our weekend only honeymoon four years earlier in London and to go on a second honeymoon down in Florida. After arranging for Pat, Bruce and Bob to get together with the Pound family while we were away, Val and I set off by car heading south through Philadelphia, Washington, Shenandoah National Park, then along the Blue Ridge Parkway in North Carolina with its lovely views. We stopped quite a lot on the way, including a couple of night stops in a motel, but planned on doing about five hundred miles a day so as to get down fairly quickly to Clearwater or Sarasota on the Gulf coast where we intended to stay for most of our holiday. We were lucky to find an excellent ground floor apartment in Sarasota right on the beach which we had practically to ourselves. It was so peaceful and lovely there lying in the warm November sunshine, we stayed for seven days. However, like all good things, it had to come to an end and we moved on south to Fort Myers and across the Everglades to Miami and Key West, before heading north on our return journey. This was via West Palm Beach and Daytona beach where we stopped for a bathe from the famous motor car world-speed-record racing sands. We also stopped at Ponte Vedra Beach on the Florida coast and stayed a few days at the luxurious Ponte Vedra Club for several rounds of golf. After that we were ready to go on to Pinehurst, North Carolina to watch the famous North-South Golfing tournament, when we watched the great Sam Snead and Jimmy Turnesa and other well known golfers play a round. We had also arranged to meet there Ruth, an American whom we used to know in England when she was engaged to John Fletcher, an old RAF and tennis friend of mine who was sadly killed in the War. It was lovely to see her again and talk about old times with John and Gus Holden.

Heading north again through Virginia we by-passed Washington and drove on through Baltimore and Philadelphia to New York. Altogether it was a wonderful trip and although a long way, it was very comfortable in our new Ford V8, but it was great too to get back to see the two little boys on Long Island after nearly three weeks away.

Not long after our return we had to move house again to one at Great Neck, but we didn't like it much and were glad it was only for a month or so. We were then able to take over a much nicer and bigger house at Kings Point from John and Joy White of our delegation who had been posted back to the UK. All four houses that we had while in New York were conveniently within a few miles of each other but the one at Kings Point was much the best. It had a good big garden for Bruce to play around in and it even had its own very small private beach on Manhasset Bay. It also had a small lily pond at the bottom of the garden which was nearly the cause of a major disaster. Val had called for Bruce to come in for lunch but there was no reply. She went out and to her horror she saw him floating unconscious on top of the pool. She rushed to pull him out, carried him into the house and wrapped him in a blanket to get him warm, and thankfully he came round. I was unfortunately at the office in New York but Pat was there looking after Bob and she called the doctor who said we were extremely lucky and that Val had only just got to him in time to save him, but that he would be all right now with no after effects – thank God. Obviously it was a terrible shock for poor Val and the rest of us and, needless to say, I had the pond fenced around the next day. There was little more that we could do, and it wasn't long before my posting back to UK came in for April.

Before then, however, we were able to fit in another week's skiing in January at our favourite 'Hob Nob' at Stowe in Vermont and also a very pleasant weekend in March up in Maine with the Jonklaas family at the country house they had recently bought there. It was in a glorious position right on the rocky coast, high up and with a marvellous view out to sea. However, it was fairly basic and needed a lot doing to it, which they planned to do, including updating the outside loo which consisted of three 'thunder boxes' in a row of different sizes for the husband, wife and child! It was quite a long drive up from Long Island but we went with the Jonklaases and their son Tony, and had quite a few pit stops where Ernest produced drinks from the boot of their car.

That was in the spring but before then and after we had moved to Kings Point we had a lot of snow in the winter and Bruce, who loved the snow, joined in digging us out of the drive on many occasions. There was one particular time when Val and I had been out to dinner and when on our return we couldn't get the car into the drive, we had to wade in through several feet of snow. Incidentally, driving back late that evening I had been exceeding the speed limit, despite Val's protests, and sure enough I was stopped by a couple of motor-bike speed cops. I opened the window as one of the cops came up to the car and he must have heard Val saying, 'I told you so, etc.,' and giving me stick, as he just looked at me and said, 'Is she your wife?' And when I said, 'Yes,' he said, 'Bad luck! You may now carry on, but slowly,' and left us without further todo.

At weekends sometimes Miss Peggy Richardson, one of our secretaries at the office and a relation of General Morris, whom we had got to know well, used to come out to stay with us at Kings Point and join in playing around with Bruce in the snow.

By the time March came around, the work of the UN Military Staff Committee was coming to an end with a final report by four of the Delegations (the British, American, French and Chinese) proposing a United Nations Military Force consisting of Army, Navy and Air Force contributions by several of the major UN countries. Unfortunately the Russians continued to say '*Niet*' to it all, which was a great pity as I believe it would have been invaluable to the UN in its major task of trying to maintain peace throughout the world.

Finally, our very enjoyable two year tour with the United Nations Military Staff in New York came to an end and Val and I and the family all returned on the Cunard White Star liner *Caronia* in April 1949 to Southampton. This was a good smooth crossing and very comfortable as I was entitled to a first class passage, and we met up at Southampton with the bulk of our luggage and the car which we had sent on a few days earlier. This was ideal, and we drove up to Traddles for part of our leave with my parents and later to Tutnall Mount near Alvechurch for part of it with Val's parents.

JOINT PLANNING STAFF, MINISTRY OF DEFENCE (MAY 1949–JULY 1951)

My new posting was to the Joint Planning Staff at the Ministry of Defence in the rank of Group Captain again which I was glad to hear. Obviously the first thing to do was to find a house to live in. As it happened, my brother Douglas was renting a small house at No. 10 Broadhurst, Ashstead in Surrey and had been posted to Fontainebleau near Paris and was moving out, so we were able to take it over from him temporarily until we could find a house of our own.

Ashstead was quite convenient for me to commute to the Ministry of Defence with a good train service to London every hour, so we decided to look for a house in that area. After a few months, in September 1949 we bought Karel House, Skinners Lane in Ashstead. It was a fairly small four-bedroom house but large enough to house us all including Pat the nannie, as we still needed help with Bruce and Bob, who were then about 3 ½ and 1 ½. There was a quite a good garden and about two acres of

Val in front of Karel House in Ashstead, bought in 1949

land and it was only a ten minute walk for me across the common to the station. It was also only a few hundred yards from the Ashstead Squash Club, though we didn't discover this until after we had bought it!

The job at the Joint Planning Staff (JPS) was a very important one reporting to the three Service Directors of Policy and indirectly to the three Service Chiefs of Staff for whom we prepared papers and briefs. These required quite a lot of research with other Service departments and were often wanted at short notice. It often meant working late and occasionally at weekends with my Navy and Army colleagues, Captain Tothill RN and Col. Thompson, who was a para and had been wounded and taken prisoner at Arnheim.

In our second JPS team we were lucky to have two excellent officers in Wing Commander (later Air Chief Marshal) Bob Hodges and Lt. Col. (later General) 'Monkey' Blacker which was a great help. It was a very interesting period with the introduction of the US Marshall Plan, the formation of the North Atlantic Treaty Organisation (NATO) and the Cold War with the Soviet Union.

Living near London I readily got back to my sports routine that summer with various RAF tennis matches at weekends and golf at

Leatherhead and the RAC Country Club. In the RAF Tennis Championships I lost, I think to A/C A. G. Roberts, the new Champion and one of the many young aspirants to our Davis Cup team who were doing their National Service in those years after the war. I played in the Inter-Services too which the RAF won again in August that year.

Val and I were also away a number of weekends with the children either to Tutnall Mount or Traddles as their grandparents were always wanting to see their family. As the 1949/50 squash season came round, both Douglas and I again won the Army and RAF Championships respectively, as we had done thirteen years earlier! However, this time I managed to beat him in the Inter-Services match, getting my revenge for the last time we played each other in 1937. Altogether between 1935 and 1952 Douglas won the Army Squash Championships six times and I won the RAF five times, once before the war and four times afterwards. The Inter Services Squash match had thus become quite a family affair! Early in 1950 we also played in the same squash team together representing our old school Charterhouse in the final of the Public Schools Londonderry Cup, but we sadly lost to Tonbridge after one member of our team led 8-3 match point in the final game of the final match!

Douglas wins the Army championship again and Brian wins the RAF championship in the same season, setting up a record that will be hard to beat

At weekends that summer of 1950 we spent rather more time on the house and garden and playing with Bruce and Bob who were growing up fast. Otherwise there was nothing special as far as I remember, except that on 1 July I was promoted to substantive rather than acting Group Captain.

SASO NO. 3 GROUP, BOMBER COMMAND (JULY 1951–MAY 1954)

After two years in the hard working environment of the Ministry of Defence, I was posted in 1951 to be the SASO of No. 3 Group at RAF Mildenhall, Suffolk in Bomber Command. I was pleased to get nearer to the operational front line with stations under command at Marham, Wittering, Honington and Upwood equipped with Avro Lincolns and the converted B15 Washington four-engined bombers, and RAF Wyton the Photo Recce Centre. Before going there I was able to do a flying refresher course at RAF Manby to familiarize myself with the Lincoln and also the new jet aircraft the Meteor and Canberra, with which the Group was to be re-equipped before long.

In July 1951 we let our house at Ashstead and moved with the family up to Mildenhall. Pat, the nannie, had left us the previous year but we had been lucky to get a lovely Norwegian girl, Mette Ohlsen, as a 'mother's help' who came with us. Mette had been due to go as mother's help to my new Navy colleague's wife, but she was so attractive Mrs Pennefather said she wouldn't allow her in the house! Val, I'm glad to say, was more trusting, or more desperate! so Mette had come to join us.

The AOC of 3 Group was a well known character called Bill Hesketh but after a few months changed to AVM Bill Brooke, an equally delightful boss. The HQ was a fairly small new building on what had become a USAF base on the airfield at Mildenhall. This worked very well and, as SASO, I was entitled to a Group Captain married quarter. This had a decent garden and was only five minutes walk from my office which was ideal. I thoroughly enjoyed the job and flew round a lot in either the Avro Anson, the Airspeed Oxford or the single-engined Percival Proctor communications aircraft on regular visits to all the stations, and Val and I attended many of their station functions. I also went on a number of the practice exercises in a Lincoln or Washington so that I knew what I was talking about when discussing matters with the aircrew. There was much liaison and competition with all the No. 1 Group Stations in

Lincolnshire and Yorkshire which helped to keep us on our toes, and we were in constant touch with the staff at Bomber Command HQ.

I was able to get away occasionally in August and September to play in some of the RAF tennis matches and in the RAF Championships and Inter-Services, and we took the boys on a good holiday by the sea at Frinton. Val and I also played a lot of golf on the well known nine-hole course at Royal Worlington near Mildenhall. We were also able to use the squash court on the American base, which was conveniently at the bottom of our garden, so I kept pretty fit and won the RAF Squash Championships again that year beating G/C Cecil Beamish, the RAF Head Dentist, in the final.

Our next door neighbour was the USAF Base Commander (Col Thomas) and his wife with whom we got on very well and we were able to join in many of the American social functions in their Officers' Mess which was a very happy bonus. We had our own small 3 Group Officers' Mess which was very pleasant but our numbers were very few. Particular friends at the time were Peter and Annette Brothers. He was on my staff as Wing Commander Ops but had been a Battle of Britain fighter 'Ace' during the war.

Unfortunately at this time Val's mother became very ill and we went over to Bromsgrove several weekends to see her, though sadly it was not very long before she died and Val's father Joe moved into rooms in a hotel nearby from where he could keep an eye on his business in Birmingham. Later, after a month or two he sold his business and he came to live with us at Mildenhall, though he wasn't too well and before long had to go into a nursing home in Cambridge where we were able to visit him regularly before he too died. Around then, after about two years with us, our attractive mother's help Mette decided to return to her home in Bergen and we were all very sorry to see her go. With all the attention and frequent cat-calls from the Americans on the base, I think she felt she had had enough, and said to Val that she had never thought that there would be 'too many men around'! Luckily we managed to get another very good mother's help, Jean Sparks, who got on very well with Bruce and Bob and remained with us for the rest of our time at Mildenhall and then later, rather romantically, married my batman John.

On 6 February 1952, HM King George VI died and his daughter Princess Elizabeth had to return hurriedly from Kenya, where she was on a Commonwealth tour, to take over as Queen. Nearly a year later on 1 January 1953 there was a very nice surprise for me when I was appointed an ADC (Aide de Camp) to HM The Queen – a great honour and privilege, though perhaps not as exciting as it might appear, as it was only an honorary appointment and there were six other ADCs at Group Captain level from each of the Services and normally one was seldom called upon to do anything. However, in our case, we were fortunate to have to take part in the Coronation proceedings on 2 June that year. We had seats in Westminster Abbey and marched behind the Royal Carriages on the Coronation Parade round London. In the evening we were invited to Buckingham Palace with our wives to the Royal Banquet which was superb. On the day of the Parade we all had to form up early in the morning at the Wellington Barracks, Birdcage Walk, and were led off to join in the parade from the Palace just behind The Queen Mother's carriage to Westminster Abbey. Luckily it was fine initially, but as we came out of the Abbey there was a very heavy downpour and we all got soaked. For a while the sun came out and we dried off before unfortunately more rain came while we marched round the rest of the Royal route – up Whitehall to Trafalgar Square, down the Mall past the Palace to Hyde Park Corner, then to Marble Arch, down Oxford Street, Regent Street and Pall Mall to the Palace again, and finally to where we started from, Wellington Barracks. Quite a long and tiring march of over five miles but on the whole very enjoyable with all the cheering and singing from the crowds lining the route, and it was lovely to be able to look forward to taking Val later that evening to the fabulous BP Banquet attended, of course, by all the Royal Family and VIPs attending the Coronation.

A little later in July Val and I flew down for another great occasion, The Queen's Coronation Review of the Royal Air Force at RAF Odiham which was organized by the Chief of Air Staff (ACM Sir Dermot Boyle).

It was a wonderful summer all round with much cheerful news including the successful climbing of Mt. Everest for the first time by Edmund Hillary and his Sherpa Tenzing. There was also a general feeling throughout the country of a new and exciting Elizabethan Age ahead of us.

In the RAF tennis field I was rapidly being overtaken by the good young National Service airmen such as Roger Becker and John Barrett who were all coming to do their two years with the RAF. The word had got around that the RAF would look after them better, certainly for tennis. While Chairman of the RAF Tennis Association I had arranged for any good players, if it was immaterial to their job, to be posted near London so that they could get away easily when off duty for plenty of practice and RAF matches, provided they behaved and worked hard while on the job. This seemed only sensible to me and it worked very well. My brother Douglas, who was Chairman of Army Tennis, tried to do the same but was let down by his first choice for this special treatment and the Army thereafter didn't bother and so they all came into the RAF.

Nevertheless, that summer one or two of us older ones still managed to get into the RAF team for the Inter-Services and Gus Holden and I had succeeded in winning the RAF Doubles championships against John Barrett and Colin Hannam, which was a good win and certainly unexpected. Later that winter I was beaten in the RAF Squash Championships for the first time since 1937 by Corporal Catherine, later a squash professional. It was also my last time as I was then aged forty and two of my squash friends in their forties had had heart attacks and had died in the squash court fairly recently. Val also put her foot down! 'Anno Domini' was evidently catching me up. Skiing was still OK, however, and it was not long before we were off again in January 1954 with Joan and John Hartnell-Beavis for two weeks in Zermatt while my mother kindly looked after Bruce and Bob for us. She loved to have them and said they were so much nicer when their parents weren't there too!

When we first went to Mildenhall in 1951 we had put Bruce into a day school in Newmarket to which he was able to go on a school coach from Mildenhall. He seemed to enjoy this though he got a bit confused in maths as they tried to teach him to add up in a different way from that which he was used to. When Val asked him who his best friend was he said rather breathlessly 'Wallypetanda' but did not know his surname! Sometime later when watching on sports day he pointed his friend out who was a small black American boy which I felt augured well later for a good anti-racist attitude! After a while Val had also found a small kindergarten school about a mile down the road which she took Bob to in the mornings.

During that summer my AOC Bill Brooke was posted to be Vice-Chief of the Air Staff (VCAS) and sensibly decided that before going he must qualify first as a jet pilot. He went on a Meteor conversion course at RAF Marham but, after going solo, tragically killed himself in an accident having failed to switch the oxygen on and consequently losing consciousness at high altitude and diving out of control into the ground. This was a great blow to everyone but was sadly not uncommon with a few senior officers in those days converting on to jet aircraft, as they were not used to climbing up so rapidly.

I was left for a month or two running the Group which gave me great confidence and made me feel for the first time that there was no reason why I should not be promoted further myself to Air Rank. A new AOC, 3 Group, however, was appointed and I was lucky to get an old friend and ex-RAF squash player AVM Hudleston, an Australian from Perth, WA as my new boss. I took the opportunity to fly him around to visit all our 3 Group stations and he began to enjoy the job, though it was a slight step down for him after his last appointment as Deputy to General Norstadt, the Supreme Commander of NATO, at Fontainebleau near Paris. I also took the opportunity to beat him up at squash in our local court!

Gradually the Group was re-equipping with the latest jet bomber, the Canberra, to replace the ageing Lincolns and I decided to do a Meteor Jet conversion course myself at RAF Marham before doing a Canberra conversion at RAF Bassingbourn. We were also due to open the following year a new station at RAF Gaydon, with a special long 10,000 feet runway to take the new 'V' bombers, the Valiant and the Victor. When the AOC was considering who to appoint to command the new station with the exciting 'V' bombers I couldn't help suggesting myself and happily this was agreed! So I pressed on with my conversion to jets.

In December there was some important function at RAF Marham and the AOC, Teddy Hudleston, decided to fly there in the Anson, taking with him his wife Nancy and Val and me all dressed up to the nines. Later, as we came out after the concluding official lunch, Teddy Hudleston said, 'Brian, I expect you would like to fly us back.' I naturally said 'Yes, of course,' but when I looked at the weather I saw it had clamped down with cloud on the deck with nil visibility. However, I

Canberra jet aircraft

reckoned there would be no problem taking off and after a few minutes we would be above the cloud, and we could be talked down for the landing at Mildenhall. Off we went but when above the cloud I tried to contact Mildenhall I found the intercom had gone u/s and I could get no reply from anyone. All I could do was look for a gap in the cloud, keeping a close account of my course and time on each leg. There was nothing doing and I was not in a happy position with my AOC and our wives on board in all their finery! Luckily I had seen the Met. forecast early that morning and remembered that hopefully the weather would be better near the east coast, so I managed to warn the worried AOC and headed east towards RAF Wattisham where thankfully I was able to land and we returned to Mildenhall by car! These are the sort of alarming incidents which inevitably occur sometimes with flying.

In February 1952 we were going on our skiing holiday, again with Joan and Johnny H-B to St Moritz, but this time we had a cheap charter flight from Southend Airport to Basle before going on by train. On arrival at Southend there was fog or low cloud and although the weather the other end at Basle was fine the pilot refused to take off. Johnny and I both felt that, although not good for landing, the weather was OK for take-off and the aircraft would be above the cloud in no time. We therefore tried in vain to persuade the pilot and after much waiting around we decided to ring up the head office of the charter firm to inform them of the position. This we did, pointing out that we were both senior RAF pilots and would have no hesitation ourselves about taking off in the present circumstances. Eventually the head office accepted our word for it and spoke to the pilot and told him to take off! It was very naughty of us to say the least to throw our weight around like that but it worked and we got to Basle quite safely and in time to catch our train on to St Moritz – after a good *wienerschnitzel* in the Bahnhof restaurant. On the return flight the pilot, a different one, nearly overran the runway at Southend and only just stopped short of the ditch. This was an example of the poor standard of many of the pilots who were then flying the cheaper charter flights after the war.

The next year, 1953, the RAF Ski Association had decided to leave St Moritz to the Army and move to Chamonix in France, and we went there with other Air Force friends, W/Cdr Dick and Margie Jones. It was a nice hotel there but the skiing more limited and we usually went in a coach to Les Houches where there were some very good runs. The British Ski Club representative was also very helpful and took several of us on long cross-country runs, including to Megève, which was most enjoyable.

After that all went happily at Mildenhall with summer holidays at Frinton-on-Sea and RAF Tennis which was won by Flying Officer N. R. Lewis, a member of our Davis Cup team, who with his partner LAC Jones beat me and Squadron Leader Ted Frith in the doubles finals. Then in August at the Inter-Services Championships the RAF had their fifth post-war victory, winning 11 out of a possible 12 rubbers.

The next winter, while we were still at Mildenhall, I unaccountably got pneumonia though my AOC Teddy Hudleston put it down to him giving me a hard game of squash a few days earlier and taking a game off me! Anyway, we had to postpone our annual skiing holiday until March when Val and I went overnight by train to Sestriere in Italy. It is fairly high at 6,000 feet and some of the ski slopes at 9,000 feet so there was a good chance of plenty of snow as late as March. As it happened there was a heavy fall the morning we arrived of two feet of snow which in fact delayed our arrival at Sestriere by a couple of hours We stayed at the rather luxurious Hotel Duce d'Aosta, of an unusual round tower shape, which was excellent in every way and with dancing after dinner every evening which was fun. The next day Val and I were skiing on the well known Sises run when a man stopped abruptly next to me and said, 'You must be Brian Burnett, aren't you? You beat me 6-0, 6-0 at the Junior Tennis Tournament at East Grinstead many years ago and I've never forgotten it!' It was Peter Forbes, a first class skier who was there with his wife Carmen and who from then on took Val and me in tow most days on some lovely soft snow runs through the woods which was super.

RAF GAYDON (1954–56)

When we got back to Mildenhall I started handing over my SASO job at 3 Group to Air Commodore Candy of the Royal Australian Air Force (RAAF) before going on to complete my Meteor jet conversion course at RAF Marham and Canberra conversion at RAF Bassingbourne in May. Finally then the whole family moved to RAF Gaydon at the end of May 1954. Wing Commander 'Vick' Willis, who was to be the W/Cdr Admin. and was a batchelor, had moved in to the Officers' Mess there and, as there were no married quarters yet he had kindly booked us in to a very nice large flat in a lovely country house called Bitham Hall owned by Mrs Worral at Avon Dasset and only a few miles away from Gaydon. It had a superb view overlooking their garden and in the distance to Edge Hill. We settled happily there while I drove in daily to start taking over command of the station which was all brand new and still largely under construction. I was able to keep an eye on the work on some of the new buildings as well as the general layout of the station which I was obviously interested in.

In the meantime, some of the aircrew instructors and technical personnel were gradually being posted in to set up the facilities ready for the Valiants' arrival. I had been asked earlier who I would like as the W/Cdr Flying/Chief Instructor and I was lucky to be given my first choice who was W/Cdr Bob Hodges. I had known him earlier, of course, in the JPS in the Ministry of Defence and he had recently commanded the special Canberra record speed flight to Australia. The other aircrew instructors and the W/Cdr Engineer were also mostly specially selected for their jobs as the introduction of the RAF 'V' Force and the RAF's future 'nuclear deterrent' was naturally considered so very important. There was much preparatory work to be done including getting the Valiant simulator going. Inevitably the date for delivery of the first Valiants receded so we had a couple of Canberra B1s and Meteor 7s to enable everyone to keep their hands in on local flying. I loved flying both the Meteor and the Canberra, so managed to do quite a lot myself.

There were no sports facilities on the new station, though I had two tennis courts marked out on the parade ground which could be made available. Otherwise, one was dependent on local facilities in Leamington Spa or Warwick or the golf course at Tadmarton near Banbury where some of us used to play. Val used to ride a lot, helping Heather King (wife of an old Charterhouse friend of mine and a W/Cdr in the RAF Equipment Branch) exercise their horses at Little Compton where they lived not far from Banbury. Val also bought a pony to get Bruce and Bob riding and kept it in a stable at a house nearby. Unfortunately the pony went lame before long, so I'm afraid that was not a great success.

After his school in Newmarket, Bruce had been to what we thought was a good pre boarding school called Southey Hall near Leatherhead, which was run by Denis Fussell, the brother of my old tennis friend Dick Shaw's wife. Unfortunately it packed up after Bruce had only been there a couple of terms, so we had moved him to a school near Maidenhead called St Pirans. This was only a few miles from Traddles and my parents quite enjoyed having him nearby so that they could easily go to watch their grandson when playing games. Bruce stayed on there and for Bob there was a small privately run school in one of the houses in the village of Avon Dassett which seemed very satisfactory for a short while anyway.

It was also very convenient, within walking distance, and enabled Val and him to get to know more of our neighbours. At Bitham Hall Mrs Worral had a daughter and two Army sons in the Guards who were often there, and a third son called Tony who worked on a farm near Banbury and was very keen on rugger. He was pretty good, I think, and a big man who was known as the 'runaway tank'! He was very kind to Bruce and Bob and used to give them rides on his farm tractor. Claud, the second son, was married with three attractive young daughters called Kate, Mary and Miranda, two of whom were about the same age as Bruce and Bob so that was rather nice when they were at Bitham Hall which was quite often.

That summer, whilst waiting for the Valiants to be delivered, I was able to carry on with much of my RAF tennis and in October playing with Neil Cox in the Old Carthusian team we won the D'Abernon Cup for the Old Boys Tennis Competition. Early in 1955 I played my last first class squash match. I was wanted to play for the RAF against Oxford University but as I hadn't played for several months I only reluctantly agreed provided I could play low down in the order at No. 5 string. However, when I arrived for the match I found I had to play No. 1 against the Oxford captain who was half my age and had won all his matches the previous year. After a long struggle I was thoroughly exhausted but managed just to win 10-8 in the fifth game! Afterwards, while having a bath in the next door cubicle, I heard Daniels (Graham I think it was) muttering, 'Fancy being beaten by an old b----- like that in my first match of the season!' It took me also several days to recover so as neither of us seemed to get much enjoyment out of it I decided that at nearly forty-two it should be my last competitive squash match – which it was.

Eventually on 8 February 1955 we got delivery of our first Valiant and there was much activity with everyone needing to get converted, including Bob Hodges and the instructors themselves. The situation was eased as more Valiants – three a month – arrived and the conversion of aircrews for the first operational squadron proceeded smoothly, so I was then able to get converted briefly myself and I must say the Valiant was a magnificent aircraft to fly. As expected, the station at that time was besieged by VIP visitors from the Air Ministry, including the Secretary of State for Air, Viscount de Lisle, as well as staff officers from Bomber Command and Group, so we were all kept very busy with briefing and showing them round. Another visit of interest was a group of air cadets

Vickers Valiant at low level over Labrador

from Cheltenham College with the Headmaster, the Revd Plentreith who I took for a flight in a Canberra to a fairly high altitude above the cloud. He came for tea with Val and me afterwards and, when he was about to go, he said he had to get back as the Bishop was coming to dinner. I said he could now tell the Bishop he had been nearer to God than him, and he said he would!

By the summer of 1955 the Valiant Conversion Unit at Gaydon was going well and the first Squadron, No. 138, had formed at RAF Wittering. Unfortunately in July there was a tragic accident when one of their Flight Commanders (S/Ldr Chalk I think) soon after taking off dived out of control into the ground killing all the crew. Until then we had had no problems of any kind with the Valiant and Sir George Edwards, the Chief Designer (later Chairman) of Vickers-Aviation Ltd., was convinced the accident must have been due to 'pilot error'. Those of us who knew the Squadron Leader as an excellent pilot were equally convinced that there must have been some technical fault. The AOC felt the Court of Enquiry was so important he wanted a Group Captain, rather than the usual Wing Commander, to chair it. As the only Group Captain with any experience of the Valiant at all I was more or less automatically selected, but I insisted on having one of the other Valiant flight commanders, S/Ldr David Roberts, who I knew was very good technically, on the Board of Enquiry with me. The Vickers chief test pilot (Trubshaw) represented the aircraft firm. A number of different possible causes of the accident were considered and failure of the aileron control was the most likely, though Vickers would not agree. I decided, therefore, that we would do an air test ourselves under similar circumstances but at high altitude so that there would be plenty of time to recover control if necessary. This was accepted though Vickers felt that, as the official test pilots, they should do the air test and let us know the result. This they did and the air test confirmed our view that there had been an electrical fault in the aileron trimmer actuator and there had been nothing the pilot could have done about it at low level. This was naturally comforting as far as the aircrew were concerned but the accident was partly due to the single pole electric wiring throughout the aircraft and this meant expensive modifications to all the Valiants. However, I think this probably saved many more aircrew lives during the Valiant's ten years or so in service.

Later that summer of 1955 the married quarters at Gaydon had progressed well and Val and I moved into one of the new ones. We had enjoyed our time living out at Bitham Hall, but it was better for me to be on the station and it was useful to have a batman to help Val in the married quarter. We were later able to get away for a couple of weeks' summer leave when I took the family down to Sway in the New Forest where, for the second year in a row, we rented a private house called Crossways. From there it was easy to drive to the beach at Milford or Barton-on-Sea, though we actually preferred a very quiet small beach on the east side of Lymington which you had to walk across a field to get to and consequently we nearly always had it to ourselves. We were fortunate at Crossways to be able to keep on the existing cook help. She was very good though Val was warned that she sometimes had an epileptic fit which didn't last long if we stood her on her head! Luckily we didn't have to put this to the test.

Back at RAF Gaydon all was going well and by the end of the year we were able to take some more leave over Christmas, when Val and I went to Zermatt taking Bruce and Bob for their first time when they were ten and eight years old. Unfortunately this was not ideal for beginners as the nursery slopes were mostly in the shade, but it was fun taking them up higher and trying to ski with them between our legs in a heavy snow plough. Anyway, they both got hooked on skiing and have been almost every year since. They have also both said that taking them skiing so young was the best thing I had ever done for them!

The Valiant conversion training continued to go well in 1956 and the converted crews moved on to their squadrons at RAF Wittering. I continued to enjoy my time as the Station Commander, and the many VIP visitors to see the Valiant never ceased. I also managed to persuade the Works and Bricks Department to fund a number of improvements to the facilities on the station more in keeping with its important role, and this too kept me fairly busy.

The next thing that happened was a new appointment for me to be the Director of Bombing and Reconnaissance Operations at Air Ministry in the rank of Air Commodore. This was great news and, although sorry to leave Gaydon which had been one of my favourite command appointments, promotion to Air Rank was not to be denied. I had to get busy to hand over the station to Group Captain Brian Young, an old friend who had recently done the Valiant conversion. Val and I had to get busy to get our house at Ashstead back and arrange a school for Bob. Fortunately we were able to get the tenants out of our house at Ashstead before long so we moved back there in good time before I was due to take over my new job at Air Ministry, and we arranged for Bob to join Bruce's school at St Pirans as a young boarder.

DIRECTOR OF BOMBER AND RECONNAISANCE OPERATIONS. AIR MINISTRY (1956–57). NUCLEAR WEAPON TEST AT CHRISTMAS ISLAND

As Director of Bomber and Reconnaisance Ops I came under AVM Ronnie Lees, an Australian, who was Assistant Chief of Air Staff operations (ACAS Ops). One of my earliest jobs on his staff was to go with him to observe the air test of Britain's first thermo-nuclear bomb from a Valiant at Christmas Island. The RAF had had some experience of testing atomic weapons at the Monte Bello islands and the range at Maralinga in Australia, but this new operation called 'Grapple' was to be our first test of the higher yield nuclear bomb. For this, and several following tests, Christmas Island on the equator and in the middle of the Pacific Ocean had been selected, presumably because its remoteness would involve fewer problems of radiation etc. There were, of course, many other problems, particularly the distances to be covered for supplying all the necessary equipment for building up a new temporary tented camp, a new runway and hard standings for the Valiants and the many other aircraft involved, as well as the weapons assembly shed, decontamination centre, Joint Operation Centre and so on.

The distances for the supply route were indeed enormous – 1,200 miles from Honolulu and a further 2,400 miles from San Francisco, or alternatively, 4,000 miles from New Zealand or Australia, or 6,000 miles

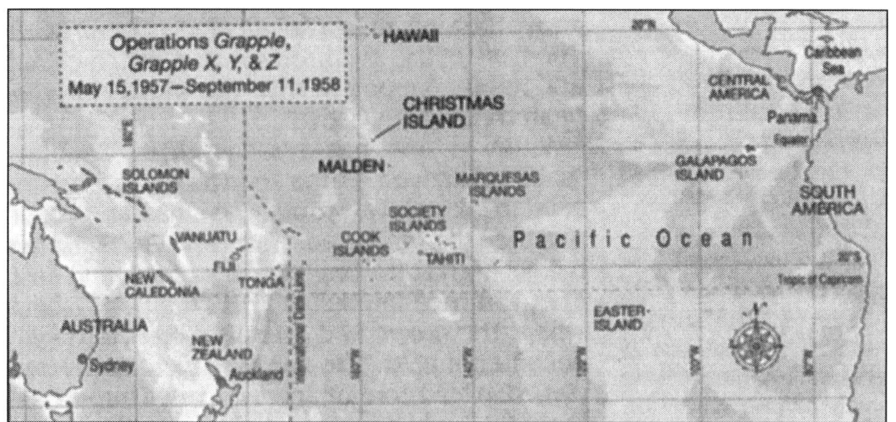

Map showing location of Christmas Island

from Singapore. The main target area, Malden Island, was also some 400 miles further south-east of the Christmas Island base.

Christmas Island itself was quite small – barely the size of the Isle of Wight in England – and had been under British sovereignty since Captain Cook discovered it many years ago. There were only very few inhabitants from the Gilbert Islands who could fairly easily be evacuated if necessary. The Americans had used a small coral landing strip there during the war which we were able to make use of and they were very helpful in allowing us to have staging posts on the way at their air bases at Travis (San Francisco) and Hickham (Honolulu).

The Task Force Commander (TFC) for Operation Grapple was an old Spec 'N' friend of mine, AVM Wilf Oulton, and Ronnie Lees and I flew out together on 3 May in a Hastings aircraft, stopping on the way at RAF Aldergrove in Northern Ireland, then across the Atlantic to RCAF Goose Bay in Canada, then to Travis Air Force base (AFB) (San Francisco) and Hickham AFB (Honolulu) before reaching Christmas Island in the Pacific. There we landed on 9 May on the old wartime coral strip which was being used by the Hastings, Shackletons and some of the other aircraft while the new runway was being finally prepared for the Valiants.

The RAF Chief Scientist (Bill Cook) and the various 'boffins' and other experts from the Atomic Weapons Research Establishment (AWRE) in England were already there when ACAS (Ops) and I arrived. We were met by Wilf Oulton the TFC and taken down to the tented camp which had been built on the North Shore, the driest part of the island and alongside the beach. Being on the equator it was very hot so a good swim before supper was very welcome. It had to be inside the reef, of course, because of the many sharks surrounding the island, but the snorkelling was wonderful and it was an ideal start before we met up with the others in the Officers' Mess tent.

Wilf Oulton and his 'Grapple' team had done a wonderful job in building up the camp from scratch and getting all the many detailed arrangements organized in such a short time – little more than a year. Much heavy equipment had to be shipped in by the Royal Navy for the Army Sappers to build the new runway for the Valiants and the other operational facilities as well as the huts and tented accommodation for a Task Force of about 4,000 personnel eventually. At Malden Island also a small landing strip had to be made and ground shelters provided for the camera and recording equipment of the AWRE scientists.

By the time Ronnie Lees and I arrived the Task Force was virtually ready to go ahead with the first of the RAF live nuclear tests. The bomb was to be dropped from a Valiant flying at 45,000 feet to explode at 6,000 feet about a mile off the south-east point of Malden Island. The bomb was ready to be loaded on one of the two Valiants standing by in their shiny white heat reflective paint, and the four Canberra crews were ready to do their job of flying through the nuclear cloud to collect the samples required by the scientists at AWRE. Regular rehearsals were carried out (without the nuclear bomb!) to ensure no last minute problems, and while these were going on Ronnie Lees and I had a good chance to have a look around and we were taken on a helicopter flight round the island which was most interesting and helped us to get a better idea of the whole set-up.

When the time came a few days later on 15 May and the weather and wind direction was favourable enough for the TFC to give the decision to go ahead, ACAS (Ops) and I were taken off in the VIP Hastings with the other official visitors to go to our observer position at the same height but about twenty-six miles west of the planned bomb burst position. The TFC and Chief Scientist (Bill Cook) paid a quick visit to Malden Island, where the recording equipment was being prepared, and were then taken by helicopter to the Control Room on HMS *Narvik* about twenty miles north of the target area. In the meantime the Deputy TFC (A/Cdre Ginger Weir) remained at the Joint Operations Centre at Christmas Island to control all aircraft movements from there. All units involved in the operation were in communication with the TFC, and the countdown of the Valiant captain (Wing Commander Ken Hubbard) on his final run in at 45,000 feet was relayed to everyone concerned so that appropriate action could be taken. When the words 'Bomb gone' came over the loudspeakers, as instructed, everyone turned their backs towards Malden Island, shut their eyes and covered them with their hands. Despite this after about a minute there was a sensation of brilliant light and a flash of heat and it was not until a few seconds later still that we were told we could turn round to have a look at the amazing, awesome sight of the rapidly rising nuclear cloud with its top spreading out sideways to form the well known mushroom shape. It was a little while later still that the Hastings we were in received an enormous bump from the resulting shock airwave even at the twenty-six miles or so that we were away from the bomb burst. The Shackletons were then busy taking photographs of the nuclear cloud at the lower levels as it grew larger and kept on rising rapidly. A PR Canberra was also doing this at higher levels so that an estimate of the size and rate of growth of the cloud could be made, leading to a rough estimate of the yield of the bomb though this was best done more precisely later from the nuclear cloud samples which Air Commodore Wilson of the RAF Medical Branch and his B6 Canberras collected about half an hour later when they actually flew through the nuclear cloud. Happily, as anticipated, the instant level of radiation and the cumulative dosage as they flew through were well within the permitted safe limits, but nevertheless after landing back at Christmas Island they taxied straight over to the decontamination centre for a shower and clean clothing to ensure they were clear of any contamination. The records from the instrumentation sites were able to be collected quickly and flown back to AWRE in England for further analysis together with the canisters with cloud samples from the Canberras.

The news of this successful drop of Britain's first nuclear bomb was, needless to say, very well received by the Prime Minister and all at home at the Ministry of Defence and was the cause for considerable relief and celebration on Christmas Island by Wilf Oulton, the Task Force Commander, and his 'Grapple' team. After a well-earned 48-hour break, however, the latter had to start preparing for the second test in two weeks' time although many of the key personnel had to return to the UK.

Ronnie Lees and I left two days later on 17 May after a most interesting and fascinating week on Christmas Island which I will never forget. We returned to Honolulu in one of the Hastings and then on to England by various airlines via San Francisco, Washington and New York, calling in on our opposite numbers in the US Air Force. We eventually got home a week later on 24 May after three weeks away.

THE SUEZ OPERATION

The next major event I was involved with was the Suez Operation when the Egyptian dictator Col. Nasser nationalized the Suez Canal for which Britain, under an international convention, was responsible for guaranteeing the free right of transit to all shipping. This provoked the Suez Crisis in which Britain, France and Israel eventually attacked Egypt to restore the status quo.

Britain had unfortunately evacuated the Canal Zone a couple of years earlier, so a special Task Force had to be organized for the job operating from British bases in Cyprus and Malta. Canberra squadrons were ready straight away but the Valiants had to be quickly switched to their conventional bombing role before deploying to Malta ready to bomb the Egyptian airfields. Together with ground attack aircraft from Cyprus, the plan was that they would take out the Egyptian Air Force and provide complete air superiority for the launch of our attacking ground forces. This was not expected to take very long, although there was a little bit of uncertainty because the Egyptian Air Force had been re-equipped with a number of Russian aircraft and there were a few Russian pilots there as instructors. Communications were extremely poor in those days but our forces concerned, which we had prepositioned in Cyprus and Malta, were kept informed satisfactorily. I remember particularly that morning when the CAS (Sir Dermot Boyle) rang for me and I rushed upstairs to find ACAS (Ops) Ronnie Lees also about to go in, when we were told by CAS: 'We have the decision to go.' There had been so much indecision before as to who and what should be attacked, that my first reaction was to say, 'Who against, Sir?' to which he replied, 'You may well ask; but it is Egypt!' So we immediately had to inform all concerned to go ahead that night. Ronnie Lees got through to Cyprus, on the teleprinter I think, but I had to get through to the AOC in Malta using very guarded plain language. That was not the end of our communications problems, however, because no sooner had G/C Bob Hodges and the Valiant aircraft taken off from Malta that evening than a message came through from the PM at No. 10 to say the Americans were evacuating Cairo on the road to Alexandria which went close by Cairo West airfield (one of the targets) and we were on no account to bomb it, because of the risk of American casualties. So we had to get through again to Malta to tell them to recall all the Valiants, already half way there, and then re-fuel them and issue different target maps excluding Cairo West. What a way to start a war! Fortunately all the Valiants got their recall message and set off again from Malta but this time, instead of Cairo West, the Valiants bombed one of the other Cairo airfields, unknowingly demolishing the hangars in which the American Ambassador's communication aircraft were kept. I never heard the end of that! Otherwise all went well; all bombs fell within the airfields concerned and although as expected there was not sufficient weight of bombs to put the airfields out of action for long, the ground attack aircraft from Cyprus were able to go in the next morning at low level to take out any remaining aircraft on the ground. So the Paras and ground forces were able to go ashore virtually unopposed and in very short time had almost reached Suez at the southern end of the Canal.

During this period one of the Air Commodore (Ops) had to be on duty at the Air Ministry overnight, and I slept every alternate night on a camp bed in my office. Most nights the Minister of Defence used to come over quite late to be briefed on the day's operations. One night though, in the early hours, I was woken up by a messenger with an urgent signal from Mr Khrushchev of the Soviet Union. It was obviously intended for the Prime Minister and, if I remember correctly, in the signal they threatened that they would walk into Hungary unless we stopped immediately and pulled out of Egypt. I sent this, of course, straight away to No. 10 with instructions to waken the Prime Minister if necessary. I can't help thinking that this, together with the strong American opposition from General Eisenhower who I believe threatened oil sanctions, may have influenced the Government and Anthony Eden, who himself was not very well at the time, to call a halt to the campaign, although British troops had already reached Port Said and the main aim of regaining control of the Suez Canal had almost been achieved satisfactorily. All the British forces had to be withdrawn and the Canal left under Nasser's control with only inexperienced pilots to guide shipping through the Canal. Although a complete military success then, as far as it was allowed to go, the Suez operation was a political disaster and undoubtedly led to the fall of Anthony Eden as Prime Minister.

After that, with the Cold War still on, our bomber forces were able to return to England and get back to their main role of maintaining Britain's nuclear deterrent. Happily I was able to do a bit of refresher flying myself at RAF Wittering on the Canberra and Valiant aircraft. Otherwise things were fairly quiet and I was able to get back to some of my usual RAF tennis. In December, over Christmas, Val and I took the boys skiing again – this time to Kitzbühel in Austria. The boys improved a lot despite not very good snow conditions and I made up a bit for the latter by doing rather well in the evenings at the casino there and winning almost enough to pay for our holiday!

My next posting then came through to attend the Imperial Defence College (IDC) course starting in January 1958.

IMPERIAL DEFENCE COLLEGE (1958)

The course at the IDC, in Belgrave Square, London, was for senior officers with potential for further advancement, and was regarded as a year's sabbatical to give future commanders time to relax and think, and to consider world affairs and matters beyond the purely military before going on to other important appointments. On my 1958 course there were as usual representatives not only from the Navy, Army and Air Force but also from the Foreign Office, Commonwealth Relations Office and others from the Civil Service as well as from the United States, Canada, Australia, New Zealand, India and Pakistan. There were a total of seventy students, fifty from the UK and twenty from overseas with General Sir Geoffrey Bourne as Commandant and three 2-star Senior Directing Staff and one Civil Servant as instructors. Lectures from the Chiefs of Staff, Ministers and VIPs from all walks of life were usually arranged in the mornings with extensive discussion periods. In the afternoons the students were split up into small groups of well balanced experience to consider other prescribed matters. Many visits were organized to service establishments and industry, and during the summer extensive tours arranged for different groups of students to countries abroad, including the USA and Canada, South Africa, the Middle East, India and Europe. Although not my first choice, I was detailed for the European tour which turned out to be very good value and most interesting.

In April 1958 the RAF celebrated its 40th Anniversary and I attended the large banquet that was laid on at Fighter Command HQ for all Air officers, with The Queen and most other members of the Royal Family, and the CAS (ACM Sir Dermot Boyle) and all members of the Air Council being present.

Before going on the European tour I was able to fit in some leave and drove down to Grasse in the south of France with Val and the boys to stay with my brother Douglas and his wife Andrée. While I went off on the IDC tour, Andrée kept the family on at La Thébaïde so they were able to enjoy the rest of their summer holidays with their cousins, George, Dany, Vivy and Siby, picnicking and swimming most days in the sea from different beaches along the coast. That was very lucky and I flew back to England leaving Val with the car there.

My European tour started on 19 August from RAF Northolt when we all climbed on board a Hastings of RAF Transport Command in which we were to be flown round everywhere to Norway, Sweden, Denmark, Germany, Italy, Yugoslavia and France. This was all very good and easy and we were greeted and briefed everywhere by senior officials and Ministers.

In Oslo we heard much about the German wartime occupation and the Norwegian Resistance activities and we were taken right up north to the Norwegian border with Russia. In Stockholm we were most impressed with the efficiency of their Air Force with their underground hangars from which aircraft could take off straight ahead to save time taxiing as well as being less vulnerable to ground attack – also their underground submarine shelters under the rocky coast. In Copenhagen too we heard a lot about the German occupation and the Danish Resistance. In Germany we went to Berlin first, where one could still see the extensive wartime damage from the bombing and where we had a most interesting briefing and discussion with Herr Willy Brandt, the former Chancellor who had got out of Germany himself to Sweden, I believe, at some stage during the war. We then went on to Bonn, the German capital at that time, for further talks. I can't remember much about the Italy visit apart from CENTO discussions and the usual sight-seeing in Rome and a visit to Naples and the beautiful islands of Capri and Ischia. After taking off from Naples we persuaded the captain of the Hastings to fly low over Vesuvius so that we could look right down into the red hot crater, which was fascinating. We then landed in Belgrade in Yugoslavia where we all stayed in the hotel where General Montgomery, at that time still the Deputy C-in-C of NATO, had been staying the week before to say a friendly farewell, I think, to Tito. However, he had discovered that his room was bugged and so left suddenly in high dudgeon! In case we too were being 'bugged' we enjoyed saying a few rude words near the pictures for them to listen to. Nevertheless, our visit the next day was nothing but very friendly, mostly to do with agriculture and farming, when we were being taken around the country. The next visit to France was mainly to NATO HQ, then at Fontainebleau, and was remarkable for the detailed briefings by the US General Norstadt and other senior officers there.

Altogether the tour was very interesting and good fun, and we enjoyed later writing a full joint report which we put over to the rest of the course when we were back at the IDC. This was also done by the other tours so the whole course could benefit from all of them.

It was good then to get the family back home from the south of France and finish the rest of the course quietly in Belgrave Square. As the year progressed and the course was coming to an end, our RAF postings were discussed with us by the Air Secretary, Air Chief Marshal Sir Denis Barnett. I was being earmarked for the post of Air Officer Administration (AOA) at Bomber Command HQ with the rank of Air Vice-Marshal. Although slightly disappointed at first, as I had hoped for a command rather than a staff job, I was told that the admin. experience at this stage of my career would be beneficial. I could see this and promotion to AVM was not to be sneezed at anyway, so I happily accepted.

On the whole it had been a very good and enjoyable year and I had made many long lasting friends and contacts, which I found very useful at times in the future.

8

BOMBER COMMAND

AIR OFFICER ADMINISTRATION (1959–61)

After another enjoyable skiing holiday over Christmas with the family at Zermatt, I then reported to HQ Bomber Command near High Wycombe on 10 January 1959 with the Acting Rank of AVM. I was taking over as AOA from AVM 'Willy' Merton who was being promoted to be Chief of Staff of Allied Forces in Central Europe and my new C-in-C was the well known Air Marshal Sir Harry Broadhurst of wartime fame who had commanded the British Ground Attack aircraft throughout the North African campaign and the Second Front in Europe. I had known him briefly before when I was Director of Bomber Ops and was delighted now to be on his staff. He was an excellent C-in-C and once you knew what he wanted he let you get on with it without interfering all the time. I also knew well the SASO AVM 'Iron Jaw' Jack Davis and the AOC No. 1 Group, AVM Gus Walker, and AOC 3 Group AVM 'Bing' Cross, so it didn't take me long to get closely involved in providing the HQ Administrative backing for the rapidly building up Valiant, Vulcan and Victor deterrent forces. In the first few months I flew myself around in the Communications Flight Anson visiting all the sixteen main stations so as to get to know the Station Commanders personally and this was good.

We sold our house at Ashstead and Val and I and the boys (when not at school) had in the meantime moved into No. 10 Bradenham Beeches, one of the senior married quarters near the Officers' Mess. This was excellent with a lovely rose garden and space for the boys to bicycle and play with our new little poodle dog, called 'Rusty Lugs' by the boys because although originally rusty coloured all over he had gradually turned white except for his ears! As an AVM I fortunately rated two batmen living in upstairs and this was a very useful help to Val,

With Bruce and Bob at Bradenham Beeches

particularly as she taught one of them, Maurice, to cook and paid for him to have private cooking lessons in High Wycombe.

There were two tennis courts and a squash court at the Officers' Mess which we all used regularly and at weekends we often visited my parents at Traddles which was only thirty minutes away, or they visited us.

Some time early that summer Sir Harry Broadhurst was posted to NATO HQ at Fontainebleau and Bing Cross moved down from 3 Group to take over as the new C-in-C with AVM Micky Dwyer taking over from him at Mildenhall. However, there was no change in policy and the Command continued to build up its deterrent forces, with the addition of Thor missiles at RAF Feltwell and North Luffenham under joint British/American operational control. Bing Cross was an old friend so we got on well together and at weekends played a lot of golf at which he was much better than me and had to give me a lot of strokes to make a good game of it.

Unfortunately early in July my father had a nasty fall and had to go into hospital in Maidenhead with a badly damaged hip. Although he was in quite a lot of pain, at the age of eighty-four the doctors did not want to operate as they felt his heart was not strong enough. As a result he gradually seemed to get more frail, so we postponed going abroad as planned for our summer holiday in case he didn't last much longer.

However, a few weeks later he suddenly appeared to get better, so Val and I and the boys went off to Le Coq sur Mer and the lovely sandy beaches on the Belgian coast. We knew the Du Vivier family who lived near there, so were looking forward to plenty of tennis and golf as well as sea bathing. No sooner had we got there, however, when my brother Douglas rang to say Dad had died on 22 August but luckily he was able to cope with all the funeral arrangements and so on. However, I got through to our Communication Flight at Booker airfield and persuaded the F/Lt CO to do a practice training flight to Ostend airport in the Anson and fly me back, so I managed to get home the following day to help Douglas and our mother. It was all very sad and we just had a quiet family cremation at the Reading crematorium, consoled to some extent with the thought that he had had a pretty good innings at the age of eighty-four. After a couple of days at home, I got the Communication Flight to arrange another training flight to take me back to Ostend from where Val collected me for the rest of our family holiday which we much enjoyed with lovely sunny weather. Fortunately Douglas was able to stay on a few days at Traddles helping to clear up Dad's estate. We suggested that when we got back Mum should come and stay with us and this she did for a few days but she preferred to stay on in her beloved Traddles where she did have staff help. She also had our old family friend Vee staying there, although he was not too well and had soon to go into a nursing home in Maidenhead where I used to visit him regularly.

That summer of 1959 there were a number of VIP visits to our Bomber Command Stations which I had to attend; an example I see from my log book is that Val and I flew up to RAF Scampton for The Queen Mother's visit to 617 Squadron on 14 May and again on 13 June for the Trooping of the Colour, then to RAF Upwood for Princess Alexandra's visit to 35 Squadron. On 19 June there was the Bomber Command Athletics Championships so there was nearly always something going on requiring my attention which was very enjoyable and involved flying myself to and fro to the different airfields, and Val was often able to come with me.

One of the smaller jobs I enjoyed doing as AOA was to help get decorated the new Officers' Mess dining room. First of all I organized a new painting of HM The Queen by the well known artist Norman Heppell, who obtained the necessary sittings with her in her Order of the Bath robes which was a great success. I also arranged for portraits of Marshal of the RAF Lord Portal (ex C-in-C and CAS) and of ACM Sir

Arthur Harris (Bomber Harris the famous war-time C-in-C) as well as a wallpamur painting by a well known London artist of the famous bombing of the Mohne Dam by Wing Commander Guy Gibson and his 617 Squadron.

In January 1960 I took Val and the boys on holiday skiing at St Moritz, staying again at the Albana Hotel on the RAF scheme. There we met up with some old squash rackets friends, Peter Brochie and David Vaughan, with whom we skied quite a lot and had great fun. After that, 1960 was a slightly quieter year although the continual VIP visits to the bomber stations kept me busy; and in the summer I was invited to join Air Marshal Sir Hugh Constantine, C-in-C of Flying Training Command, in a separate Service Investigation into RAF Administration at Command level. This involved many interesting meetings and discussions with Commanders-in-Chief, and included a visit to RAF Middle East Command in Cyprus when we flew out via Geneva and Athens and back via Ankara and Rome. It all ended up in a fairly lengthy report but I can't remember whether any of our recommendations were accepted or not!

In June 1960 I played for the second time in what had become a very enjoyable annual golf match for the Air Officers against the Aircraft Industry at Wentworth Golf Club. It was a great gathering of senior officers and, although the standard of golf was far from brilliant, it was always great fun and very interesting meeting many of the aircraft designers, test pilots and others. I was lucky to play in it for four or five years.

Around that time I was rung up by Herman David, Chairman of the All England Lawn Tennis Club, at Wimbledon inviting me to join the Committee. I wasn't sure whether I would be able to spare the time but the C-in-C, Bing Cross, who was very keen on all sports, said there was no question about it – I *must* accept and make time, So I did, much to my enjoyment later on! While in that job, with his backing, I was able to get away fairly easily for meetings at Wimbledon and London.

In July 1960 my substantive promotion to Air Vice-Marshal came through happily and later in the year in December I accompanied the C-in-C in a DH Comet of RAF Transport Command via Keflavik in Iceland to visit our 'V' Bomber low flying training base at RCAF Goose Bay in Labrador. From there we went on to visit HQ USAF Strategic Air Command and then Vandenberg AFB, where the USAF allowed us use of their Thor Missile test firing base for our periodic testing of one of the Thor missiles with which Bomber Command were now partly equipped. It was fascinating to see the missile go off out over the Pacific and great to know that they worked! Eventually we flew back in the Comet, via USAF Offutt AFB and Strategic Air Command HQ and Goose Bay again, in time for Christmas and for me to take the family on our annual skiing holiday for two weeks in January 1961 to Zermatt.

After that I began to think of my next appointment – hopefully in Command and hoping I might be able to take over No. 3 Group, which I knew and felt I could do well. The year proceeded as usual, so I made a special effort to get into full jet flying practice on the Canberra at RAF Bassingbourne and the Valiant at RAF Gaydon in the hope of persuading the C-in-C to ask for me for 3 Group. Happily this was finally agreed and a straight swap was arranged for October with AVM Micky Dwyer who would have done his time there by then, and he took over from me in due course as AOA at Bomber Command HQ.

In the meantime I carried on in the AOA job which kept me pretty busy as usual and in the Birthday Honours that summer I was awarded the CB and made a Companion of the Order of the Bath, which was a nice surprise. In June it was soon Wimbledon time and I took two weeks' leave to attend it every day. Val and I stayed conveniently nearby at the RAC Country Club at Epsom, of which I was an Honorary Member as a member of the International Lawn Tennis Club (ILTC) of Great Britain. We found this very convenient and pleasant, and we sometimes played a few holes of golf in the morning first before going to Wimbledon. It was an excellent introduction to my first year on the Committee at the Championships. Apart from playing in the Championships in 1946, I had, of course, been there before for occasional days when I could get tickets, including the rather disappointing Ellsworth Vines v 'Bunny' Austin final in 1932. However, 1961 was a good year as far as I can remember, with Rod Laver winning the Men's Singles after two years as runner-up and Angela Mortimer beating Christine Truman in the Ladies' Final. It was a remarkable year too in that there were two English ladies in the Final.

After Wimbledon was over I managed to fit in a bit more Valiant flying up at RAF Gaydon preparatory to going to take over 3 Group in October. Val was delighted then to be going back to the Mildenhall area where she knew lots of friends, and where she knew we would enjoy living in the AOC's Residence (The Old Rectory) at Barton Mills near her favourite well-known golf course Royal Worlington. Fortunately it was also only about one hour away from Haileybury College where both Bruce and Bob were now installed, and therefore easy to visit or take them out at weekends. Before going to 3 Group, however, I still had two weeks' leave left and we all went down in August by car to stay with Douglas and family at Grasse to enjoy the south of France sunshine and sea bathing, and to see my mother who was now living with them. She had decided about a year earlier to leave Traddles and to go and live with Douglas and Andrée at La Thébaïde where she had a small suite on the ground level built on for herself. Vee, our old family friend, who used to live with us at Traddles had recently had to go into a nursing home and had died, so there was nothing to keep her there and she was letting the house in case Val and I might want it later. It had been my family home for thirty years but we decided sadly against it as we were still moving around in the RAF, and felt it would be better to sell it for her, which I did later.

AOC 3 GROUP, BOMBER COMMAND (1961–64)

I finally got to take over 3 Group in October 1961 and arranged in January to be converted on to the Handley Page (HP) Victor by Wing Commander Bob Wilson at RAF Honington. At the end of January 1962 I flew out with him on a two week trip to visit one of our Victor squadrons rotating through the Middle and Far East. We flew first to Akrotiri in Cyprus, then on to Bahrein in the Gulf, Gan in the Maldive

Victor Bomber

Islands, and on to RAAF Butterworth. There I spent next morning with the Victor squadron and in the afternoon was taken on a very interesting trip in a Sycamore helicopter, when we landed vertically between very tall trees to inspect one of the Army training camps in the Malayan jungle. At Butterworth I stayed with the Australian Group Captain Station Commander in his house right near the beach, and he persuaded me to go in for a swim before breakfast the next morning. I did – but didn't like it much because the sea was swarming with sea snakes. But that didn't seem to worry him and he just picked them up and threw them over his shoulder! After that we flew on in the Victor to RAF Tengah in Singapore where I called on the Air Commander, AVM McGregor, and stayed a couple of days before flying home to RAF Honington via Gan, Nairobi in Kenya, Khormaksar in Aden, and Luqa in Malta. It was a great trip round the various Middle and Far East stations used regularly by my 3 Group Valiant and Victor squadrons.

We got home early in February 1962 in time for me to take Val on our winter skiing holiday to the Hotel Bristol at Wengen for a change. That started badly as Val had her suitcase taken by mistake at the airport. However, the bag she was left with fortunately had an address on it at Grindelwald, so we were able to ring up and arrange a swap at Scheidegg, which was at the top of both the Wengen and Grindelwald ski lifts, the next morning. That was extremely lucky – it might have gone somewhere a hundred miles away. All went well after that, and we skied a lot up at Scheidegg with some old friends, Peter and Gill Young, who were staying at Grindelwald and whom we happened to meet by chance up at Scheidegg.

In April that year, I had to give a lecture on Bomber Command at the USAF Staff Academy at Maxfield Field in Alabama, so I flew out again in a Victor with Bob Wilson. We took the opportunity to visit en route one of my squadrons carrying out low flying training at RCAF Goose Bay, before proceeding to Maxfield Field where the lecture and discussion went well and I stayed a couple of days. We then returned via Kindley AFB in Bermuda where Bob and I had a round of golf on the wonderful course there, and I called on the Governor (General Sir Julian Gascoigne) who, as I mentioned earlier, had been a kind of ADC to my father in London in 1932 to help look after the Indian Princes from Hyderabad and whom I had got to know quite well then. He was keen to look over the Victor and I showed him round it the next morning when he came to see us take-off for Lajes in the Azores on the way back to RAF Honington.

BKB and Governor General Sir Julian Gascoigne in front of a Victor at Kindley AFB, Bermuda

My SASO at 3 Group was the ace RAF fighter pilot of World War II Air Commodore Johnny Johnson, who for a change was being given experience in the Bomber field. He was a surprisingly good staff officer too and fortunately was quite capable of looking after 3 Group while I was away on some of the extended flights overseas. He was also good fun to have around and had a ribald sense of humour. The well known legless Group Captain Douglas Bader was a great friend of his and used to come and stay at Mildenhall when we used to play golf together. My friend AVM Gus Walker, who was AOC 1 Group, also often stayed with us and, on one occasion when we all played golf at Royal Worlington, Johnny said to me, 'Sir, we ought to be shot if playing together we can't beat those two b-----s with only two legs and three arms between them!' I am glad to say we did, but only just!

May/June 1962 was a very busy time for me visiting all the 3 Group Stations, especially the Thor missile bases which were new to me. There were many QRA (Quick Reaction Alert) exercises also. These were tied in with my official AOC Inspections, Bomber Command Sports Day at RAF Wittering and VIP visits of the Secretary of State for Air, HRH

Princess Margaret, Field Marshal Montgomery and the NATO Defence College to four of my stations.

Towards the end of June, however, the Wimbledon Championships were again coming up and I took two weeks' leave so as to attend every day and pull my weight on the Committee. This year, 1962, Rod Laver was the Champion for the second time and Janet Susman of the USA won the Ladies Singles. Val and I thoroughly enjoyed the Championships again, meeting so many friends from overseas and attending the various hospitality events such as the ILTC pre-Wimbledon dinner, the Garden Party at Hurlingham, the LTA Dinner Dance on the first Saturday and some of the official cocktail parties in the evenings. In fact there was never a dull moment. Val and I were happy staying again at the RAC Country Club for the whole of the period. This year too, HM The Queen came, for the first time I think, and had lunch with Princess Marina (the President) and the Committee in the Members' Dining Room. There was unfortunately an annoying incident during one of the matches on the centre court when a lady climbed over the barrier from the front row of seats and paraded with a larger banner in front of The Queen in the Royal Box. I can't remember what the banner said, and the lady was fairly quickly escorted away by the Referee (Col. Legg), but I think the incident may have rather upset The Queen. The Championships finally ended with the usual Champions' Ball at Grosvenor House with the two champions starting the dancing together.

After that we were back to Mildenhall and 3 Group flying, with VIP visits at least once a week to see our nuclear deterrent force, a CENTO staff visit to the Reconnaisance Wing at RAF Wyton, the Imperial Defence College (IDC) to RAF Cottesmore, HRH Princess Marina to RAF Honington to present standards to No. 55 and 57 Squadrons. And I think it was at some time around about then that the Shah of Iran, who was a pilot, came to visit Cottesmore and was taken for a flight in a Victor. By then we were being equipped with the Victor Mark II which was a great improvement, and much more powerful with a take-off like a fighter aircraft. Crews were being rapidly converted. It didn't take long to switch from the Mk IA to the Mk II and I see from my log book that I did my conversion at the end of July with a Squadron Leader Bryan at RAF Wittering. This was preparatory to taking No. 139 Victor II (Jamaica) Squadron to Jamaica for the Independence celebration in August 1962.

On the outbreak of World War II Jamaica had asked what they could do to help Britain, and had decided to provide the money to pay for a

Blenheim Bomber Squadron which became known in the RAF as 139 Jamaica Squadron, now equipped with Victor II aircraft, and was based at RAF Wittering under my command. When their Independence celebrations came up they asked for their squadron back! It was agreed that I should take it over there for the week of their celebrations which HRH Princess Margaret was attending on behalf of The Queen. At the beginning of August I flew out with three of the squadron aircraft via Goose Bay to Palisadores the Jamaica airport at Kingston from where in the next few days we did a number of low flights over Kingston and the island to show them their aircraft. One day Princess Margaret told me she was worried as one of the low flying Victors looked as though it was coming in her bedroom window! Anyway all went well and we were given an excellent welcome. Wing Commander Plenderleith, the CO of the squadron, and I were taken on a lovely drive over the mountains to have lunch one day with the chap who had organized the wartime squadron arrangement. He had a lovely house high up on the north shore overlooking Ocho Rios and the sea. Our Secretary of State for Commonwealth Affairs was also in Jamaica and there were several official functions with the Jamaican Prime Minister that I attended before the final evening celebrations. These were fairly normal, with the nostalgic hauling down of the British flag and up with the new Jamaican flag, and then of course the usual speeches and all the wonderful fireworks which went on for what seemed forever. The next day we took our leave and the Squadron flew back via Kindley AFB in Bermuda and RCAF Goose Bay in Labrador to RAF Wittering. It had been a great trip which I had been lucky to be on.

We got back about the middle of August and I was able to take the family for a summer holiday at Grasse with Douglas and Andrée. Instead of driving all the way, this time we put the car on the overnight train to Lyons where we arrived about 7.00 a.m. and then had an easy drive on to Grasse. As usual it was a very good, sunny and relaxing holiday with Vivy and Siby there, and Douglas and Andrée looked after us marvellously.

After that we were back to normal at Barton Mills in September with numerous visits, for example to RAF Odiham for the SBAC Display, RAF Wyton for Battle of Britain Day and an Air War Course visit, RAF Honington for a Norwegian Ministry of Defence visit – many of these requiring special briefing from me and the Station Commander. The Group was also involved in a special 'Micky Finn' dispersal exercise.

Finally on the last weekend of the month I flew Val down in the Anson to RAF Booker for the Bomber Command Ball for which we stayed with Bing and Brenda Cross at the C-in-C's residence, Springfields, before flying back the next morning.

In 1963 I was lucky to get a very interesting and enjoyable visit to Mexico City. This arose because the CAS of the Mexican Air Force (General Fuerro) had invited the USAF to send some of the B25s, I think, to take part in their 50th Air Force Anniversary celebrations there, but the Americans had refused because of the problems associated with the high altitude of Mexico City. So General Fuerro had rung our CAS (ACM Sir Thomas Pike) to invite the RAF instead, and he rang me to ask whether we could do it with our Victor IIs. After checking details I rang back to say, 'Yes, certainly; and I would plan to take three Victor IIs myself from RAF Wittering,' and this was agreed for the end of January 1963. Before then I took Val and the boys for a super weekend over the New Year with the Thompsons at Holbeach Hurn and a fortnight's skiing at Zermatt. After that I flew with S/Ldr Bryan and three Victor IIs to Mexico via RCAF Goose Bay and Offutt AFB in the USA. On landing at Mexico City Airport we were met by General Fuerro and our British Ambassador (Sir Peter Garran) who very kindly had me to stay with him and his delightful Australian wife.

The next morning we showed the general public round the aircraft and then took the Minister of Defence, General Fuerro and Sir Peter Garran for a flight in the three Victors round the City. They were greatly impressed by the performance of the aircraft in using only about half the runway to take off despite the thin air at the altitude of about 8,000 feet! In the afternoon we were taken sight-seeing outside the City and in the evening to a marvellous *Folklorico* musical show. The following day the Mexican Air Force gave a large lunch party for their anniversary Air Day with many speeches and presentations, when I gave an RAF Shield to their Minister of Defence and a Bomber Command plaque and model of a Victor Bomber to General Fuerro to mark the occasion. The next morning I laid a wreath on their Independence Monument and in the afternoon, being a Saturday, General Fuerro invited me for a game of golf. He was only quite a small man but when he drove off the first tee I was amazed to see the ball go some 300 yards or more, then much to my surprise, my drive did too! It was, of course, the thin air at that altitude that did it and I had to get accustomed to using a much shorter club than usual. It was good fun and quite exciting, and I managed to just win. The next day we made our farewells and took off to fly low as requested, over the Presidential Palace and their Parliament Buildings where they would be looking out for us. Unfortunately there was mist and fog over the City so it was impossible to identify the buildings and, although we flew all round before leaving, I understand they didn't see us and were disappointed. It was a pity, after otherwise a very successful visit when the Mexican Air Force was greatly impressed by the RAF Victor 'V' Bombers. It had been a very interesting trip for those of us lucky to go on it, and a good experience of landing and taking off under those high altitude conditions. On the return flight we stopped off at Nassau in the Bahamas for a dinner with the Governor and then spent a couple of days at Goose Bay where the crews did some low level flying training. Unfortunately when we got back to RAF Wittering there was thick fog and we were diverted to RAF St Mawgan in Cornwall from where I returned to London on the night train as I had an important appointment the next day. Finally, the following week I reported to CAS (Tom Pike) and left him in his office the Mexican Air Force plaque which General Fuerro had presented to me for the RAF.

After getting back to normal at 3 Group after leaving Mexico there were the usual many VIP visits including the NATO Parliamentary visit to RAF Marham and General Lemnitzer (Saceur) to Bomber Command HQ and RAF Scampton to see the Vulcans of No. 1 Group. Other visitors to 3 Group Stations were the NATO Defence College and the Swedish Chief of the Air Staff. All of these had to be briefed and given a demonstration of our quick reaction take-off capability and it was important that people should know about it. With the build up of Bomber Command with its Victors and Vulcans and Thor missiles as the main British nuclear deterrent there was naturally increasing interest in its capabilities. To be effective the deterrent had to be known to be capable, if necessary, of getting off the ground in time before being attacked itself as well as getting through to the target against the enemy defences. Hence the need for QRA (Quick Reaction Alert) using dispersal airfields and the low flying exercises (best carried out from RCAF Goose Bay) in case it was considered best to go in at low level beneath enemy radar cover. So much practice and many exercises were constantly carried out to ensure this quick reaction and to get the V Bombers airborne within the 3-5 minutes which was all the warning we would get for a nuclear missile attack, for example, from the Soviet Union. The Cold War was still on in Europe and then we had the Cuban

Crisis when Fidel Castro and Soviet technicians were installing nuclear missiles on the northern coast of Cuba aimed at the USA, and the US Navy was blockading further shipping to Cuba. President Kennedy had actually been on television at that time, I believe, to reveal that the world was on the brink of war, and there was a constant risk of conflict until Khrushchev finally gave way and agreed to remove the missiles and Soviet 1L28 bombers from Cuba. During this time there was a period when Bomber Command was dispersed and actually brought to five minutes readiness and occasionally to cockpit or three minutes readiness when a number of crews were actually sitting in their aircraft ready to go. With the Thor missile force there was less of a problem but during this period the C-in-C of Bomber Command and his No. 1 and 3 Group Commanders had to be on telephone call from Whitehall the whole time. Incidentally it was the first time that I had a telephone in my car! It certainly *was* a very worrying time.

Later in July 1963 at Wimbledon Chuck McKinley of the US won the Men's Singles and Margaret Smith of Australia the Ladies'. We stayed down again at the RAC Country Club and it was all very enjoyable as usual and Val appreciated again her two days in the Royal Box as the wife of a Committee member.

In August the RAF were invited to take part in the Toronto Air Display in Canada and with W/Cdr Robinson I flew over there with two of the Wittering Victors and landed at Toronto airport, where we were based together with the many other aircraft taking part. I managed to get Val invited too and she was flown over in one of the RAF Transport Command Comets that were also taking part. We were able to spend a couple of nights over the weekend with my great friends Bill and Hope Pigott in Hamilton not far away, which was a nice bonus. I let the Wing Commander and his crew fly in the Display and Val and I had seats in the front row of the stands along the Toronto lakeside front where the excellent Air Display conveniently took place over Lake Ontario.

Not long after we got back, my boss (Bing Cross) was posted from C-in-C Bomber Command to be C-in-C Transport Command, and ACM Sir John Grandy took over from him at Bomber Command HQ. This led to many C-in-C visits to all our stations which kept me busy on return from Toronto, but I was able to get away for a couple of weeks' leave at the end of August to take the family on another lovely holiday to Grasse, to stay with Douglas and Andrée again, before the boys had to go back to school.

Back at home in November I attended a 50th Anniversary Reunion Dinner at the Royal Aero Club for winners of the Britannia Trophy, with Sir Alan Cobham, the well known aviator, as guest speaker and I think one of the earliest winners of the trophy forty years earlier. I had been a joint winner of the Trophy in 1938 with the other members of our Long Distance Record Flight and it was a great evening with them and a number of well-known flyers and past winners. In January 1964 a LRDU 25th Anniversary Dinner had also been arranged at the RAF Club for our Long Distance Flight Record, and again it was great to meet up with our old colleagues, particularly as it was sadly the last time nearly all of us could make it.

For our skiing holiday that winter Val and I took the boys to Zermatt again early in January 1964 and that was wonderful as usual. In the meantime I had been invited to take a flight of our Victor IIs to New Zealand in February to represent the RAF at their RNZAF Day Celebrations at Ohakea airfield north of Wellington so, after our skiing holiday and a bit more Victor flying practice at RAF Wittering, I set off with one of the Flight Commanders (S/Ldr Bichard) with three Victors on 5 February. En route we called in at Akrotiri in Cyprus, Nairobi in Kenya, Gan in the Maldives, Buttterworth in Malaya and Tengah in Singapore before going on to Darwin and Brisbane in Australia (where the Victor IIs had not been before) and we finally landed at Ohakea a few miles north of Wellington in New Zealand. There we were met by their CAS (AVM Ian Morrison), an old friend who had been at the IDC with me in London in 1958. While the aircraft and crews stayed at Ohakea for servicing by some of our ground crew who had followed us to New Zealand in a Britannia of Transport Command, I was taken away by Ian Morrison to stay with him and his English wife (Dinnie) at their house in Lower Hutts. It was good to see them again and on the Sunday Ian took me off to play golf.

The following day I was driven, with a RNZAF Squadron Leader as escort, to Wairoa and Nuhaka on the east coast of the North Island for a traditional Maori welcome, including the delightful nose-rubbing greeting by two of the Maori maidens! We were then driven through the lovely countryside past Lake Waikaramoana to Lake Taupo where the Morrisons had a small lodge. I was being put up at the local country lodge not far away and where the Canadian CAS (AVM Larry Dunlap) was also staying the weekend for fishing. The next day we were taken out on the lake by the Morrisons in two small motor boats and we fished and

Maori welcome

trawled for a couple of hours or more, without success. Lake Taupo was, of course, famous for the number and size of trout that were normally caught there, so it was very disappointing from that point of view although otherwise lovely on the lake. We also borrowed waders and were taken to try in the well-known River Tongariro but there again we had no success. We were due to leave the next morning about 9.00 a.m. but before going to bed that evening I said to Larry Dunlap, 'I can't go back to England having fished in Taupo and never having seen a fish, so let's get up early and go out on Taupo for about an hour before breakfast.' Rather reluctantly he agreed, and the New Zealand Squadron Leader with us kindly laid it all on, so off we went again the next morning in our motor boat and fished and fished again without success, and finally decided that there weren't any fish in Lake Taupo and gave it up! On the way back to the shore, however, we were trawling and suddenly first Larry Dunlap got a bite and then I did, and in the end we caught several large trout that we took back with glee to have cooked for breakfast. We then drove happily down to Ohakea for the Air Display rehearsal and later that evening a dinner with the New Zealand Air Board. The next morning Ohakea was crowded with thousands of visitors and there were hundreds queuing up on the ground to look round the Victors. The flying display took place in the afternoon and all went very well including the Victors.

It was altogether a wonderful ten days that we had in New Zealand and we finally started home on 24 February with the Victors, each flying a different route to Adelaide, Perth and Darwin to show the aircraft to more of the Australians. After that it was Singapore, Gan, Aden and Malta before we got back to RAF Wittering and, although it had been a marvellous trip, it was good to get home to Val and the boys after a whole month away.

April and May 1964 were busy for me at 3 Group HQ with the annual AOC Inspections of all my stations. We also had quite a few friends to stay with us at The Old Rectory – the Margessons from Toronto, Joan Bearder, Bill and Jean Hobson and Douglas and Andrée and my first cousin Helen Luard. The boys were home part of the time on holiday too and I see from my diary that on both 9 and 10 April I had to go and pick them up about 01.00 hours after a dance nearby! So they seemed to be having a good time and we had quite a bit of golf together at the weekends.

In May 1964 my mother flew back from Grasse to stay with us for about a month. She was over eighty then, but in very good form and while Val and I played golf she used to still do very good water colour paintings, some of which I still have in my dressing room at Heather Hill. I collected her, of course, from Heathrow on arrival and took her back by car and in due course, with her agreement, I sold Traddles quite well for her. While she was with us we got Bruce and Bob out for two weekends from Haileybury so she enjoyed seeing quite a bit of them, as well as meeting all our local friends who we had to dinner parties with her.

Wimbledon soon came round again and I managed to drive down to attend most days though I couldn't, as before, take the whole two weeks off and stay down for it. This year it was Roy Emerson's and Maria Bueno's turn to win. It was Fred Stolle's second time as runner-up and Bueno beat the previous year's winner Margaret Smith, and they were both excellent hard fought finals.

Incidentally around the middle of May I was invited for an interview with CAS (now ACM Sir Charles Elworthy (Sam)) when he told me, in confidence, that he wanted me to be his Vice Chief (VCAS) in October to take over from my Australian friend Air Marshal Sir Wallace (Digger) Kyle. This would mean promotion for me to Air Marshal which was a super surprise as I was still only fifty-one. Before she left to go back to Grasse at the end of the month I couldn't help telling my mother who was of course delighted. I think she knew that it would probably entail a knighthood before long. I hope so anyway as I remember her telling Douglas and me many years ago that she had chosen our names, rather optimistically, with that possibility in mind! Val was thrilled too, of course, and we contacted the Kyles (who also knew) to see if we could take over their flat, 7a Inverness Gardens, in Kensington. We agreed to buy them out of the rest of their long term lease on the flat but could not get in until they moved out in November. For the interim period we rented a flat in Queens Gate Place from our friends AVM Sir Alan and Pam Boxer who were shortly retiring, and this worked very well.

While we were in the middle of moving and handing over at 3 Group to AVM Denis and Ann Spotswood, my mother suddenly died and I flew down to Nice for a couple of days with Douglas and Andrée for her funeral at Grasse. It was all very sad but she had had quite a good and happy innings at eighty-one, and I was so glad that she had been able to come and stay with us only recently at Barton Mills for a good long visit.

I then returned to finish handing over and moving out of The Old Rectory on 5 August. We were very sorry in many ways to leave Barton Mills and 3 Group which had really been my most enjoyable RAF appointment so far, but it was great to know myself that I was to be promoted to Air Marshal. It seemed rather silly but we still couldn't at this stage tell anybody else where we were going, and it was a bit awkward at the various farewell parties and dinners. It was only after we had already moved down to London that the appointment was made public and I then received the following telegram which I thought was rather nice from my SASO, Air Commodore Harry Burton, who had taken over the previous summer from Johnny Johnson – 'For VCAS Designate from SASO and Staff of 3 Group. Congratulations on new appointment. We are all basking in reflected glory:

Thank God the truth is now exposed
Your staff are now at sweet repose
It's nice to know we have on call
The Honourable Member from Mildenhall!'

Incidentally, Harry Burton had been one of the first prisoners of war after being shot down over Germany to escape back to England. It had been a remarkable effort as he had managed to hang on under a train for about three hours, I believe, while it was speeding along heading north towards the Baltic. He eventually hid on a boat to Sweden and then somehow got back to England in 1940.

My appointment as VCAS incidentally got a certain amount of publicity because it meant that all the members of the Air Council would, for the first time, and probably ever, be graduates of either Oxford or Cambridge Universities – ACM Sir Charles Elworthy, Walter Cheshire and Jack Davies of Cambridge and Chris Hartley and myself of Oxford. Quite a credit to the University Air Squadrons which we had all joined before the war.

By the middle of the month (August 1964) I was free to take a couple of weeks' holiday and we put the car on the train overnight to Lyons and then drove down with the boys for our usual summer holiday at Grasse with Douglas and Andrée. On return to London I started to take over from Digger Kyle and joined him on his farewell world tour as Acting Air Marshal. He had been allotted the VIP Comet from The Queen's Flight and was able to take his wife Molly and me, and a couple of other passengers who were indulging part of the way.

9

VICE-CHIEF OF THE AIR STAFF

VCAS DESIGNATE (SEPTEMBER–OCTOBER 1964)

We flew from RAF Northolt to Lyneham on Saturday 19 September and left there early on the Sunday morning for the RAF Staging post at Ascension Island, refuelling at Sal in the Cape Verde Islands on the way. At Ascension there was a good runway built by the Americans during World War II that they used for Maritime Reconnaisance. It is a small volcanic island but with one quite high hill with a small signals establishment on top; and there, much to one's surprise after driving up through varying degrees of tropical vegetation, one found what looked like a small English farmhouse, a grass tennis court and a stone archway with a lovely large blue clock which had been presented by Queen Victoria! There were also a few old cannons that had been there for defence of the island in the old days, and to stop the French from using it as a base from which possibly to try to rescue Napoleon from St Helena. After dinner and an interesting talk with the Administrator later that evening we left early the next morning for Luanda in Angola and then on to Livingston in Rhodesia (now Zimbabwe) where we stayed the night at the Victoria Falls Hotel.

In the morning we walked round to have a good look at the falls which were a wonderful sight, and I wasn't surprised that the indigenous Africans called them '*Mosi-oa-Tunya*' (the smoke that thunders). Later that day we flew up the Zambezi River to see the Kariba Dam before going on to land at Salisbury (now Harare). There we spent most of the next day with the small but very efficient Rhodesian Air Force and their CAS (AVM 'Raff' Bentley). In the afternoon after calling on the Prime Minister (Mr Ian Smith), who had been a Wing Commander with the RAF during World War II, Digger and I had a very interesting session with him for a good hour on all his UDI problems at that time. That evening we flew overnight to Mauritius (for refuelling only) and then on to our RAF Staging Post, Gan. There we had a bit of a rest and a good swim before taking off again at midnight – this time to Cocos Island for refuelling, before going on to land at Perth, Western Australia, which was Digger's home town and where we were met at the airport by lots of Kyles who took him and Molly away for the weekend. The next day we called on the Governor of WA (Major General Sir Douglas Kendrew, the well known ex-England rugger captain). While there I met up with several old friends from when I was in Perth twenty-five years earlier, including 'Smithers' and the Lidells with whom I had a lovely afternoon on Cottesloe Beach which brought back many happy memories. On the Monday Digger, Molly and I had lunch at Government House, which would have been of particular interest to the Kyles if they had known then that he was going to be Governor there eleven years later after retiring from the RAF.

On leaving Perth, Digger took on board the Comet his daughter Cherry who was coming home after a holiday in Australia, and it was good to have her with us in the main cabin. Our next stop was Melbourne for a day and then Canberra for two. I was glad there to have the opportunity to meet the Australian CAS (AVM Val Hancock) and also our military representative Rear Admiral Davies, both of whom, with their wives, kindly invited me to dinner. Over the next two days we called in to Port Moresby, Kuching in Sarawak and Labuan in North Borneo where we were met by the AOC, FEAF (Air Marshal Peter Wykeham) and A/Cdre Sandy Johnstone (the local Air Commander). The next morning we had an interesting trip on a river boat in the jungle to see some of the problems our forces had had to contend with during the Indonesian Confrontation with Malaysia. That afternoon we flew to Singapore where we stayed at Air House with Peter Wykeham and his wife for a couple of days of meetings and briefings, as well as a very good lunch party on the Sunday on the Air Commander's launch out at sea, and a dinner party that evening with Vernon and AVM Frank Headlam at Cluny Road.

After that we flew up to Kuala Lumpur for a quick visit to the British High Commissioner in Malaysia (Sir Antony Head), and stayed a night with him there before flying on up to Hong Kong. There we were met at RAF Kaitak by the AOC (A/Cdre Crowley-Milling) who took us off to stay at Air House with his wife Lorna. The next day we called on Lt. General Sir Denis O'Connor (Commander British Forces Hong Kong) and then Sir David Trench (the Governor) both of whom I knew well from the Imperial Defence College (IDC) in London in 1958. We were then all taken on a very enjoyable trip around the harbour and islands in the Governor's yacht.

The following day we started on the way home, stopping at Guam in the Marianas and Wake Island, the USAF Bases that played such an important part in stopping the Japanese in the Pacific in World War II. Next stop then was Hickham Air Force Base in Honolulu where we stayed a couple of nights at the lovely Hawaiian Beach Hotel, then on to Vancouver for the weekend before going on to Toronto and Ottawa, where Digger and I had meetings arranged with an ex-RAF Group Captain who was in charge of de Havillands (Canada) Aircraft Company, to discuss their latest training aircraft. From there we flew down to Washington for a meeting with our USAF opposite number at the Pentagon and then overnight, via Gander for refuelling, to RAF Lyneham. It had been a wonderful four weeks' world tour which was very useful for me later, but I was very glad as always to get home to Val on 17 October.

VICE-CHIEF OF THE AIR STAFF, AIR MINISTRY (1964–67)

After the weekend in London, I had a couple of weeks in the VCAS office with Digger Kyle calling in on CAS, the Air Minister (Lord Shackleton) and the Under Secretary of State for Air (Merlyn Rees) and meeting my Air Commodore Directors of Policy and Operations. I also visited the HQs of Transport, Fighter and Bomber Commands. I then finally took over as VCAS on 9 November 1964 and was very conscious of my new responsibilities for all RAF Policy and Operations under CAS – particularly as he went on leave a few weeks later, and left me to represent the RAF at a couple of Chiefs of Staff meetings and a Defence Council Meeting with the Prime Minister at his office in the House of Commons. In the meantime, Bruce had left Haileybury and had been commissioned as a Pilot Officer in the RAF Navigation Branch, and I was delighted he was following in my footsteps as I was sure he would enjoy life in the RAF. At the end of November Val and I moved into the flat at 7a Inverness Gardens which was excellent, and very conveniently we were able to park our car easily outside the front door. Bob was still at Haileybury but enjoyed being in London, I think, during his school holidays, so that was all very satisfactory. He was in any case due to go up to St Andrews University before long.

1965

It was clearly going to be a very busy job for me as VCAS and when I called in on our Secretary of State for Air, Lord Eddie Shackelton said, 'I've been told you are a hard worker, which is just as well as you will need to be!' We had all noticed earlier how exhausted Digger Kyle had seemed to be at times whilst he was VCAS. Fortunately apart from the Indonesian Confrontation with Malaysia in the Far East, there were no major operations to worry about, but there was endless discussion about the roles of the three Services and the Government's desire to cut expenditure on defence. In particular, the questions arose as to how best to maintain our nuclear deterrent and whether our possible future requirements overseas could best be met by land-based aircraft or aircraft carriers. This led to many meetings and discussion papers which had to be vetted thoroughly and which one had to go through carefully before attending the meetings, usually the next day, when one was representing the RAF view and, so to speak, fighting the RAF corner.

The pressure or amount of work was such that although it was a bit of a risk taking some of the Top Secret papers home to work on after dinner, one was forced to do it. I remember one occasion when Sam Elworthy (CAS) asked me what time I had got to bed the previous night. I said about 3.00 a.m. and he said, 'Well, you did better than me – I was nearer 4.00 a.m.!' Val frequently used to come down and drag me off to bed in the early hours. I tried getting up early to do the work before breakfast, but it was difficult then to allow enough time and when I did that I sometimes ended up insufficiently prepared when it came to the meetings later that day. That was just not on. Regrettably that was the form most of the time, but happily there were a number of occasions at official luncheons or receptions in the evenings when one could relax before getting on with the paperwork and preparing for the important meetings the next day.

These social functions were fun but also very useful in enabling one to get to know personally some of the other service defence ministers and Cs-in-C, as well as all the High Commissioners and Air Attachés of the Commonwealth countries and our allies. Other more important and interesting social functions were an Air Force Board (AFB) Reception for the Anglo/US Relations Committee at Lancaster House, an AFB lunch for the Australian Air Minister and later dinner with the Australian High Commissioner, and a Defence Council Reception by the Lord Mayor at the Banquetting House; also an AFB Benefactors' Dinner for Sir Frank

Whittle, the inventor of our first jet engine, and a dinner for Sir Martin Baker, the inventor of the parachute, to celebrate the recent 2000th life-saving ejection. In the meantime ACM Sir Harry Broadhurst, my old C-in-C of Bomber Command, had retired and was working as a Director of the Hawker Siddeley (HS) aircraft firm, and he was very hospitable to some of his old RAF colleagues in inviting us and our wives regularly to the ballet at Covent Garden. He also saw to it that we were invited to the Grand National by Sir Roy Dobson, the Hawker Siddeley Managing Director. For this we met for a champagne breakfast on the train with a number of colleagues followed by an excellent lunch party at the races and ending up with dinner and more champagne on the train back to London. Quite a party!

Fortunately, as a member of the Air Council I was entitled in London to the use of a Service car and driver who was able to drive me to and from the office in Whitehall and take me to any of the official functions. This was invaluable. Another very great privilege was being able to use the VIP Communications aircraft of The Queen's Flight or Transport Command, in particular the Comet or Britannia for visits to the Far East. Without this facility it would certainly not have been so convenient or even possible to visit all the places we needed to get to. For shorter trips in the UK we were able to use the BAC 125 jets of 32 Squadron from Northolt and occasionally to call on a helicopter of The Queen's Flight using the Battersea helipad by the Thames, which often saved much valuable time.

On 1 January 1965 my substantive promotion to Air Marshal came through and my appointment as a Knight Commander of the Order of the Bath (KCB) – one of the nicest honours as it was one that could be shared with one's wife, and Val became a Lady! It was not long before my investiture by The Queen took place at Buckingham Palace on 16 February which was quite exciting.

At the end of January I attended a 2ATAF meeting in Germany for a couple of days, then had to return to give a lecture to the Senior Officers War Course at Greenwich before attending CAS's annual conference with Cs-in-C, which was a great gathering of old friends. Following that we went on our annual skiing holiday to Val d'Isère with Bob. Bruce was still busy doing his navigation training and could not get away for long enough, but he used to come down occasionally and stay at the flat at Inverness Gardens and I used to take him when I could on a Sunday to play tennis at the All England Club.

When I attended, on behalf of CAS, my first Defence Council meeting in January, I hadn't realized that the Service Chiefs were only there for advice if asked for it, and weren't supposed to speak otherwise. When I thought that they were about to make the wrong decision on the matter of providing spares for Vampires or Shackleton aircraft for the South African Air Force I rather bravely piped up from the back of the room to say so, much to the consternation of all concerned. However, the Defence Minister (Mr Healey) was very good and said, 'Prime Minister, I think we should hear what the VCAS has to say.' So I had my say and am glad the decision was changed! However, the next day I was sent for by Lord Mountbatten (CDS) and torn off a colossal strip for intervening without being asked. I think he must have felt he had been made rather a fool of and should have intervened himself. Anyway, we got the right decision! Incidentally this happened to me again several months later, but I then adopted the official (rather silly) procedure at that time of having to write a little note for the Defence Minister asking permission to speak and passing it up the line to him via the CGS, CNS and CDS. So I wrote my little note for the Defence Minister saying, 'I don't think the PM has ever been to Singapore and doesn't appear to realize there are a number of different Service bases there. Can the Service Chiefs explain?' Again I am glad to say Mr Healey supported me and all three Service Chiefs were then asked for their comments regarding the PM's plan to mothball what he called 'the Singapore Base'.

That summer Douglas and Andrée came to stay for ten days and it was good to be able to return some of their Grasse hospitality. In May also I played in the Air Marshals/Generals/Admirals golf match at the Royal Berkshire Golf club which was always good fun, and Val and I were invited to a splendid Guildhall Reception as well as an HMG Reception for the Canadian Defence College and another for the SEATO Delegates at the Savoy. We also flew to Paris for the annual Air Show as it was 'their turn' to hold it in 1965. I was still also the President of the RAF Squash, Tennis and Skiing Associations so had to keep in touch with them every now and again for their annual meetings and championships. There were also the regular All England Club and Wimbledon Championship meetings which I had to attend, so there was never a dull moment!

The Wimbledon Championships were now coming round again too, and living in London made it easier for Val and me to go most afternoons to entertain our guests and attend the various meetings and functions expected of me as a Committee member. Roy Emerson, the No. 1 seed, won the men's singles for the second time in straight sets. Unfortunately for Fred Stolle it was his third successive defeat in the Wimbledon Singles final. He had the consolation, however, of having won the Men's Doubles twice with R.A.J. Hewitt in previous years. That year though the Doubles title went to John Newcombe and Tony Roche (more Australians) for the first of many times. In the Ladies' Singles, Christine Truman did well again to get to the semi-finals but was beaten by Margaret Smith, who also went on to get her revenge against Maria Bueno in two close sets, reversing the previous year's results. Altogether it was a very enjoyable Wimbledon as usual.

In July there was a farewell party which we attended at St James' Palace for Lord Mountbatten who was retiring as CDS and handing over to General Sir Richard Hull. We also went to the excellent Fighter Command Summer Ball and the Royal Tournament at which I had to take the salute one evening. In August we had three very pleasant weekends, one with the Melhuishes in Kent who took us to the Glyndebourne Opera, another with Gus and Brenda Walker at Brancaster for golf, and the bank holiday weekend with the Thompsons at Holbeach for tennis and squash. In September we also had a golfing weekend with Bing and Brenda Cross in Wiltshire and another with the Pertwees for tennis and bathing at Frinton-on-Sea. It was lovely to get into the country for some exercise and away from the noise and bustle of London for a few days.

On Battle of Britain weekend I was invited to RAF Biggin Hill Open Day on the Saturday and flew there and back with Val from Battersea in one of The Queen's Flight helicopters which was rather exciting, and on the Sunday we attended as usual the annual Battle of Britain Service in Westminster Abbey. That evening our old friends Rupert and Venetia Hogan came to dinner with us and stayed the night. Other events of note later that year to which we were invited were a Battle of Britain (B of B) Guildhall Reception by the Lord Mayor of London, a B of B Ball at the Dorchester with Rolls-Royce, an RAF Regiment Dinner, a B of B Dinner at Fighter Command, an HMG Reception at Lancaster House for the Norwegian National Defence College, the British Legion Festival of Remembrance at the Albert Hall, the Park Lane Fair Charity reception of which I was President that year and which The Queen Mother attended, and another Covent Garden opera with Harry Broadhurst. At the beginning of October we also managed to fit in three weeks leave again in the south of France with Douglas and Andrée. So it went on, with again never a dull moment.

1966

This year started off in much the same vein with a dinner for me with Sir Harry Broadhurst at the Vintners Hall with the Worshipful Company of Coach and Harness Makers and lunch with Bing Cross for the England versus Wales rugger match. In February I had to give another lecture at RN Greenwich for the Senior Officers War Course, then there were more dinners with C-in-C Fighter Command, the Italian and Swedish Air Attachés and with USAF General Hardy at the Columbia Club, an English Speaking Union Ball for George Washington's birthday and a Commonwealth Relations Office cocktail party at Marlborough House – to all of which, I am glad to say, Val was able to come with me. Early in March we took two weeks leave to go skiing at Wengen again and only got back just in time for Sam (CAS) to go visiting the Far East for four weeks leaving me in charge at the office. On 6 April Bruce was due to have his Passing Out Parade at RAF Stradishall and I was invited

Bruce gets his wings from Dad

to take the Parade and was a proud Dad in presenting him and his fellow officers with their Navigator's Wings. That evening there was the All England Club Annual Dinner when J. C. Masterman was the guest of honour and I had to propose the toast to the guests on behalf of the Club. J.C. was a well known and outstanding athlete who had represented England at hockey, squash and tennis and had been a don at Oxford University whom I knew and played squash with when I was there. I was therefore only too pleased to do this, but to have to make two different speeches in one day I found a bit much! I was delighted that the next weekend was a quiet one over Easter though it was soon followed by CAS's Annual Conference with Cs-in-C and two more speeches at the Joint Services Staff College at Latimer and as guest of honour at the Oxford University Air Squadron dinner.

At CAS's Conference with C-in-Cs in April Sam Elworthy was pleased to announce that we on the Air Staff had won the case for land based bombers rather than the more expensive option of aircraft carriers, and he asked me to give a presentation to the Cs-in-C on our case showing how with the range of the F111 aircraft we could meet all our likely requirements from our existing bases in the Middle and Far East. The Navy had, of course, argued that aircraft carriers were more flexible but even if we got a third carrier, which the Navy wanted, they could not guarantee that more than one would be operationally available at all times. That meant this option would be very expensive if we were to have enough of them to meet all potential requirements, and Mr Healey and the Defence Council had accepted the Air Force case and confirmed the order for the American F111 aircraft which they had decided on rather than our Vickers TSR2. Later, of course, on grounds of expense, the numbers were reduced again and finally cancelled altogether. The other sad outcome of this matter was that the Chief of Naval Staff (Admiral Sir David Luce) decided to resign which we in the RAF thought was unnecessary and a great pity.

In May I had arranged to book the VIP Comet for a visit to the Middle East, and as Bruce was between RAF courses I was able to take him with me officially as my ADC. We set off from RAF Lyneham on the 10th for Luqa in Malta, then on to Idris and El Adem in Tunisia and from there to RAF Akrotiri in Cyprus where I spent a couple of days visiting Dhekelia and Episkopi. There Bruce and I were able to meet up with our cousin Dany and her husband Colonel Hugh Johnstone who was based out there. However, I stayed over the weekend with the AOC AM

'Splinters' Smallwood and his wife at the lovely Air House not far from RAF Akrotiri and the AOC flew me round the island in his Whirlwind helicopter. On Monday we took off again in the Comet for the Persian Gulf to spend a day each at our RAF bases at Bahrein, Sharjah and Masirah before going on to RAF Khormaksar at Aden. There the Station Commander was G/C Mike Beetham (CAS several years later) and the AOC AVM Andrew Humphrey (also CAS and CDS later). I knew the latter well and he and his wife Agnes kindly had me to stay with them at Air House. The next day I was taken up country in a Whirlwind helicopter to where some of the troubles had been and I spent most of the day there before returning to Khormaksar.

The following morning we set off in the Comet again for Nairobi in Kenya, where I was met by the AOC Air Commodore Charles Simpson, an old friend who had served under me many years earlier at RAF Mt. Hope in Canada. He and his wife Gillian kindly took me off to stay with them in Air House on the outskirts of Nairobi. They didn't seem to have any RAF problems to put to me and, as the next day was a Saturday, they took me to the delightful little racecourse there where they had their own horse running. On Sunday we flew to Jeddah for a quick visit with the British High Commissioner to Saudi Arabia before going on later to El Adem and back to RAF Lyneham the following day. It had been an excellent two-week trip and incidentally a very good and interesting experience for Bruce.

It was not long after we had got back, and Bruce was continuing with his Navigator/Bombing training at RAF Lindholme when we had the nasty shock of Bruce's crash landing on 13 June after a mid-air collision between the Varsity aircraft in which he was on a routine training flight and a private Cessna plane. Thankfully, apart from bruises and severe cuts about the face he was all right and had apparently put up a very good show in helping three of the crew to bale out and then, when the aircraft was too low for him and the Captain to bale out, he had gone back up to the cockpit to help the pilot to crash-land the aircraft. Two of the crew who had baled out were OK but the third was found dead in his parachute, and the two people in the Cessna were also unfortunately killed. Poor Bruce had to have his nose stitched on again, with twenty-seven stitches I believe! but otherwise he had been extremely lucky and done very well in the circumstances. Val and I were naturally keen to see Bruce after his accident and the C-in-C of Bomber Command (our old friend Digger Kyle) invited us to stay with them for the weekend at Springfields and arranged for Bruce to come down to see us at Bomber Command HQ.

Bob in the meantime had left Haileybury and had been to a crammer in London to help him get the necessary qualifications for university. Whilst waiting to go up to St Andrews on 5 October he had got himself a temporary job during the summer at a prep school near Horsham in Surrey – teaching cricket of all things! He was never any good at it. However, it was good for him and I think he quite enjoyed it.

It was now Wimbledon time again at the end of June and I managed to go most days and Val every day with different guests in our seats. This year Emerson was surprisingly defeated in the quarter-finals by O. K. Davidson (another Australian) who then lost to Manolo Santana of Spain in five close sets in the semi-final. Santana, a delightful player to watch and very popular, then went on to beat R. D. Ralston (US) in three sets in the final. In the Ladies' Singles Mrs Billie-Jean King, who had been in the final as Miss Moffitt three years earlier, beat Maria Bueno, a previous winner on three occasions, in a good three-set match.

July was back to normal at the Ministry of Defence with the usual meetings with Commands and a HMG Reception for King Hussein at Lancaster House. I had a golfing weekend at the RAC Country Club and another with the Pertwees at Frinton-on-Sea. With CAS away for a week in Canada and then on leave for a fortnight I was pretty busy at the office, and then we had Uppy and Ginny Moorhead from America to stay for the Prentice Cup match at Wimbledon between Oxford and Cambridge and Harvard and Yale over the weekend of 12/13 August. We also had a golfing weekend at Brancaster with Gus and Brenda Walker and when CAS got back from leave at the end of the month Val and I flew down to Grasse for our summer holiday with Douglas and Andrée for a couple of weeks in September. At the end of the month we had a weekend with Viv Crone at Barton Mills where we played some golf at Royal Worlington and met up again with many of our old friends near Mildenhall. Viv came to stay with us in London a week or two later.

CAS was away again in France for a week at the end of September but was back in time for the Commonwealth Air Staff meeting and then an AFB lunch for the Netherlands CAS (General Wolff) and AFB dinner for General and Mrs Hardy of the USAF and another Defence Council Reception at Lancaster House which Val and I also attended. We also went to an interesting dinner on 30 September given by the Guild of Air Pilots and Navigators at the Royal Festival Hall for Sir Alan Cobham, to celebrate the 40th anniversary of his flight to Australia and back, when he had landed his small float plane on the Thames outside the Parliament buildings at Westminster!

Bob had by now got himself a mini-van to drive around in and at the beginning of October had gone off in it to St Andrews University. Bruce was still finishing his training in England before being posted to a Canberra Bomber Squadron at RAF Tengah in Singapore early in the New Year 1967 which he was much looking forward to.

At the beginning of November I paid an interesting visit to Fighter Command and RAF Fylingdales, our early warning establishment on the north-east coast, before CAS flew off on the 4th for a visit to India for a week with three days in Aden on the way back. I unfortunately had to take his place at short notice to give his lecture to the IDC; with the senior officers on the course all looking forward to CAS himself, I found this rather nerve racking and difficult as I only had a few short notes of Sam's to work on.

It was my turn then to visit the Far East and as well as Geoff Street, my VCAS Secretary, A/Cdre Gerry Wade the Director of Bomber Ops and A/Cdre Alan Frank the Director of Operational Requirements, I was able to take Val with me in the VIP Britannia, so over the weekend of 19–20 November 1966 we flew to Nairobi, stopping in Malta briefly on the way. In Nairobi I stayed the night with the AOC Air Commodore J. C. McDonald and had talks with our High Commissioner before visiting some of the RAF flying instructors who were there helping to train pilots in the small Kenya Air Force. We then had another quick visit to the Nairobi Game Park before, after dinner, flying on over-night to RAF Gan in the Maldives. It was extremely hot there but Val came round the station with me, including visiting the Airmen's Mess and the hospital, before rushing to the sandy beach and the sea for a lovely swim and snorkel inside the reef. After that it was an early night for another early start the next morning for a seven and a half hour flight to RAF Changi in Singapore. The C-in-C of the British Forces there now was my recent boss at Bomber Command (ACM Sir John Grandy) and he and Cécile kindly had us to stay with them at Command House over the weekend. I attended various briefings with him and they gave a large dinner party for us one evening and an excellent swimming and lunch party on the Sunday on the 'Admiral's Barge' out at sea. Early on the Monday we flew on up to Kuala Lumpur in Malaysia to meet the High Commissioner there (Sir Michael Walker), whom I knew well from when we were on the IDC Course together in London in 1958. He and his wife Enid had us to stay the night at 'Carcosa' but Michael and I did most of our official talks on the golf course that afternoon whilst Val stayed by their swimming pool!

The next morning it was on to Hong Kong where we stayed a couple of days with Denis and Lorna Crowley-Milling at Air House before flying on overnight to Guam and Wake Island in the Pacific. After a day there on the Wake American Base we flew to Honolulu for a day, before flying on again overnight to San Francisco, where we stayed the weekend and enjoyed our lobster thermador at the well known Fisherman's Wharf. On the Monday we flew down to the USAF Flight Test Centre at Edwards AFB, California, where we were met by General Manson and his wife Lucy who looked after Val while the rest of us were shown round by the General. The airfield was right out in the Mojave Desert and had an exceptionally long runway for testing their latest aircraft, including the one recently used for breaking the air speed record. Alan Frank, Gerry Wade and I all had a check out in a F111 cockpit, and I also had a go in the T27 space simulator and did a simulated docking in space which was rather fun and most interesting.

In space simulator

After that fascinating and instructive visit we flew east to Colorado Springs to visit Norad, the Combined American and Canadian Air Defence Headquarters, where we were hosted by USAF General (Herb) Thatcher and Royal Canadian Air Force Air Marshal Larry Dunlap who I had met three years earlier in New Zealand. We had two days in Colorado Springs so also had time to visit the USAF Air Academy, where all their Air Cadets were trained and where their excellent facilities rivalled ours at Cranwell. Then on to Washington to have brief talks with my USAF opposite number, before we flew back overnight to land at RAF Lyneham about 11.00 a.m. on Saturday 10 November 1966 when we were met by Bing Cross who was by then C-in-C Transport Command and his wife Brenda. Altogether it had been a very successful three week world tour and it was a marvellous support to have Val with me who was very popular playing her part in visiting various hospitals and airmen's wives at the different bases; and she thoroughly enjoyed it all too, I'm glad to say.

After getting back things were fairly quiet in November and December and Bruce and Bob were staying with us quite a lot in London. Bruce's

On return to RAF Lyneham with the full Britannia crew

twenty-first birthday was due on 27 December and we all went to a dinner dance at the Savoy to celebrate that and his RAF posting to No. 45 Squadron Canberras at RAF Tengah in Singapore on 4 January 1967.

1967

Early in the New Year there were a number of changes with farewell AFB dinners for Lord Eddie Shackleton, ACM Bing and Brenda Cross on retirement and CAS ACM Sam and Audrey Elworthy on stepping up to be Chief of the Defence Staff as a Marshal of the Royal Air Force. Hugh Johnstone, Dany's husband, came to stay with us in London for a few days before he too retired from the Army. In February and March I seemed to get involved more with being invited to the Inter-Services rugger matches, and the England v France and Scotland matches at Twickenham at the weekends which I much enjoyed. At the Ministry of Defence Denis Healey kept us pretty busy with endless defence reviews, but Val and I were able to catch up with quite a lot of return hospitality in the evenings with the Pertwees and David and Caroline Thompson coming to stay a night at our flat, and the Broadhursts, Crosses and Elworthys and others to dinners which kept Val busy.

Other interesting receptions which we attended around that time were the Soviet Military Attaché's Reception at the Soviet Embassy in Kensington Palace Gardens and an HMG Reception for the Canadian National Defence College. In March we went on our annual skiing holiday to St Moritz again with our friends Joan and John Hartnell-Beavis, which was great fun as usual.

Soon after we got back at the beginning of April there was a big CENTO meeting of Military Staffs at Lancaster House at which I was the leader of the UK delegation. This took up a whole day and a half, including the Opening Ceremony, morning and afternoon sessions round the table, an official lunch at Admiralty House and in the evening a launch trip from Westminster Pier down the Thames to Woolwich and the Royal Artillery Mess for a Guest Night dinner. A final session at Lancaster House the next morning was followed by a lunch with the Iranian Ambassador. Other receptions for the CENTO delegates followed during the next day or two with the US and Turkish Ambassadors and the London Air Attachés, and I went to see them off at London airport on Sunday 9th after a busy few days.

Towards the end of the month I flew with Val to RAF Wildenrath for a six-day visit to RAF Germany where we stayed a couple of nights with the C-in-C AM Denis Spotswood and his wife at Air House and visited RAF Laarbruck and RAF Bruggen. On the Saturday I had a game of golf with Denis at Bruggen before we flew on to RAF Gatow in Berlin where we stayed with the Station Commander, Group Captain Howard Lewis, and his wife Joan for a couple of days when we toured the centre of Berlin on the Sunday. I had an extremely interesting visit to 'Brixmis' on the Monday before we flew on to visit RAF Gutersloh and RAF Geilenkirchen and then back to RAF Northolt and England in time to go with Val to the opera again with the Broadhursts and to the Anglo-American Ball at the weekend. Later in the month my great Canadian friends Bill and Hope Pigott from Hamilton, Ontario came to London for a week when we saw quite a lot of them including lunches and dinners, which were fun, talking about old times and friends at RAF Mount Hope twenty-four years earlier. At the end of May Bank Holiday weekend, I had a couple of good rounds of golf at the Royal Berkshire course with Sam Elworthy in the Admirals/Generals/Air Marshals annual match and then caught the train up to Lincolnshire to join Val at Holbeach Hurn where she had gone ahead by car for the weekend with the Thompsons.

It was around March, before he retired as CAS, that Sam Elworthy told me I was to be promoted to Air Chief Marshal shortly and would be going in December to be the Air Secretary. I was a bit disappointed at first as I had secretly hoped I might take over Bomber Command, and it meant another three years probably in London which I knew Val wouldn't like. However there was really no alternative at that time if I was to retain 4-star rank as an ACM. My promotion to ACM did come through on 1 July and it was certainly very satisfying to have reached the top rungs of the RAF ladder at last! Val was delighted in the end and we started to look for a house in the country where we could at least go for weekends.

In the meantime I had a number of important meetings with the Indian CAS (Arjan Singh), the Pakistan CAS (Nur Khan), Air Marshal Al Murdoch of Australia whom I had known before the war in England on the Spec 'N' Course, and the South African CAS, for all of whom there were various receptions and lunches and a big dinner in honour of the President of Turkey and Madame Sunay, and another for the Turkish CGS (General Tural), all of which Val and I attended. There was also the annual Commonwealth Air Staff meeting and sadly the Memorial Service for MRAF Lord Tedder, as well as a reception by the German Ambassador in London and a visit to RAF Waddington in Lincolnshire by Princess Marina and to Catterick by The Queen which we attended. So we were fairly busy until Wimbledon came round again.

This year of 1967 John Newcombe of Australia won the Men's Singles for the first time, beating Wilhelm Bungert of Germany, who had ousted both our Bobby Wilson and Roger Taylor in memorable five-set matches in the last 16 and semi-finals respectively. In the Ladies Singles Mrs Billie-Jean King of the US, the previous year's winner, was the Champion again having beaten our Virginia Wade in the last 8 and Ann Jones in the Final. As usual it was an excellent fortnight which we much enjoyed.

Soon after that I had some leave and we flew down to Nice and hired a car for our two weeks' holiday with Douglas and Andrée. Bruce had gone already to Singapore and Bob was due to go and stay with his girlfriend (Helen Burnett – same name but no relation!) with her mother in Portugal, I think, but he had failed a couple of his first year exams at St Andrews and had to go back to take them again. It was due to pure idleness and not working, and so rather unkindly I made him pay for his journey all the way up to Scotland and back to retake the exams. That I think taught him a good lesson that he couldn't get away without working, which he always did in future – enough anyway to make a fortune several years later!

After we had got back to London there was a farewell reception for Field Marshal Dick Hull (CDS) and a dinner by Admiral Sir Varyl Begg (CNS) for his VCNS and my Navy opposite number Admiral Sir John Bush, which Val and I went to before going up to Frinton-on-Sea for the weekend with the Pertwees at the beginning of August.

We had previously looked at a few possible houses in the country without success, but on Sunday 13th on our way down to lunch near Haslemere in Surrey with our friends AM Sir Paul and Lady Holder (ex C-in-C Coastal Command and recently retired) we decided to look at three more. One of these, facing south with a lovely view over heather and woods for about six miles to the hills near Hindhead, we rather liked as Val always wanted to be on top of a hill. The house was small with only three bedrooms but adequate for our weekend needs from London, from where it was only an hour by train and about an hour and a half by road, rather conveniently via Wimbledon. It was surrounded by about six acres of mainly woodlands so it could not be built on or looked over and could easily be extended if we wanted to do so later. It had also recently been refurbished and redecorated with new central heating installed so that we could move in straight away. The price was very good even for those days at only £11,000, and we said we would like to think about it and would ring back on the Monday morning to confirm. After much thought the rest of the day and discussion with our friends the Holders over lunch, we decided to go for it and were surprised when the owner (Mr Darby) rang us that evening to say he hoped we wanted their house but another couple, whom they didn't like much, had been to see it that afternoon with their surveyor (who was very fussy but apparently satisfied) and they were going to go to Hampton's the estate agency the next morning with their decision to buy the house. He said that he and his wife would far prefer us to have it and that he would let us have his six-month-old satisfactory surveyor's report if we wanted. He also said that Hampton's had a 24-hour answering machine, so if we rang them that evening we would get our bid in first before the others and get possession. We thanked him very much and rang Hampton's immediately so virtually buying the house on the answer-phone, much to the annoyance of the couple who could hardly believe it when they went to buy the house the next morning! The deal was thus completed within the next day or two and it was not long before we were able to move in some of our furniture from store and make it habitable for the occasional weekend until we could settle in properly. The house was called Heather Brae but not being Scottish we changed it to Heather Hill!

In September I played again in the RAF v Aircraft Industry golf match at Wentworth – always good fun – and attended the Battle of Britain 'At Home Day' at RAF Abingdon and Gaydon, and a Bomber Command party at Springfields with the Kyles, as well as a reception the next day at Coastal Command with Val. I also attended an interesting joint Service Exercise 'Unison' at Sandhurst, which went on for several days, and an RAF Regiment Dinner at which I was the Guest of Honour. Another interesting visitor I had at the office was General Weizman of Israel, to talk about their 6-Day war with Egypt, and in October there was an Atlantic/Channel Symposium followed by a lunch in the famous Painted Hall at the RN College, Greenwich which HRH Prince Philip attended. This was followed the next day by a reception for SACLANT at Lancaster House and a week later another reception by the Defence Council for Commonwealth Advisers.

Eventually, after a CAS (Sir John Grandy's) Conference with all Cs-in-C, I handed over as Vice-Chief on 6 November to my ACAS Policy (AVM Peter Fletcher) which was nice and easy as he was already well in the picture. I then went off on a farewell visit to the Far East in a VC10 of Transport Command, taking Val with me, via RAF Muharraq and RAF Gan. We flew to RAF Changi over the weekend and then had three good days with the Air Commander (AVM Hughes) staying at Air House with him and his wife Elizabeth who gave a dinner party for us and took us for a sail around Singapore on their beautiful 35-foot yacht. Bruce was out there by then, of course, at RAF Tengah and after seeing him there we went up to Penang for a week's holiday, where he had arranged for us to stay at the lovely Penang Club. Val and I then went on to Kuala Lumpur for a couple of days with Sir Michael and Enid Walker, the British High Commissioner, before returning to Singapore. Whilst there we took Bruce and his Canberra crew out to dinner one evening before flying home in the VC10 over the weekend via Gan and RAF Akrotiri in Cyprus. This was all just prior to taking over my new job as Air Secretary in Adastral House, Air Ministry.

10

AIR SECRETARY (DECEMBER 1967–MAY 1970)

Although Air Secretary doesn't sound a very exciting job, and it was only introduced as a new appointment in the RAF in 1957 with ACM Sir Denis Barnett, the Air Secretary was responsible for the career planning, promotion and appointment of all RAF officers of Squadron Leader and above, and was consequently regarded as one of our important 4-star posts as in the case of the Army and Navy. It involved quite a lot of detailed work in selecting the right people with the right experience for the different jobs and meant looking a number of years ahead and planning accordingly. After the Vice-Chief job it was a very interesting and pleasant change without the same pressure of work, and we decided to keep on the flat in London.

I finally took over on 7 December from ACM Bill Macdonald and could look forward to a few quiet weekends and the Christmas break to settle in properly at our weekend house, Heather Hill, near Seale, Farnham, Surrey. We soon joined the golf club at Hankley Common near there where we had a couple of Air Force friends, who persuaded us to join there rather than the slightly nearer Farnham golf course. We were lucky to get in straight away and Val and I played most weekends when we went down to the country.

1968

In January Bob went back to St Andrews and I attended CAS Conference with Cs-in-C and we had the Hughes from Singapore to stay as well as our cousin Hugh Johnstone for a week in February. As we were still due a couple of weeks' leave, we went in March to Zermatt for skiing. Bob and his friend from St Andrews (Christopher Smith) were able to come too during their Easter holiday which was great fun and I see from my diary we had nine glorious sunny days out of twelve which was marvellous.

At the beginning of April there were a number of functions to celebrate the 50th Anniversary of the Royal Air Force – a wreath laying ceremony at Lord Trenchard's statue (the Father of the Royal Air Force), an RAF Association Jubilee Festival, an RAF Anniversary Concert at the Royal Festival Hall, and an RAF Golden Jubilee Banquet and Royal Reception for all senior officers at Fighter Command HQ at which The Queen and nearly all members of the Royal Family were present. About a week later there was a big reception and dinner for the RAF by the Lord Mayor at the Guildhall.

One weekend later Val and I drove up to Scotland to visit Bob and his friends at their digs called 'Rockard' at St Andrews University. We had a round of golf on the Old Course there and at Carnoustie with him. Val and I then went on to Gleneagles for a round of golf there before staying a night at Peebles and driving back to London after a very enjoyable long weekend. The rest of April and May were fairly quiet, though I was quite busy with Promotion Boards and visits to Coastal and Flying Training Commands. Our friends the Pertwees came to stay one weekend for the first time at Heather Hill and we enjoyed seeing again for dinner one evening Bill and Hope Pigott from Canada and Frank and Vernon Headlam from Australia, who were over in London. On the 31st we again had the annual Admirals/Generals/Air Marshal's golf match at the Royal Berkshire Golf Club. I never knew who won! but it was always great fun with many old friends.

June was much the same though I had to fly up to RAF Manby in Lincolnshire to talk to one of the courses there at the Flying College. I also had to give a talk to the Joint Services Staff College at Latimer in Buckinghamshire and speak to the RAF students about their postings. The third week of June was always Ascot races and Val and I were kindly invited again by Harry and Jane Broadhurst to join their Hawker Siddeley party one day with several other old Air Force friends.

Wimbledon this year of 1968 was very special being the first year of Open Tennis and there was much excitement and speculation with the return of the professional circuit of great players like Laver, Rosewall, Hoad, Roche, Gonzales and Segura. Although John Newcombe was the holder then of the Men's Singles, Laver and Rosewall were seeded 1 and 2 but Roche beat Rosewall in the 4th round and went on to reach the final before losing in three sets to Rod Laver, who after five years as a professional had returned to prove himself the best player of his generation. In the Ladies' Singles, Billie-Jean King won for the third year in a row, beating our Ann Jones in a very close three-set semi-final and Judy Tegart in two close sets in the final. Val and I were able to go every day – Val with a friend in our seats and me in the Committee Box – and I see from my diary that I managed to get seats for Bob and his girlfriend Helen on seven days so we did very well.

In July I enjoyed a visit to RAF Wyton with Val to the new Standard Presentation to my old wartime 51 Squadron, and we went one evening to the Royal Tournament and two other evenings to the Columbia Club with the USAF Generals Clyde Box and John Hardy. We also stayed one weekend with our friends Joan and Johnny Hartnell-Beavis at 'Sadleirs' in Lymington, and another weekend our old friend Gus Holden came down to stay with us at Heather Hill, for some golf and bridge. Weekends in August were also fairly busy with one at the Thompsons at Holbeach Hurn for tennis on their lovely private grass court, when we also attended the RAF Cadets Graduation at RAF Cranwell and fitted in a round of golf on the Sunday with Viv Crone and a friend at our old favourite golf course at Worlington on the way back to London. The following weekend there was a great gathering of RAF friends at the wedding of the daughter and son of two Air Chief Marshal friends Digger Kyle and Walter Cheshire, and the next weekend we spent with the Pertwees at Frinton for tennis, bathing and a dinner dance at their tennis club. Other weekends we usually spent at Heather Hill with golf and bridge with Joan and David Smith, or Elisabeth and Paul Holder. In September I played in the RAF v Aircraft Industry golf match at Wentworth Golf Club and went to the SBAC Air Show at RAF Farnborough. There I was invited to the Hawker Siddeley tent which was very enjoyable and the next evening to the SBAC Dinner at the Dorchester Hotel in London. A few days later I had to pay an official visit to AFCENT (Allied Forces Central Europe) at Brunsum in Holland and I flew over with Val and we stayed the weekend with Brenda and Gus Walker (the Deputy C-in-C) which was fun, and we had a couple of rounds of golf with them there. I remember they had a wonderful Alsatian dog who behaved immaculately, stood still on the golf tees and as soon as Gus had driven rushed off to find the ball in the rough or wherever! They came to stay with us in November in London for CAS John Grandy's Conference of Cs-in-C and later for the weekend with us at Heather Hill.

Around that time there were farewell dinners at Admiralty House for ACM Digger Kyle (then C-in-C Strike Command) and ACM Kiwi Broughton (AMSO) who were both retiring from the RAF and also for Merlyn Rees (Under-Secretary of State for Air) who was to take over as Minister of State for Northern Ireland. There was also an Air League lunch at the Mansion House that I attended, and Val and I went to a USAF Anniversary party at which The Queen Mother was present. Finally towards the end of the year I was appointed President of the Old Carthusian Society (my old school Charterhouse) and I was also made Chairman of the Inter-Services Skiing Association. We therefore went to Zermatt in January 1969 and Val presented the skiing trophy to the Royal Navy who, rather surprisingly, beat the two other Services that year. For Christmas we had stayed at home at Heather Hill where Joan and Johnny Hartnell-Beavis and Gus Holden joined us for a couple of days and we had some golf and bridge. Despite all the golf I had been playing I was still only a poor handicap 13 to which I had been reduced from 15 after winning the local 'Rabbit Trophy' competition at Hankley Common! My short game was not too bad but I had a terrible golf swing and couldn't hit the ball very far, so Val insisted on giving me a series of golf lessons as a Christmas present. I enjoyed them though I am afraid they didn't do my handicap much good. Incidentally one evening when we were down at Heather Hill we got our next door neighbour Grannie Taylor (aged 101) to come and play bridge with us and Bob (aged 21). Actually the old girl was jolly good but very impatient and kept urging her partner to play quicker and bid up! Quite amusing at her age! Before that, on Sunday 8 December Val and I had an interesting visit to St George's Chapel, Windsor Castle for a Thanksgiving Service and Dedication of a pair of silver candlesticks which the CAS presented to The Queen on behalf of the Royal Air Force.

1969

In 1969 work in the office as Air Secretary continued much as before with Promotion Boards for officers of Squadron Leader and above and a number of interviews to discuss careers and appointments. This involved visits to the Staff Colleges at RAF Bracknell, the Joint Services at Latimer and the Air Warfare College at RAF Manby, as well as the Commands including RAF Germany and HQ Shape. I had always been interested in people so enjoyed this work, particularly as I felt I was gradually getting to know a large proportion of officers in the RAF. Some of the interviews were more difficult than others. It was obviously pretty good when one was able to tell people they were going to be promoted and going to good new jobs, but with the general cut-back in the size and shape of the Forces I had to tell a number of senior officers that there would be no further promotion for them and that they would have to retire early. This was not so good, particularly as many of them were friends, but fortunately at that time I myself was due to retire two years earlier than the normal fifty-seven for an Air Chief Marshal and it helped to be able to tell them this.

Easter weekend in April we spent in the country at Heather Hill with lots of golf and bridge and Bob came down from Scotland to join us. The long Whitsun weekend was similar and the Kyles and the Walkers (Gus and Brenda) came to stay at Heather Hill.

In June 1969 I had the honour of being appointed one of the two Senior Air ADCs to The Queen – I had been an ordinary Air ADC from 1953–57 but this had ceased on my promotion to Air Rank – and on this occasion I had an interesting interview with Her Majesty at Buckingham Palace on 27 June. Wimbledon was already with us and I took the opportunity to tell The Queen how much we were all looking forward to seeing her for lunch and the Ladies' Final on 4 July, which she had already accepted. Unfortunately later she had to cancel and got Princess Anne to take her place, but this was not a great success as she didn't really want to come or seem to enjoy it much and has never been again since, unfortunately. Incidentally, Dan Maskell, our Club Pro, used to give her and Prince Charles tennis lessons on the Court in the garden of Buckingham Palace and Dan used to say how promising Princess Anne was and that she could be really good if she wanted to be. Sadly, however, from our point of view she seemed to prefer her riding.

At Wimbledon Rod Laver won again for the fourth time, beating John Newcombe in the Final, and he went on to win his second Grand Slam that year. In the Ladies' Singles Ann Jones did very well, beating Margaret (Smith) Court, a previous two times Champion, in the semi-finals and Billie-Jean King, the Champion for the last three years, in three sets in the Final. It was a good Championships and fortunately Val and I were able to go every day.

From 15–18 July there was a State visit to The Queen and Duke of Edinburgh at Buckingham Palace by President and Madame Kekkonen of Finland. As was normal in those days, a senior serving officer was attached to a visiting President's suite for the period of the visit and on this occasion I was fortunate to be chosen. To meet them on arrival by air at Gatwick I accompanied HRH Princess Alexandra and her husband, the Hon. Angus Ogilvie, on the train to Gatwick, together with the Lord in Waiting (Lord Hamilton) and Lady in Waiting (Lady Margaret Hay). When the aircraft had landed the Princess went on board to greet them on behalf of Her Majesty.

There was then some slight delay as it appeared that Madame Kekkonen was not feeling very well and needed some assistance; but they finally descended and the President reviewed the RAF Guard of Honour. Princess Alexandra then introduced the rest of the meeting party before we and all the Finnish retinue embarked on the special train to London. At Victoria railway station, The Queen and the Duke of Edinburgh, the Prince of Wales, Princess Anne, Princess Margaret and the Duke of Kent were all there to meet the President and his wife who were then conducted to their carriages for the Royal Procession to Buckingham Palace. The Queen, President Kekkonen and the Prince of Wales were in the first carriage, with Madame Kekkonen, the Duke of Edinburgh and Princess Anne in the second, and Princess Alexandra, Angus Ogilvie and the Master of the Household in the third carriage. The Ambassadors, Ladies in Waiting and the rest of all the retinue were in the remaining four carriages. I was in the seventh carriage with some of the Finnish party. It was a lovely day luckily, so was great fun trotting along in the open carriages, escorted by the Household Cavalry, with the route of the Procession lined by contingents of the three Services and crowds cheering madly. There was a welcoming lunch party at Buckingham Palace for everyone, though Madame Kekkonen had to retire to her room. Later that evening The Queen gave a magnificent State Banquet in honour of President and Madame Kekkonen to which Val and I were also invited. Unfortunately Madame Kekkonen still did not feel well enough to attend, and when Val and I were talking to someone over a drink before dinner The Queen and the Queen Mother came to join us and The Queen said to Val, 'Mummy and I have just been tucking the old girl up in bed!' And giggling away she went on to say, 'The story has it that she took several sleeping pills by mistake instead of tranquilisers before flying!'

My duties on attachment to the President's suite for his visit were not very arduous. He was a tall fine looking man who when young had represented Finland in the Olympic Games at either the hurdles or high jump or both. He spoke English perfectly and was extremely nice and all I had to do was to report each morning to Buckingham Palace where I was given a good cooked breakfast and then, when the President's programme had been settled, escort him on his various visits, one of which was in a helicopter of The Queen's Flight from Kensington Gardens to the de Havilland aircraft factory at Hatfield. That evening the Lord Mayor of London (Sir Charles Trinder) gave a big reception and banquet in honour of President Kekkonen at the Guildhall to which Val and I were also invited. On the 17th the President and Madame Kekkonen left Buckingham Palace with the suite in attendance and drove to St James' Palace in another carriage procession – rather smaller this time with only four carriages (with me in the third) but with an escort of Household Cavalry and the usual glamour and splendour of these occasions. At St James' Palace the President received all the Commonwealth High Commissioners and the Chefs de Mission of the Diplomatic Corps, and later left for Claridges Hotel where they stayed another day and where they felt they could return some hospitality. This they did, and there was a splendid reception and dinner at the Finnish Embassy for The Queen and Royal Family and everyone involved in their State visit. They also gave presents to all those attached to their suite, and I received a lovely purple vase with a silver base, on which the Finnish crest and white rose are engraved, and most surprisingly I was also awarded the 'White Rose of Finland' Star and neck decoration.

After all that excitement everything was back to normal – including my breakfast! After a weekend with the Pertwees at Frinton and supporting the RAF in the Inter-Services Tennis at Wimbledon, we flew to Nice for a couple of weeks holiday with Douglas and family at Grasse, which as usual in August was lovely and sunny and the Mediterranean warm enough for swimming – particularly after the North Sea at Frinton!

Back in London in September and October I had to make several visits to Bomber Command (now named Strike Command), and for talks to the Joint Services Staff College. I also went to Australia House to meet AVM Colin Hannah, the future CAS of the RAAF. There were also a few personnel matters in the Far East which needed my attention so I decided to fly out there at the end of October and booked the VIP Comet, so I was able to take Val with me and one of my Directors (Air Commodore Baker) to help with interviews and talks on officers' careers.

Val and I set off on Sunday 26 October 1969 flying from Northolt to RAF Lyneham, where we stayed the night after dinner with Bob and

Elizabeth Hodges (now the C-in-C of Transport Command). We then took off early the next morning in the Comet with S/Ldr Bichard and his crew for RAF Luqa in Malta, and after a day there with the AOC we flew to Nairobi in Kenya. We had a whole day there before flying on overnight to RAF Gan in the Maldives. Val and I were lucky as there were a couple of bunks in the VIP Comet so we were able to lie down and have quite a good sleep. We had another whole day looking round at Gan but with time for a bit of rest on the lovely beach including a swim and snorkeling which was ideal before flying on to RAF Changi in Singapore. There we were met by the Air Commander AVM (Nebby) Wheeler and his wife Elizabeth who took us off to stay the weekend with them at Air House, where there were a number of parties around their swimming pool with other friends, including Bruce from RAF Tengah whom they kindly invited to join us. The next two days were taken up with visits to the Air HQ and the three RAF Stations of Changi, Tengah and Seletar as well as to the British High Commissioner (Sir Arthur de la Mare) and Admiral Sir Peter Hill-Norton, the C-in-C at Far East Command HQ. Incidentally, 4 November was Val's and my Silver Wedding anniversary for which Bruce and Bob gave us four silver table napkin rings engraved with the family crest and our four initials; and we took Bruce and his crew from Tengah out to dinner with us in Singapore that evening. Val and I also did some shopping and bought a lovely Blue Rhapsody Noritake china dinner service to take home.

The next day we flew on in the Comet to RAF Kai Tak, Hong Kong where Val and I had a day and two very pleasant evenings staying with the AOC (Air Commodore (Birdie) Wilson) and his wife at Air House. After that we started on the way back via Kuala Lumpur where Val and I stayed with Sir Michael and Enid Walker (the British HC) and we had a round of golf with him there. After that our route home was via Gan again, then the RAF bases in the Gulf, Masirah, Sharjah, Muharraq and RAF Akrotiri in Cyprus where we had a couple of days including the weekend with the C-in-C Near East, Air Marshal (Splinters) Smallwood and his wife (Jeanne) in the lovely Air House there. He flew Val and me in his helicopter to the north of the island again from the helipad at the bottom of their garden which was interesting, and while in Cyprus I talked to many of the officers on their careers and promotion prospects, as I did at all the other bases we had called in at. To the C-in-C (Splinters) himself I had to give the rather unwelcome news that he was going to have to leave his present delightful appointment and return shortly to London as the Vice-Chief of the Air Staff. He and his wife were loving it out there in Cyprus and were very disappointed to be short-toured in Command and to have to return to the Air Staff in Whitehall, even though it meant promotion in due course to 4-Star Air Chief Marshal rank.

The other Air Rank appointment which was arranged by CAS while I was away was very surprisingly my own. He, Sir John Grandy, wrote to me in Cyprus on my way home to say I was wanted to take over from Admiral Hill-Norton as C-in-C Far East Command instead of Nebby Wheeler as originally planned. I rang to thank him but to say I really didn't think I could as when having to tell a number of senior officers that owing to the cut back they would have to be retired early, to soften the blow I had told them that I too would be retiring early next year. I didn't feel as Air Secretary I could go back on this and accept another appointment of two years which would take me over the official retiring age. John Grandy said he realized this and had discussed the one or two alternatives that I had suggested, if Wheeler was not to do it, with CDS (Sam Elworthy) who definitely wanted me to take on the job and said that service needs must come first. So that was that and I had to agree. Val was not too pleased at first as she was looking forward to me retiring, but she knew that I would enjoy having a top Command at last and in the end she quite looked forward to it.

We finally flew back in the Comet to RAF Lyneham after a very useful and enjoyable three-week tour covering most of our RAF bases overseas. We were so lucky in those days to have the use of the VIP Comet or Britannia or VC10 which made life so much easier and without which we would have had difficulty visiting many of our overseas stations.

On return to UK in November it was back to work in the Air Secretary's office plus the usual visits to the Staff College at Bracknell, the Air Warfare College at Manby and Flying Training Command for talks to officers on careers and postings. As the year drew to a close I unfortunately went down with bad flu though I got well enough in time to enjoy a pleasant quiet Christmas at Heather Hill where Gus Holden came to join us for some golf and bridge – also Joan and Johnny Hartnell-Beavis.

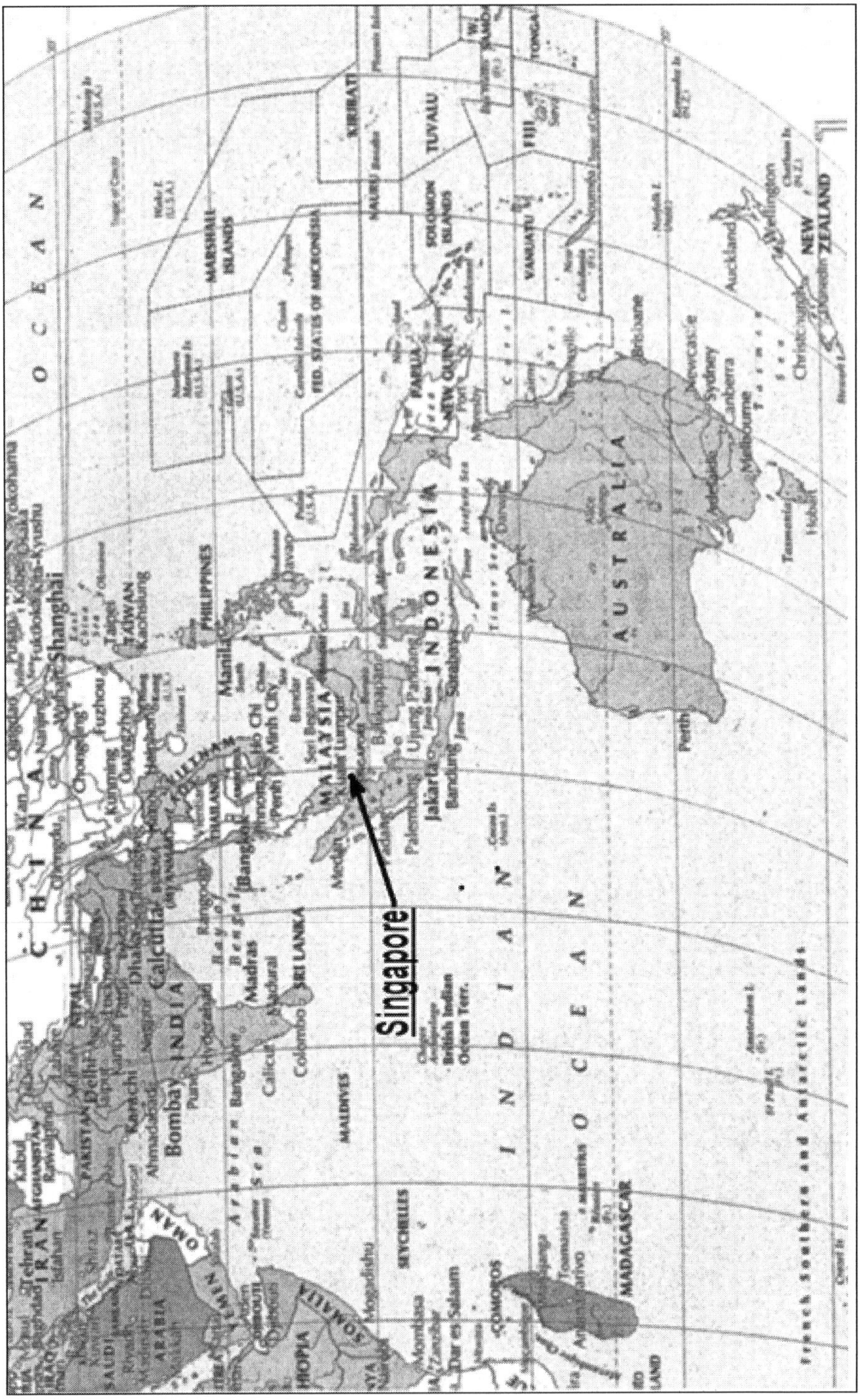

Area covered by Far East Command

11

C-IN-C FAR EAST, SINGAPORE

1970

In the New Year's Honours List in 1970 I was delighted to be appointed GCB, a Knight Grand Cross of the Order of the Bath, one of the more senior honours – for which I later had the pleasure of the Investiture by The Queen at Buckingham Palace. This entitled me to my armorial bearings which I discussed at length with Sir Conrad Swan, Garter King of Arms, who had dug out an old one of the Burnett clan with our family crest, but recommended adding supporters, to which I was apparently entitled, on either side and also any additions that I would like to make it more personal. Val and I had a lot of fun choosing eagles as bearers and a small picture of a long range Wellesley on one side and a blue tennis racket on the other (see picture on back cover). The latter made it unique, I think, though I got the idea from Lord (Willie) Whitelaw who had put a golf club on his! All this would go on a silken banner over one of the stalls in the Order of the Bath Chapel in Westminster Abbey when I eventually got one a few years later when 'Bomber' Harris died. When I die my banner will be returned to my next of kin, but a small metal plaque with my name on it which has been put in my stall will remain in perpetuity, which is rather a nice thought. My stall is on the left hand side in the second row nearest the altar.

Later, after my new posting to Singapore had been confirmed, at one of the All England Club regular meetings I took the opportunity to offer my resignation from the Committee as I would be abroad from the next May for about two years and unable to attend the necessary meetings. However, this was not accepted by Herman David, the Chairman, and the Committee kindly agreed to carry me, so to speak, until I returned to UK. I continued, in absentia, to maintain a close interest in all the Club and Championship affairs and Herman did in fact consult me by post on one or two matters whilst I was in Singapore. On RAF tennis and squash, however, I did hand over the Chairmanship, as I did also of the Combined Services winter sports whose annual meeting I attended in February before flying out to Geneva for two weeks skiing in Verbier. There we ran into our Holbeach friends David and Caroline Thompson again and enjoyed skiing quite a lot with them.

Val and I had, of course, been thinking ahead about our posting to Singapore and what we needed to do about possibly letting our house at Heather Hill and selling our flat in London. We had decided to sell the flat as it was only on a very short term lease and Bruce was abroad in the RAF and Bob at St Andrews University and usually staying with friends during the holidays. Regarding the house, in the end we decided to lend it to Group Captain Howard Lewis and his wife Joan whom we had stayed with once when he was stationed at RAF Gatow in Berlin and who was now posted to the Air Ministry and wanted somewhere for a year or two while looking for a house in our area. By the time we would have paid tax on any rent we felt it would hardly be worth it and we were sure the Lewises, whom we had got to know quite well, would look after the house much better than someone we didn't know. They agreed in exchange for free rent to buy us a few garden tools, such as a mower and garden roller and chainsaw which we needed. It all worked out perfectly and they were ready to move out by the time we returned in January 1972. Selling the flat was more of a problem. It was officially sold, for the price I had paid for it, within a week but it then fell through and only finally was sold a week before we left for Singapore. As to what we needed to take with us to Singapore I thought the best thing to do was for me to fly out there for a couple of days to stay, if we could, with the Hill-Nortons in Command House. He welcomed this and said, 'Certainly, come and case the joint!'

I left RAF Brize Norton on a Transport Command VC10 scheduled flight on Friday 20 February returning overnight on Monday 23rd. The Hill-Nortons very kindly looked after me over the weekend, showed me around everywhere and briefed me fully on the C-in-C job. As I expected, all essentials were provided at Command House and the only extras they suggested we should take out were some large pictures to put on the extensive walls of the house as well as a few of our personal ornaments and so on to make the large sitting room feel more like our own. I also arranged for Transport Command, when space was available on a scheduled flight towards the end of May, to fly out my car so that we could be free to travel about out there when we wanted. Most of our larger pictures at home were water colours painted by my mother and these would fade badly in the Singapore climate and therefore were not suitable; so Val went out and bought a number of very good reproduction oil paintings by David Shepherd and other painters which we took out and had framed locally in Singapore. We couldn't afford originals!

At the office I gradually prepared to hand over to Air Marshal (Tubby) Clayton as Air Secretary at the end of March, so I had plenty of time for a full briefing at the Ministry of Defence on my new job, as well as for a few farewell parties, before moving out of the flat and getting all our furniture down to Heather Hill. Finally, the week before Val and I were due to leave, our heavy luggage was collected to be flown out to Singapore ready for our arrival and we handed over our little dog Rusty Poodle to our Air Force friends the Pringles, who had loved him and looked after him once before and were going to again while we were abroad. On Bank Holiday Monday we handed over our house to the Lewises and set off for RAF Lyneham from where we flew in the VIP Comet the next morning to Akrotiri and then Muharraq and Gan before landing at Changi in Singapore on Friday 29 May 1970. En route in the aircraft I had a short hand-over talk on the RT with Peter Hill-Norton who was also in mid-air somewhere over the Gulf on his way home after leaving Singapore in a VC10.

C-IN-C BRITISH FORCES FAR EAST COMMAND SINGAPORE (MAY 1970–SEPTEMBER 1971)

The area covered by Far East Command stretched from the Beira Patrol, East Africa, through Mauritius, the Seychelles, the Maldives, Sri Lanka, India, Nepal, Pakistan, Burma, Thailand, Vietnam, Cambodia, Malaysia, Japan, the Philippines, Indonesia and Singapore to Australia, New Zealand, Fiji and the Pacific islands (see page 172).

On landing in the Comet at RAF Changi on 29 May we were met by my Air Commander Nebby Wheeler and Elizabeth and the Station Commander Group Captain Honley as well as Major General Pat Howard-Dobson, my Chief of Staff, and his wife (Bar), my PSO (Lt. Col. Alan Findlay) and my Army ADC (Capt. Reggie Lawson-Tims). The Wheelers then took us off to lunch with them at Air House before delivering us later to Command House in Kheam Hock Road. There we were welcomed by Colour Sergeant Parry (Colours) and all the staff of

Met on arrival in the Comet at Singapore by the Wheelers and General Pat Howard-Dobson

Command House

With Val outside Command House at Singapore, as new C-in-C Far East

twenty-one, including drivers and gardeners, and we were able to unpack and settle in. This was relatively easy, having 'cased the joint' myself only two months earlier and with the help of the Warrant Officer Chief Steward and Heng my excellent batman, who had served the three previous Cs-in-C, and Ah Muhn who looked after Val.

The next morning I was driven to the Far East Command HQ at Phoenix Park where I was welcomed in full dress uniform by a Three Service Guard of Honour with the Army Commander Lt. General Sir Peter Hunt, Vice Admiral Derek Empson the Fleet Commander, Air Vice-Marshal Hennock SASO (representing the Air Commander) and Mr Reg Hibbert, my Political Adviser. Afterwards I was then given a full briefing on all aspects of the Command at that time. Later that evening I was officially dined in at the Phoenix Park Mess. In the next few days I called on our British High Commissioner (Sir Arthur de la Mare), the Singapore Minister of Defence (Dr Goh) and Mr Lee Kuan Yew the Prime Minister, as well as the Australian and New Zealand High Commissioners (Mr Parkinson and Mr Francis). Sir Michael Walker, our BHC in Kuala Lumpur, also came to see me and I then later flew up to meet the Malaysian Prime Minister to discuss our plans. At that stage our

Guard of Honour welcome at Phoenix Park HQ

Mr Wilson's Labour Government policy was to withdraw all British Forces from the Far East and my main task, sadly, was to gradually wind up our Far East Command and take everyone home. The British withdrawal after so many years in the Far East was far from popular locally and there were many regrets and much goodwill. Fortunately, however, from my point of view in particular, the Labour Government in London was defeated before long by Mr Ted Heath and the Conservatives, and there was a change of policy which made my job much more interesting. It was now to organize a small UK, Australian, New Zealand (ANZUK) force in conjunction with the Malaysian and Singapore Armed Forces, which would take over from my Far East command at the end of the following year 1971.

In the meantime I had a number of important visits to make. First of all to the Army who were conducting a major exercise at that time called Bersatu Padu in the Malayan jungle, and I spent a couple of days and nights up there with Colonel Alexander and his No. 40 Commandos. I was particularly interested in what they called 'Booby Trap Alley' and was most impressed with the tough conditions which the Army had to put up with, including sleeping out on the ground in the jungle, often

Visit to Exercise 'Bersatu Padu' in Malaysia

with snakes crawling over them. Incidentally I also met up there for the first time the Australian Minister of Defence (Mr J. M. Fraser) who was visiting the Australian forces taking part in the Exercise.

My next visit then was by helicopter to the RN Base and I was taken by Commodore Templeton-Cotill (Top Cat!) the Chief of Staff in a launch to board HMS *Plymouth* where I was welcomed by FO2 Far East Fleet, Rear-Admiral Terry Lewin (later the Chief of Defence Staff at the time of the Falklands War) who showed me round the ship and introduced many of his officers and crew, with whom we had one of the last Navy tots of rum! – this had recently been cancelled, sadly. After that, it was a very good lunch on board before returning to my HQ at Phoenix Park.

In those early days there were several other visits to make to Army Units including the Gurkha Rifles up in Penang and the War Dog School and No. 18 Signals Regiment, and also the RAAF Base at Butterworth. Therefore I was pretty busy – and so was Val who was a bit taken aback when she was told by the ADC on our arrival that we were due to have two dinner parties for twenty-four arranged for the following week to meet some of the more important people. However, with two cooks in Command House she was told not to worry, to keep out of the kitchen and that all she had to do was just agree the menu with the Chief Steward! The ADC would then brief us on the guests, whom Colour Sgt. Parry would introduce on arrival. That was fine and all worked very well. This was just as well as there were many visitors from overseas staying with us all the time, necessitating one or two large dinner parties every week. It was very warm, of course, which Val and I didn't mind but fortunately we had air conditioning in all the bedrooms and in my office in the house, as well as in my office at the HQ. Otherwise the house was very much 'open plan' and we had most of our ordinary meals outside on the terrace and we usually sat upstairs in a large balcony room with the windows open wide on all sides. I couldn't help remembering that it was from that very room that General Percival, the then Army Commander, had walked out to surrender to the Japanese in 1940.

SEATO MINISTERIAL CONFERENCE, MANILA (JUNE 1970)

At the end of June General Sir Leonard Thornton, the New Zealand CDS, came to stay for a couple of days before we flew up together in the Comet to Manila in the Philippines for the South East Asia Treaty (SEATO) Ministerial Conference, which was attended by our British US of S Sir Anthony Royle, instead of the Foreign Minister. We stayed in the InterContinental Hotel where the conference was also held. The security was very tight with armed guards on every landing which surprised us, until we heard next morning that two dead bodies had been thrown over the hotel garden wall! Apart from that it was a very interesting visit to Manila for four days and we went to a big reception at the Palace given by President Ferdinand and Imelda Marcos. Bob was on holiday from his job with Cooper Brothers in London, and had indulged out to Singapore with RAF Transport Command to stay with us at Command House, so he was able to come too and in Manila was kindly looked after by our Military Attaché there.

VISIT TO AUSTRALIA AND NEW ZEALAND (JULY 1970)

A week after we got back to Singapore, I had a visit lined up to go to New Zealand and Australia in connection with their armed forces under my command. Unfortunately Val had sprained an ankle badly playing badminton and was unable to go with me, so Bob was lucky again and came with me in the Comet as an extra ADC! In Wellington I was met and kindly looked after by the British High Commissioner Sir Arthur

Meeting with Sir Keith Holyoake and Sir Arthur Galsworthy

Galsworthy and his wife. During the next couple of days I had meetings with the New Zealand Prime Minister Sir Keith Holyoake, as well as their CDS (General Bill Thornton) and CAS, my old friend AVM Ian Morrison. After that we flew to Canberra where I had meetings with the Australian Chiefs of Staff as well as their Defence and Prime Ministers. There Bob and I stayed with our Defence Adviser in Canberra (Captain 'Slab' Wilson RN, and his wife Joan) who proved a very useful contact in Australia while I was in Singapore. Incidentally at a dinner with our High Commissioner in Canberra I was amazed to find myself waited on by my ex-batman of 1960 at Bomber Command! Maurice had finished his National Service and left the RAF and gone to Australia and made himself invaluable apparently in running people's dinner parties for them in Canberra including the British High Commissioner's. We had clearly taught him well!

After Canberra we had a couple of days in Sydney and Perth on our way back to Singapore, so Bob had a good trip round.

HQ FAR EAST, SINGAPORE

On return we had Lord Carrington, our new Defence Minister, and his wife Iona, to stay for a couple of days. I joined him for his meeting with

Lee Kuan Yew and the Singapore Defence Minister to discuss the recent change in policy. At the same time we were visited by a party from the Imperial Defence College (IDC) in London for briefings, and we had a cocktail party and dinner for them all at Command House. The Carringtons were delightful guests and Val enjoyed showing Iona round to meet some of the wives and visit the British Military Hospital. The following week we had a meeting of the various High Commissioners of the area, an HQ Far East cocktail party at Phoenix Park and a Far East Air Force Ball at RAF Changi which was most enjoyable. Most Sundays we took a party of friends and visitors on the so-called 'Admiral's Barge' (named, I don't know why, *Uriah Heep*!), which was at my disposal, for a picnic lunch and cruise round the island with a bit of bathing and water skiing which was always great fun. For the latter we also had the use of Bruce's small motor boat which we took over from him in Singapore when he was posted home a few days before I went out there. I was no good at water skiing myself but Val managed to get up occasionally! Bob was very good, particularly on one ski, and I enjoyed watching him and the others and just having a swim myself. Val and I had also been made

Lord Carrington, Minister of Defence, and his wife Iona come to stay

honorary members of the delightful Singapore Island Golf Club where we often played on Saturdays.

Our next visit was to Bangkok and we stayed with Lady Pritchard at the British Embassy although the Ambassador was unfortunately ill in hospital. I was looked after by our representative there (G/C Tug Wilson) who had arranged a press conference for me when I was able to explain the new British policy of retaining a small force in the Far East together with our Australian, New Zealand, Singapore and Malaysian allies so as to help promote confidence and stability in the region.

When asked whether the UK would help Thailand to control the infiltration by communists across their borders, I said the Thai/Malaysian forces should be quite capable at the present stage of handling this problem themselves, and that any further help, if necessary, would have to come from the SEATO organisation as a whole. The next day all the papers came out with the headlines 'British C-in-C says Britain won't help'. This led to a stream of telegrams to me from Whitehall, needless to say, and shows how very careful one has to be in what and how one says it to the media for fear of being misrepresented.

On return to Singapore we had a welcome visit by AMP (ACM Sir Andrew Humphrey) and his wife Agnes, also by Admiral John S. McCain (the US C-in-C Pacific) with his wife Roberta and her identical twin sister (Mrs Willis). The three latter usually travelled around together and when someone asked the Admiral, 'How do you manage to tell the difference?' he replied, 'Gee, that's their problem!' He was a very keen tennis player and I always arranged a tennis four for him on the Command House court with two of our other RAF representative players who were stationed in Singapore at that time (G/C Robin Lees and W/Cdr Jackson) and occasionally Nebby Wheeler, and my ADC, whenever he visited. This was fairly frequently as the Vietnam war came under his command and he had to spend much of his time in the SE Asia region. He had a son, Jack, who was serving in Vietnam then and who had unfortunately been shot down and taken prisoner. As the son of the US C-in-C he was given a very tough time, which must have been extremely worrying for them all. I am glad to say, however, that he survived. He has recently been defeated in the US Presidential Election of November 2008.

After the McCains had left, Val and I had a delightful Saturday at the Races with the well known Singapore character Tan Sri Runme Shaw, followed by a dinner and film in the private cinema at his house. There

I met again the Australian Defence Minister (Mr Fraser) and his wife, who had done rather better than Val and I had betting on the horses!

VISIT TO HONG KONG AND JAPAN (SEPTEMBER 1970)

In September we flew up in the Comet to Hong Kong for a two day visit to RAF Kai Tak and HMS *Tamar* when we were met by the Commander of British Forces there, Lt. Gen. Sir Basil Eugster and his wife. They took Val and me to stay in Command house where they showed us proudly where the British Union Jack flag had been buried in the garden for the duration of the war when the Japanese took over. Later the next day we flew on to Osaka in Japan for Expo 1970. The British Consul Mr Robert John and his wife kindly had Val and me to stay and showed us all round the Expo, which we found fascinating and mostly very good though sadly we found the UK Exhibition most disappointing. The next day we all – including Reg Hibbert (political adviser), Alan Findlay (PSO) and his wife ('Bumble'), Reggie (the ADC) and Bob who had come on the trip with me – went sightseeing temples in Kyoto and stayed a night in a hotel there. We then flew up from Osaka to Tokyo, where Val and I stayed at the British Embassy with our Ambassador Sir John Pilcher. The following day was taken up with meetings and talks for me with all the senior Japanese service people, plus an official lunch with the British Ambassador. In the evening there was a dinner with the Chairman of the Japanese Joint Staff Council (Admiral Itaya) and his wife for all of our party, when we all had to remove our shoes and sit on the floor with legs crossed. Val found the Admiral's socks a bit much next to her food! but we were all waited on by geisha girls and it ended up with dancing and a good evening had by all. The next morning sight-seeing in Tokyo and a similar lunch party with geishas, with some of our party dressed up in Japanese clothes, had been arranged for everybody, but I'm afraid I escaped and had a good game of golf on one of their excellent golf courses nearby with one of their naval officers. Altogether it had been an excellent and very interesting trip, much enjoyed by all my staff as well as Val and Bob.

On our return from Japan we stopped off for a night in Hong Kong, where we met up with Rex Sterry, the All England LTC Vice-Chairman who was on holiday in the Far East. He was due to come to stay with us in Singapore so I was able to give him a free ride in the Comet for which he was very grateful, but he always used to tell the story afterwards of how we played bridge with Val and Bob on the aircraft and he had got the C-in-C 3 down doubled and vulnerable at 30,000 feet over the South China Sea!

SINGAPORE

We gave a dinner party for Rex while he stayed a few days with us at Command House, and he thoroughly enjoyed my small swimming pool which I had had constructed there in the garden near the two avocado trees. Incidentally these trees, incredibly, seemed to produce excellent avocados taking it in turn, one tree one year and its mate the next! All the ladies thought this was a very good system. The swimming pool, by the way, had been a great bone of contention and had been turned down for Command House by the Air Ministry on a number of previous occasions. The Naval Commander had one (built by the Japanese, I think, when they were there during the war) and the Air Commander also had one at Air House, and I felt that one would be a great help to me as C-in-C in that very warm and humid climate. The Air Ministry came back firmly 'no' so I arranged privately for plans to be made for a very small pool – not much more than a paddling pool – to be built into a bank on one side and by Chinese labour only so as to keep the cost down. It would be enough to dive into and help keep cool and the cost would be minimal, so I tried again for approval but without success. Finally I said, 'OK, I will pay for it myself,' and gave the order to go ahead. That seemed to shame the Works Department into agreeing, though there were the inevitable questions, including in the House of Commons, about it! I certainly found it invaluable as did nearly all my many guests at Command House during the next year and a half. After work in the office at HQ I often used to come back to Command House and, after a quick dip in the pool to cool off, continue with some of my work in the shade down there under the avocado trees.

Around that time, Air Chief Marshal The Earl of Bandon (Paddy, but also known as the 'abandoned Earl!') was staying with the Wheelers at Air House prior to presenting their new standard to No. 103 Squadron at RAF Changi. Paddy Bandon, like the Atcherley brothers, was one of the great characters we had in the RAF before World War II and his visit to Changi as expected was a great success and a lot of fun, although on this occasion he didn't celebrate as he sometimes did by jumping into the swimming pool in his full dress uniform!

At this time also we had a visit of a party of English MPs, led by the then Conservative MP W. F. Deedes, later Editor of the *Daily Telegraph* and well known leading columnist. I had to give them a full briefing at the HQ before they were then taken around various Service units and came to a cocktail party at Command House in the evening.

BRUNEI VISIT (SEPTEMBER 1970)

A few days later I flew to Brunei for two days to visit our forces there including the Gurkha Battalion. Val and Bob came too and we were met by our High Commissioner Mr Robin Adair, I remember, with umbrellas in a surprise tropical down-pour. A call was made by me later on the Sultan, Sir Omar Ali Saifuddin, and discussions were held regarding the hoped for retention of the Gurkha Battalion. I also took the opportunity of visiting by helicopter one of the Shell oil platforms off the coast and I enjoyed a ride driving one of the Brunei very fast motor boats which they used for coastal defence.

On our return to Singapore I had a meeting of British High Commissioners and Michael and Enid Walker from Kuala Lumpar came to stay for a night. The next day Michael joined my golf team in a friendly match against the Singaporeans.

FIJI INDEPENDENCE CELEBRATIONS (OCTOBER 1970)

The next major event was the Fiji Independence at which HRH The Prince of Wales represented The Queen. The New Zealand Prime Minister was there to represent their interests and I was invited as Fiji officially came within my Far East Command for defence. Val and I flew on 7 October in the Comet to Nandi, the Fiji international airport. The one at Suva, the capital, was not big enough for the Comet so we stayed the night in Nandi and then got a smaller aircraft to fly us across the island in the morning to Suva. We checked in at our hotel there and changed into uniform etc. ready for the Welcome Ceremonies for the Prince of Wales at Albert Park. These were followed by the always rather sad Retreat Ceremony when the Union Flag was lowered by the Fiji military forces. The next morning there was the Fiji Flag Raising Ceremony with a large number of Fiji military forces on parade, followed by some Festival of Youth entertainment and lunch at Government House. That evening there was again the Retreat Ceremony, and speeches by the Prince of Wales and Ratu Sir Kamisese Mara, the first Fiji Prime Minister, and then a wonderful display of fireworks which went on into the night. Sunday was a quiet day and on Monday Val and I were free to attend a programme of entertainment and to look round Suva. I also

Behind Prince Charles on the saluting base with Ratu Edward

took the opportunity to visit the Australian frigate HMAS *Swan*, which was in harbour, and I presented the Captain with a silver ashtray to mark the occasion. Finally Val and I attended the official State dinner given that evening by the Prime Minister, Ratu Mara. He incidentally, like me, was later made an Honorary Fellow of Wadham College, Oxford where he had been in the late 1940s.

On leaving Fiji we headed to Honolulu where I was scheduled to attend a meeting of SEATO Military Advisers, but we stopped for a night at Pago Pago on one of the beautiful Samoa Islands. We stayed at the Inter-Continental Hotel where our room was right by the beach and we had a good swim before an interesting talk over drinks and dinner with the American Administrator there.

33RD SEATO MILITARY ADVISERS' MEETING, HONOLULU (OCTOBER 1970)

On arrival in Honolulu on the 12th, we were met by C-in-C Pac Admiral John McCain with the usual reception by Hawaiian girls with leis for everyone and there was later a press conference for me regarding the

Agenda for this 33rd SEATO Military Advisers Meeting. This was to review and update SEATO military plans for the region in the light of President Nixon's recent plans to reduce the number of US forces in Vietnam, and the British change of policy and decision to retain a small ANZUK force in the Far East to help maintain confidence and stability there. The New Zealand CDS (General Bill Thornton) arrived about the same time, as did General and Mrs John Wilton of Australia, and we all then went for a quick swim on Waikiki Beach including Val and Bob, and Alan Findlay (my PSO) who had also come with me. There then followed my inevitable game of tennis with John McCain and we settled in to our accommodation in the separate VIP camp which was very convenient and close to all the other delegates. Later there was a reception hosted by Brigadier-General Felix Pestana (CMPO) in honour of all the Military Advisers and their wives, including General Yan of the Philippines and ACM and Mrs Dawee of Thailand, who had arrived by then, and the SEATO Secretary General Jesus Vargas. The next morning there was a colourful opening ceremony with a parade of US Marines and unfurling of flags. Unfortunately, there was a slight hitch when both the US and the Philippine flags refused to unfurl! However, this didn't

Met on arrival at Honolulu by Admiral John McCain with General Bill Thornton of New Zealand

stop the ceremony or the military conference going ahead satisfactorily and good humouredly afterwards! The official meetings were all held in the mornings so we had plenty of time for private talks with the other advisers, sight seeing around Pearl Harbor and a game of golf too.

On the second evening the McCains hosted a *luau* party at the Marine Officers Club with everyone in colourful Aloha dress, Hawaii sleeveless shirts and leis with some musical entertainment, singing and hula dancing. All very good fun, and on the third day, with the military meetings over and after the golf and swimming at Waikiki beach in the afternoon, the McCains gave a more formal large dinner party for all concerned, which was an ideal end to an excellent 33rd SEATO meeting with all the wonderful American hospitality.

Over the weekend we flew back to Singapore stopping for refuelling and a night at the US Air Force base Andersen at Guam in the Pacific. We finally got back to Singapore in time for a farewell dinner party for the Army Commander (General Sir Peter Hunt), who was leaving to be CGS, and another for Nebby Wheeler who was also going to Whitehall as the RAF AMSO. Bob was due to leave too and return to work in London after what must have been the holiday of a lifetime for him. He had not only enjoyed a few weeks with us at Command House and plenty of water skiing but also flown with me to Australia, New Zealand, Malaysia, Thailand, Japan, Brunei, Fiji, Samoa, Honolulu, Guam and Hong Kong before flying back to England. Quite a tour!

For the next two weeks in Singapore there was the usual round of High Commissioner meetings, briefing of the visiting MOD planners, a press conference, dinners and a weekend visit by an old RAF tennis friend, G/C Gordon Stowell and his wife Gwen who were on holiday in the Far East.

VISITS TO UK, CEYLON, INDIA AND NEPAL (NOVEMBER 1970)

In November I was invited to attend an Investiture by The Queen on the 10th for my GCB and I flew home the weekend before with Val in the Comet, taking with me my then ADC (Reggie L-T) for the last time as he was being posted to Germany. We stayed at the RAF Club in London and I had lunch with CDS (Sam Elworthy) on the Monday before the Investiture on Tuesday at Buckingham Palace which was exciting as always, particularly this time as with the GCB I was first in the presentation line. After that I attended a Chiefs of Staff meeting at the Ministry of Defence (MoD) and had separate talks with the three Senior Chiefs and a few other friends at MoD. We also got in touch with our tenants, the Lewises, at Heather Hill who seemed to be very happy there and all was well with the house. After a night with Gus and Brenda Walker in their flat at Roehampton we then flew back overnight to the Far East in a VIP equipped VC10 this time, stopping at Colombo in Sri Lanka where we were met in the early morning by my PSO Alan Findlay and his wife 'Bumble' and my new Naval ADC Lt. Richard Sanderson who had flown up the day before from Singapore in our Communications Aircraft Andover. We landed at Katunayake airport and were taken in to Colombo by helicopter for an excellent breakfast and meeting with our High Commissioner and his wife, Mr and Mrs Mackintosh. As it was the weekend we didn't stay long in Colombo and flew on in the Andover to Madras and Hyderabad in the Deccan where I was born and where I wanted to see the Nizam's College where my father had worked most of his life, ending up as the Principal of the College before retiring in 1932. I enjoyed looking round the College and seeing my father's picture in the Hall, and then we were taken to the Secunderabad Club where we had a drink and which seemed just the same as I had always imagined it, still completely anglicised. That night Val and I stayed in the Ritz Hotel which had been converted from the old palace which MJ, the younger son of the Nizam, had lived in with his bride Nilufar after their return from Europe in 1933. All was fine until the plumbing went wrong and our bathroom was flooded but I was told that this was fairly normal!

We flew on after the weekend to Delhi where unfortunately the High Commissioner was away but we were looked after very kindly and hospitably by his Defence Adviser (Major General Penrose) and his wife who had Val and me to stay with them. After making my official calls on the three Indian Service Chiefs of Staff the next morning, we were taken sightseeing in the afternoon and went to a reception by the Indian Air Force and a dinner with General Penrose. Early the next morning we flew to Agra where we were met by a very nice G/C of the Indian Air Force with his delightful wife, who were living proof of success with the Indian custom of pre-arranged marriages by parents. They both showed us round the Taj Mahal and the Red Fort and couldn't have been nicer to us and to each other!

Later that afternoon we flew on in the Andover to Kathmandu, where we had rather a hairy arrival as there was low cloud over the mountains and covering the airfield. It was bad enough to get me worried and I went up to the cockpit to ensure the pilot was playing it right, which I was glad he did!

At Kathmandu we were met by our Ambassador and Mrs O'Brien and taken off to stay in their Residence where they had a dinner party for us. The next day I made my official calls on the Nepal Government and Minister of Defence before going out into the country to visit Major-General (Bunny) Burnett (no relation) who was in charge of the Gurkha Training Establishment. The following day we were all taken in a couple of jeeps for an interesting trek through the countryside up into the mountains where the military adviser Neil and his wife had organized a splendid picnic lunch at the top from where we had a marvellous view of the Tibet mountain ranges including Mt. Everest in the distance. Come the weekend, we took off for Singapore in the Andover and had a wonderful view again from the air of the whole mountain range including Everest, before proceeding via Rangoon. Altogether it had been a most interesting trip, but after two weeks away, there was much to catch up with in our training arrangements with the Singapore and Malaysian armed forces. I was lucky, however, to have a first class Chief of Staff in Major-General Pat Howard-Dobson to continue this work while I was away.

BACK IN SINGAPORE

The President of Singapore had in the meantime died which necessitated an early visit by me to the Istana to pay my respects. I also had the fourth of my regular meetings with the ANZUK High Commissioners, and the Walkers from Kuala Lumpur came to stay again. The next weekend we had 'Splinters' Smallwood (now VCAS) and his wife to stay, when we had a dinner party for them and the new Air Commander (Nigel Maynard) and his wife Daphne and we took them all for a barge lunch party on *Uriah Heep* on the Sunday. We repeated the entertainment the following weekend when AM Foxley-Norris (Chief of Personnel and Logistics) and his wife Joan came to stay and the new Singapore High Commissioner (Sam Falle) and his wife also came for dinner. In mid-December then we took a week's leave and drove up to the Cameron Highlands for a rest and some golf there in cooler weather. We stayed in the small but comfortable Mar Lodge and made good friends of two other couples with whom we played golf and bridge some evenings.

Christmas 1970 was fairly quiet apart from a drinks party with the NCOs and staff at HQ and a dinner party at Command House. We also had a dinner with the Maynards and went to a bar-b-q with Capt. Merson of the Australian Navy who was attached to their High Commission. His wife Silvia had become a great friend of Val's and, incidentally, was the ex-wife of the well known Australian tennis player Adrian Quist whom I had known previously at Wimbledon.

With the gradual rundown of our forces in Singapore it had been decided that the 3-Star posts of Service Commander under the C-in-C should be dropped to 2-Star. In due course the Navy was taken over by Rear Admiral Tony Troup, the Army by Major-General Sandy Thomas and the Air Force by Nigel Maynard as an AVM. When Nebby and Elizabeth left, Air House was then handed back to Singapore as it was thought at that time that Lee Kuan Yew might like to live in it next to his favourite Island golf course. However, for security reasons apparently that didn't happen, but it meant that Nigel and Daphne Maynard had to go into the SASO's house at Changi which was free as the latter had also just been posted home. This house was a good bit smaller but in a lovely position at Fairy Point and they seemed very happy there when Val and I went to dinner with them one evening.

The New Year 1971 started off with a visit for several days by two senior Civil Servants, Pat Nairne (later Sir Patrick) who was Deputy Under Secretary of State at the MOD, and Michael Wilford (later Sir Michael and Ambassador in Japan) who was Assistant Under Secretary of State at the Foreign and Colonial Office (FCO). We enjoyed their stay with us at Command House and on the Sunday took them out on *Uriah Heep* for a lunch picnic and swim in the sea. Val particularly enjoyed talking with Pat Nairne who was an expert water-colour painter, and sitting on the end of the barge produced several lovely paintings in no time at all with the kit he had brought with him. It certainly inspired Val to keep up her painting later after we had retired. Another enjoyable visit then was by General Sir George Baker who had been my opposite number when I was VCAS and was now retiring as CGS. He brought with him his wife Tina and their daughter who in England used to parachute jump with her mother for fun!

After that there was the Commonwealth Prime Ministers' Conference which was being held in Singapore. Ted Heath, our PM, decided to stay the week in a hotel where he had a piano installed in his room so that he could relax and concentrate while playing between meetings. The

Foreign Secretary, Sir Alec Douglas-Home, however, stayed with us at Command House and we became indirectly involved as we had a reception one evening and a dinner party on another for some of the Conference delegates. We were also invited to a reception by the British High Commissioner (Sam Falle) for all the PMs and to a dinner which Ted Heath hosted on board HMS *Intrepid* at the Naval Base. Val also went to a lunch party at the Istana for the wives of visiting Prime Ministers. On the Sunday morning we took Ted Heath, who was a keen sailor and in his own boat *Morning Cloud* had won the tough Sydney-Hobart Ocean Race a year or so earlier, for a quick sail with AM Sir Rochford Hughes (Hughie) and his wife Elizabeth and attractive daughter Annie on their beautiful 35 foot yacht. Hughie had been the previous RAF Air Commander in Singapore but had now retired from the RAF and returned as the Air Adviser to the Singapore Government. The PM much enjoyed this relaxing sail and agreed, the day after the big conference was over, to fly round with me in a helicopter to visit some of the RAF and Army units when he took the trouble to address them all briefly. Altogether it was a very interesting and enjoyable week.

After that Val and I took a few days off over the Chinese New Year holiday (27/28 January) and went up to Frasers Hill, calling in on the Walkers in Kuala Lumpur on the way and returning in time for CDS Sam and Audrey Elworthy's farewell visit. He was now retiring after a long and successful spell at the MoD as both CAS and CDS. Later in February John Grandy (CAS) and his wife Cécile came to visit and stayed with us. John had also been the C-in-C Far East and lived at Command House three or four years earlier when they had been very popular with all the staff who were thrilled to see them again. The Grandys also brought with them their son who was a Lieutenant in the Army and was recovering after being badly wounded in Northern Ireland. Lee Kuan Yew had played golf occasionally with John Grandy when he was in Singapore and they had always got on well, so he and his wife joined us for the dinner party we gave for them. John and I then had a game of golf the next day with Kuan Yew on the new Championship Course which he had designed himself.

This was also a busy time for me in the office with various Five-Power official meetings to review progress with the integration of ANZUK and Singapore/Malaysian armed forces. There was also much social activity in the evenings. Nearly all the more senior officers on the HQ staff of the three Services had married quarters with Chinese staff so took the pleasant opportunity to have drinks and dinner parties fairly frequently.

AUSTRALIA, NEW ZEALAND, INDONESIA VISIT (MARCH 1971)

My next move was to visit New Zealand where we flew in the Comet stopping for a couple of days in Sydney on the way, and an official visit to Indonesia on the way back. In Sydney, where Val hadn't been before, we met up with an old friend of mine from my Australian tour in 1938, Josephine Hughes, and her husband Alan Williams who had driven down from Mudgee specially to see us and show us round. We had dinner one evening with them and their son and daughter which was very nice. The next day we flew to Christchurch in New Zealand South Island where I had arranged for a private visit over the weekend, and the NZ Air Force flew us down in one of their DC3 Communications aircraft to Queenstown. There we hired a car and stayed in the Franton Inn overlooking the beautiful lake. My new PSO, Lt. Col. Brian O'Rorke and new ADC Lt. R. Sanderson were with us, and on the Sunday we all went on a coach trip upcountry which was interesting and where we saw people panning for gold in the river. On our flight north again on Monday to Christchurch we flew low level and round Mt. Cook so saw a lot more of the countryside which was superb. At Christchurch airport we switched back to our Comet and flew to Wellington that afternoon.

There we were met by General Bill Thornton, their CDS, before calling on our High Commissioner, Sir Arthur Galsworthy, who kindly had Val and me to stay again. The next morning I held a Press Conference and called on all the Service Chiefs and Ministers, including the Deputy Prime Minister, before attending a Ministerial Lunch. The afternoon was spent in discussions with the Defence Council and in the evening I attended a formal Defence Council Dinner. The next day we were flown up in a DC3 to Wairoa where I was met by a Guard of Honour and inspected one of their units, before we were taken by car via Lake Taupo to Rotorua with sightseeing stops en route. There we had time to look around some of the natural hot geysers before staying the night in the International Hotel. The following morning we were flown on for me to inspect the RNZAF Base at Whenuapai before going on by car to Auckland and lunch with the Governor General (Sir Arthur Porritt). In Auckland we stayed at the South Pacific Hotel, and as the afternoon was free, I got in touch with ACM Sir Keith Park – the famous

No. 11 Group Battle of Britain Commander who had thirty-seven years earlier persuaded me to join the RAF and who now lived in Auckland. He was in great form, even remembering me from my Oxford University Air Squadron days, and on the telephone when I said, 'You won't remember me,' he said, 'Yes I do. You were a small chap with red hair and were a Tennis Blue.' Later he came round to the hotel to have a drink with us and stayed reminiscing about the RAF for hours. The next morning, which I spent touring the Naval Base, Val went to see some old friends, Anne and Johnny Stewart, at their house overlooking the lovely harbour. In the evening we went to a dinner party with the Defence Adviser at HMNZS *Philomel.* That was the end of a very enjoyable ten days in New Zealand and we started on our way back in the Comet, re-fuelling at Townsville on the north-west coast of Australia and then on to Bali where we stayed the weekend privately at the splendid Bali Beach hotel before my official visit to Indonesia.

INDONESIA VISIT (MARCH 1971)

In Bali we did some sightseeing but stayed mostly by the magnificent swimming pool round which there were also fairly frequent Balinese dancing performances, some of which in the evening we could watch from our room balcony. On the Monday morning we flew early to Djakarta where we were welcomed by Air Marshal Saleh Basarahand and our Ambassador and Mrs Combs with their Defence Adviser (Col. D. A. Jones). I then spent the day calling on the other Service Chiefs (General Panggabean, Admiral Sudomo and Air Marshal Suwoto Sukendar) with Guards of Honour at each of their Headquarters. In the evening there was an official reception with a performance of national dances, and we stayed the night in the Government guest house. The next morning I laid a wreath at the Kalibata cemetery before calling on a number of other senior Generals and Air Marshals, and visiting their National Strategic Command HQ. In the afternoon Val and I both had games of golf organized with Indonesians, and we later attended a dinner party with the Combs at their Residence. All very enjoyable and we flew back to Singapore the next morning after two weeks away altogether.

SINGAPORE (MARCH 1971)

The day after we flew back, there was a big No. 3 Commando Brigade parade with Brigadier P. J. Ovens and some 2,500 Commandos for me

Inspection of No 3 Commando Brigade with Brigadier Ovens at their farewell parade

to review. This was virtually their farewell parade as they were due to return to UK shortly and it was followed by an excellent cocktail party. We also had several dinner parties at Command House lined up to include several UK visitors and old friends such as General Sir John Mogg (Adj. General) and AM Sir Gareth Clayton (Air Secretary) as well as several distinguished Singaporeans such as Dr Goh (Defence Minister), Chief Justice Wee, Dr Yeo (Speaker), Tan Sri Runme Shaw and Tan Sri Tan Chin Tuan (Chairman Overseas Banking Corporation) and their wives. I also called one day on the new Singapore President Sheares to make my number with him.

AUSTRALIA – RAAF 50TH ANNIVERSARY CELEBRATIONS (APRIL 1971)

I heard then from CAS that the RAF had been invited to the Australian Air Force 50th Anniversary celebrations during the first week of April. Unfortunately he was not able to go, so asked me to represent the RAF and said he would send, as back-up for me, our two recently retired

Australian ACMs Teddy Hudlestone and Digger Kyle. This was ideal as they were both old friends of ours as well as being Australians originally from Perth WA. They both came out in the VIP Comet and stayed a couple of nights with us at Command House before we all flew together with Val to Australia. We had a day in hand, so I decided to go via Darwin and Alice Springs where we spent a night and then flew round to have a look at Ayers Rock before going on to Canberra. On landing at RAAF Fairbairn in the afternoon, we were met by the Australian CAS (AM Colin Hannah) and a Guard of Honour. Val and I were then taken off by the Defence Adviser Captain 'Slab' Wilson RN and his wife Joan with whom we were again staying. Later I called unofficially on Colin Hannah again to present him, on behalf of the RAF, with a silver salver suitably engraved to mark the occasion of the RAAF 50th Anniversary. The next morning we were all flown to RAAF Richmond near Sydney to attend the ceremonial parade of the two RAAF Squadrons who were being presented with new Standards by HRH The Duke of Edinburgh. After lunch in the Officers' Mess, we flew back to Canberra in time for an Air Board Reception and later dinner with the Governor General and Lady Hasluck at their Residence.

The next day I called on the British High Commissioner and met some of the BDLS officers, followed by the Australian Secretary of Defence (Sir Arthur Tange) and a meeting with the Chiefs of Staff before an Air Board lunch. In the afternoon I called on the Prime Minister and Mr Gorton (then the Minister of Defence) before having discussions with their Secretary of Foreign Affairs (Sir Keith Waller). A busy day, ending with a cocktail party and a dinner party hosted by 'Slab' Wilson and his wife. While I was out visiting, Val was taken riding in the country outside Canberra which she loved, and then to a lunch party with Lady Hannah.

The RAAF Anniversary Flying Display which we all attended, took place the next day and was a great success with enormous crowds watching. Our representation of the RAF, including Teddy Hudlestone and Digger Kyle, went down very well and was much appreciated. We finally took off later that afternoon in the Comet heading for Singapore, but this time via Perth which surprisingly is not much further than via Darwin. This enabled Teddy and Digger to have a day with their relations still living there. Val and I stayed at the Riverside Lodge hotel, but joined all the Kyle family with several of Digger's brothers and sisters on a lovely boat trip on the Swan River one afternoon. The one evening we were in Perth we all had dinner with the West Australia Governor, Maj. Gen. Sir Douglas Kendrew and his wife.

After a very enjoyable and busy week in Australia we got back to Singapore on 5 April and, after a night with us at Command House, the two retired ACMs went on back to the UK in the Comet.

SINGAPORE (APRIL 1971)

Following meetings with my Service Commanders, including a farewell dinner for Admiral Empson, I had to get busy preparing for the Five Power Defence Conference and SEATO meetings in London, for which I was having to leave only a week later. Val and I then flew back to UK over the Easter weekend in the Comet with my PSO (Brian O'Rorke), Political Adviser (Reg Hibbert) and G/C Ops (David Craig). We stopped off at Gan for refuelling and a night at Muharraq when we had dinner with Maj. Gen. 'Roly' Gibbs. That night we stayed with Mr G. Arthur, our Political Representative in the Persian Gulf, with whom I had a very interesting talk on their problems there. The next day we flew to Gatwick with only a short stop en route at RAF Akrotiri.

The first week in London we stayed with our friend Betty Rowlands at her flat in Wimpole Street which was very convenient and particularly fun for Val as I was going to be busy most of the time. In the morning my first job was to call on CDS (now Peter Hill-Norton) and attend a briefing with him for the Secretary of State Lord Carrington on the Five Power Defence Meetings. After lunch with CDS I had a further meeting with Lord Carrington before attending a Government Reception that evening at Admiralty House.

FIVE POWER DEFENCE CONFERENCE, LONDON (15–16 APRIL 1971)

This main meeting was being held in the splendid conference room at Marlborough House and started the next morning with a Flag Ceremony on the arrival of the Prime Ministers, Mr Heath, Sir Keith Holyoake of New Zealand, Mr Tun Abdul Razak of Malaysia and the Defence Ministers, Mr Gorton representing Australia and Dr Goh Keng Swee Singapore. There were also in attendance the various High Commissioners, Military Chiefs of Staff and Defence Advisers of the countries concerned, with Lord Carrington as Chairman. The meeting started with an opening speech by Ted Heath explaining the British position of partial withdrawal from the Far East but still retaining a sizeable force there in conjunction with our allies. Compared with the previous

Government's plan of complete withdrawal this was welcomed by all concerned, and I was asked as the C-in-C to give a report on progress so far with the Five Power integrated training and defence arrangements. The delegates then spent some time discussing the political framework of the defence arrangements with an interlude between the two sessions for a lunch party for senior delegates with the Foreign Secretary (Sir Alex Douglas-Home) at Carlton Gardens. That evening a large dinner party was held by the Prime Minister at 10 Downing Street to which all the wives were kindly invited. Two more plenary sessions were held the next day with a lunch for senior delegates given by CDS Dick Hull at Quaglino's and at the end of the main meetings there was a press conference. Finally, that evening HM The Queen gave a large and magnificent dinner party at Windsor Castle for all concerned including the wives, which Val particularly enjoyed.

The weekend was free and Val and I went to Lymington to stay with Joan and Johnnie H-B and were glad to meet up there again with Digger and Molly Kyle. On return to London we stayed at the RAF Club, and I spent a couple of days at MoD calling on each of the Service Chiefs and attending a CoS Meeting. One evening we were kindly taken to dinner and the theatre by Brian and Elisabeth O'Rorke and on the other I enjoyed having my SEATO Military Adviser colleagues and their wives to dinner at the RAF Club.

SEATO MILITARY ADVISERS CONFERENCE (21–23 APRIL 1971)

The next couple of days were taken up by the 34th Conference of SEATO Military Advisers of which, as the UK representative, I was Chairman. This was held in the splendid surroundings of Lancaster House and started with a welcome ceremony for the delegates, Admiral John McCain (US), Admiral Sir Victor Smith (Australia), General Bill Thornton (New Zealand), ACM Dawee (Thailand), General Yan (Philippines), Brigadier Felix Pestana, General Jesus Vargas (the Secretary General) and Major General Hay, the Chief Military Planning Officer (CMPO). There were two closed sessions that first day and a reception that evening by our SoS (Lord Carrington) followed by a dinner at the Commonwealth Institute. The next morning there was a closing session at Lancaster House, a signing ceremony and lunch at Quaglino's. After that the weekend was free, and Val and I enjoyed a dinner with our

In the Chair for the SEATO Military Advisers' Conference with G/C Neubroch and G/C David Craig behind

friends Gus and Brenda Walker and a day at Wimbledon with Rex Sterry.

SEATO COUNCIL OF MINISTERS (26–28 APRIL 1971)

After the weekend the 16th Meeting of SEATO Ministers, High Commissioners and their Defence Advisers started with an informal party given by the PM, Ted Heath, at 10 Downing Street, followed by a reception and dinner at the Guildhall in the City of London by the Lord Mayor for all the delegates and their wives. The next morning there was an Opening Ceremony on Horse Guards Parade and an Opening Session at the Banqueting House in Whitehall, but the first closed session took place at Lancaster House in the afternoon. Later that evening HM The Queen gave another splendid dinner party at Windsor Castle. The next day there were two more closed sessions of the council ending up with a big dinner party hosted by the Foreign Secretary at Hampton Court Palace on 28 April.

This marked the end of three successful and enjoyable meetings on defence matters with our Far East Allies who certainly appreciated the high level of hospitality they received while in London. Val and I enjoyed it too. I had one more job to do before leaving for Singapore which was to give a lecture to the Joint Services Staff College at Latimer. Having done this Val and I then flew back in the Comet stopping a night with AM Sir Derek Hodgkinson in Cyprus, and at Gan, before landing at Changi in Singapore on 2 May.

SINGAPORE (MAY 1971)

On the whole Val and I were glad to get back to Command House and a fairly quiet few weeks of our regular routine in Singapore, but I flew to Kuala Lumpur for a couple of days to meet the Malaysian General Ibrahim to discuss the integrated training arrangements. One evening also we had our new High Commissioner in Malaysia, Sir John Johnston and his wife, who had recently taken over from the Walkers in KL, to stay at Command House and we gave a dinner party for them and the Australian CAS, Sir Colin and Lady Hannah, who were visiting at that time. The next day I had a full meeting of all the ANZUK High Commissioners and Service Commanders who then came to lunch at Command House before continuing our meeting later. At the end of the month, on the 28th, Val and I attended a very enjoyable 25th Anniversary

With Val at RAF Changi Ball

Ball at RAF Changi with the Station Commander, G/C Honley, and his wife.

VISIT TO VIETNAM AND CAMBODIA (31 MAY–3 JUNE 1971)

In the meantime I had been invited by the American General Creighton Adams to visit his Command in Vietnam. Val and I flew up to Saigon (now Ho Chi Minh City) with my PSO (Brian O'Rorke) and landed at the airfield Tan Son Nhut. We went in a C130 Hercules aircraft of Transport Command so that I could take a full load of equipment and stores which were now becoming surplus with our rundown in Singapore, and of which the Vietnamese armed forces were in very short supply. This included many tents and blankets for the wives and families of the soldiers who, as was their custom, nearly always went with them just behind the front line. We were met with a Guard of Honour by the Commander of the Vietnam Air Force, who was thrilled with all the equipment we had brought for them, and by our Ambassador Mr J. O. Moreton and his wife. I was then taken to call on the Minister of Defence (General Nguyen Vanvy) before visiting the British Embassy. After lunch there I called on the Vietnamese Chief of Naval Operations (Admiral Tran Van Chon) and their Chief of General Staff, who both gave me briefings, before I went on to join Val at the Moretons' residence where they were kindly having us to stay while we were in Vietnam.

The following morning I called on the USAF Deputy Commander (Major General Hardin) for a briefing and then the Commanding General of the 7th Air Division Vietnamese Air Force (Major General Tran Van Min) who later took me for an official lunch by the Vietnamese Air Force at their Officers' Club. In the afternoon I paid further visits to units of the Vietnamese Air Force and then to the 1st US Army Air Brigade at Long Binn. In the evening I was invited by General Abrams to a fairly informal dinner and talks with some of his staff which was most interesting and went on fairly late. However, it was not an easy meeting for me as the Americans were clearly fed up and critical of the UK for refusing to send any forces to help in the Vietnam war, and I was expected to talk to them about how General Templer's 'hearts and minds' policy had helped to win the day in the Malaysian emergency.

The next day, a trip in a helicopter had been arranged for me and Brian O'Rorke to see a bit more of the country on the way up to Da Nang and we stopped off en route to talk to some of the Vietnam soldiers at a Defence Artillery post high up overlooking the valley. There I was most impressed with the efficiency and keenness of the young soldiers to engage the enemy whose fire we could actually hear from there. When we later arrived at Da Nang, we were met by the Commanding General of Military Region 1 (Lt. Gen. Hoang) who briefed us on the latest position at the front and took us round some of his Units. Later we met the Commander of US 24 Corps (Lt. Gen. Sutherland) for further talks and we stayed the night there with them. It was a bit of an eye-opener for me to hear about all the drug taking amongst the US troops, though perhaps not altogether surprising bearing in mind the awful conditions in which they were having to fight.

The following day, again with the helicopter, we were taken to visit the Coastal Zone and the Vietnamese Navy (Admiral Tran Van Chon) at Cam Rann Bay and in the afternoon we dropped in on the General Military Region 4 at Binn Thuy where I was given a further briefing. We finally arrived back in Saigon in time to join Val for dinner with the Moretons. While I had been away Peggy Moreton had been wonderful looking after Val and had accompanied her on a helicopter trip round Saigon and then up the coast to Qui Nhon where they visited the hospital

Talking to Vietnam soldiers at a Defence Artillery post

at the American air base and a children's convalescent home. There Val was nearly tempted to adopt one of the young children! She did, however, become a regular correspondent friend or penpal with one of them and continued for a year or so after we got back to England.

We had one more visit to make, to Cambodia, and we flew up early in the morning to Phnom Penh. We were met by their Director General of Training and the Chief of Staff of the Khmer Air Force with a Guard of Honour and taken off to visit the Kambaul Training Centre. Later, after calling on the Delegate Prime Minister (General Sirik Matak) we had lunch and talks with the charming Khmer CAS, accompanied by the sound of firing not very far away where the enemy were advancing on the town. In the circumstances we were surprised how calm the CAS and all of them were, but I was glad that afternoon to be flying back to the peace of Singapore after a very interesting five days away.

SINGAPORE (5 JUNE–5 JULY 1971)

In Singapore all was going well and it was back to the regular programme of dealing with visitors, meetings with various High Commissioners and a couple of visits to KL to discuss the integrated training arrangements with General Ibrahim. One day we attended the reception given by Sam Falle, our High Commissioner, for The Queen's birthday, and there were the usual dinner parties. I also went to RAF Tengah and got one of their Lightning pilots to take me up in one of the dual aircraft, as I hadn't flown a Lightning before, to show me how they did a high altitude supersonic interception. I found it most exciting and I thoroughly enjoyed it. Two weekends followed with our customary lunch picnics at sea on *Uriah Heep*, and at the end of the month I sent it up with the crew overnight to Mersing on the east coast of Malaysia and we drove up the following morning and took the boat out to Tioman Island, where we stayed on it and anchored in the bay for a couple of nights. The rest of the weekend was spent enjoying the swimming and water skiing and Bruce was able to join us too. He had managed to 'indulge' out to Singapore for two weeks' holiday which was lovely for all of us. The first weekend in July the Hill-Nortons came as CDS to stay with us at Command House and we had another enjoyable party with them for lunch at sea with the Hibberts, and Vernon and Frank Headlam who happened to be visiting friends in Singapore at that time.

AUSTRALIA, NEW ZEALAND AND PACIFIC ISLANDS (5–18 JULY 1971)

My next visit was to the Pacific Islands, calling in at Australia and New Zealand briefly on the way. The first part of the trip was with the Hill-Nortons in their Comet, and Peter and I did all our official calls together to the Australian Secretary for Defence and their CDS (Admiral Smith) with whom we attended an ANZAM Chiefs of Staff Meeting. On the second day in Canberra we called on the Governor General and the Minister for Foreign Affairs and had meetings with the Defence Minister and some of the BDLS Officers at the British High Commission. Val and I stayed with Rear Admiral 'Slab' Wilson and his wife who kindly looked after Val all the time, and each evening there was a dinner party hosted by either the Smiths (CDS) or the British High Commissioner to which the wives were also invited. The next day we all flew on in the Comet to Wellington where the Hill-Nortons disembarked, and we went on to Auckland for a day before flying on to Nandi in Fiji. From there we sent the Comet back to NZ for the Hill-Nortons as we had to switch to a C130 Hercules of RAF Transport Command for the smaller runways on the Pacific Islands. At Nandi Val and I stayed a couple of nights and our

British High Commissioner came over from Suva to see me there and have dinner one evening with us.

In the Hercules we flew on to Port Vila in the New Hebrides (now called Vanuatu) which in those days, until 1980, was administered as a condominium by France and Great Britain. We were welcomed by the British Administrator and had time for a swim in the sea from a lovely little beach nearby before a small reception party that evening. The next day I had a meeting with the French Resident Commissioner and was interested to hear how well, in his view, the joint administration seemed to be working. The following morning we were seen off by an Anglo-French Guard of Honour before heading north on a six-hour flight to Tarawa in the Gilbert Islands. On landing there we were met by Sir John Field the Resident Commissioner and a Police Guard of Honour. We were then taken by Sir John and his wife Irene to the Residency where we were looked after very hospitably for the two days we were in Tarawa. The Residency itself was an unusual type of official building – only a fairly small bungalow with a thatched roof but very comfortable and in a lovely position right on the beach under the palm trees and looking out to sea in the east. Tarawa had, of course, been occupied by the Japanese during the war and had to be recaptured by the Americans later, on their fight back across the Pacific. The recapture of Tarawa had been a terrible battle as the US landing craft ran aground on the reef surrounding the island, and the troops who then had to wade ashore several hundred yards were mown down in their hundreds by the Japanese machine guns before they could reach the mainland. During our stay there I visited the Police HQ and the Marine Training School and we were then taken round the island to see some of the defence positions and relics of the war which was fascinating and led to some very interesting discussions later that evening. With hindsight, it appeared that the Americans had not been very clever and that if they had done more reconnaissance first they could have virtually walked ashore on the other side of the island where there were few defences, and their casualties would have been far far fewer.

It had been a most interesting visit and we then flew south-west again to Honiara in the Solomon Islands, where we were met by a Police Guard of Honour and our High Commissioner (Sir Michael Gass) and Lady Gass who kindly took us off to stay at Government House. After lunch there I had official discussions on Far East defence matters with the HC and some of his staff, but had time to enjoy their swimming pool before a quiet dinner. The next morning I visited the Police HQ, the Department of Lands and Surveys and the Technical Training Institute but had a free afternoon with Val around the swimming pool before a dinner party at Government House that evening. A tour of the Guadalcanal battlefields the next day was of particular interest and gave me an idea of the awful terrain and conditions in which the Americans were having to fight back against the Japanese and gradually claw their way back to the Philippines and Japan itself. On the Sunday we flew to Port Moresby in New Guinea where we didn't stay long before leaving the Hercules and transferring to a VC10 which had come to fly us back to Singapore in comfort after a long and fairly arduous but most interesting tour of island hopping in the South Pacific.

SINGAPORE (19 JULY–9 AUGUST 1971)

On arrival back at Command House we were surprised but delighted to find two uninvited but very welcome guests sitting out and enjoying a cup of tea by the pool. Eddie Tuckwell, ex-Surgeon to The Queen and a nearby neighbour of ours at The Sands, was on a lecture tour in the Far East, accompanied by his sister Margaret, and had arrived that morning in Singapore. He had persuaded the Chief Steward to let them stay the weekend with us at Command House! Luckily Val and I were only too pleased and would have invited them anyway if we had known. Val enjoyed showing them round the Botanical Gardens and other places in Singapore. I was pretty busy myself at HQ catching up on developments while we had been away. Michael Hogan, son of my old LRDU friend, also came to stay the next weekend on his way to a new job in Japan, and we had our usual lunch parties on *Uriah Heep* both Sundays which everyone enjoyed. I also, later on, had some very useful talks with Lee Kuan Yew at the Istana on the proposed new defence arrangements and the timescale for the rundown of the British forces there. After that I took a week's leave, and Val and I flew up in the Andover to Ipoh in West Malaysia where my driver had taken my car, and we drove ourselves up to the Cameron Highlands where I had booked into the lovely Mar Lodge again. There we enjoyed a few days of relaxing golf in the cooler weather.

On our return from leave I had a full day's meeting with the British High Commissioners with an interval for a lunch party at Command House, and on another day I paid a long overdue visit to 1/2 Gurkha Rifles. I was then off again on another two weeks' tour in the Comet.

MOMBASA, MAURITIUS AND THE SEYCHELLES (13–22 AUGUST 1971)

This time it was to the western area of my Command and Val and I took off in the Comet with my PSO and ADC first of all for Mombasa in East Kenya, after stopping as usual at Gan for refuelling. At Mombasa we had a whole day and my main object was to check up on the BIRA oil patrol which was in the area of my Command. We were met on landing at Port Reitz airfield by the Consul First Secretary (Mr Peel), the Defence Adviser (Col. Tayleur) and RNLO (Cdr. Manuel) and taken to the Mombasa Beach Hotel. The next morning, accompanied by the DA and PSO I called on Mr Peel, then the Commissioner for Coast Province, and the Mayor of Mombasa. After that we called on Commander Kenya Navy (Cdr. Hall, RN) and went with him from the naval jetty to visit RFA Derwentdale before returning later to our hotel. I was glad to find all was well with the BIRA Patrol and there were no problems for me there.

We then had two days over the weekend when my PSO (Brian O'Rorke) had arranged for us to hire a jeep to take us round the Tsavo Game Reserve. It was the greatest fun and we were lucky to see all the wild life and animals we had hoped to. The first night we stayed in the comfortable Voi Lodge high up overlooking a water hole, which was partially flood lit and where we saw masses of zebras and elephants come down for the water in the evening. For the second night we had gone on to Tsafaris Lodge, a thatch roofed tented camp just the other side of a small but fast flowing river which we had to cross in turn in a small boat with any night bags we needed. There were a couple of camp beds in each tent and a fairly basic shower with a bucket to fill with warm water from the kitchen if required, and then pull a string to upset it over one's head! After a quick change, Val and I started to leave our tent to go along to the mess tent to have a drink but were immediately confronted by a rhino and had to beat a hasty retreat until the rhino had finished its regular 6.00 p.m. meal which was put out every evening to keep him tame. I thought they might have warned us! Eventually we went for our drink and supper and an early bed as we were leaving early the next morning for Mombasa. Luckily we weren't planning to leave Mombasa until midday because half way back the jeep broke down and we were stuck at the side of the road for a good hour or more. I can't remember how we got the jeep going in the end but Richard and PSO Brian managed somehow. In due course we took off for Mauritius. On the way we flew round to have a look at Aldabra Island where, when I was VCAS, I was always keen the RAF should build a runway so as to have an 'all-red' route to the Far East – unfortunately in that project the RAF lost out to the wild life protagonists who didn't want to upset the famous giant tortoises! Anyway, I was interested to see the layout of the island and precisely where we had planned to put a runway. We eventually landed at Pleasance Airport in Mauritius about 5.30 p.m. and were met by the British High Commissioner (Mr P. A. Carter) and his wife who took Val and me off for a quiet evening at their Residence, which was high up with a good view of Port Louis and the harbour in the distance.

The next morning Mr Carter took me to call on the Governor General (Sir Leonard Williams) at his splendid residence 'La Réduit' where I had some very interesting talks with him and later the Prime Minister (The Hon. S. Ramgoolam). After another brief call on the Mayor of Port Louis (The Hon. G. Duval) I visited HMS *Mauritius* (Cdr. Ram RN) accompanied by the PSO and ADC. The afternoon was free and all four of us went swimming in the sea with the Carters from their beach cottage on one of the many lovely Mauritius sandy beaches. The next morning we were driven round on a tour of the south of the island before going to lunch with the Governor General and Lady Williams. I had asked earlier to visit the harbour, so after lunch we were all taken on an interesting boat trip round the harbour, but there were no signs of any Russian ships. One of the reasons for my calling in on Mauritius was because of the growth of the Soviet fleet in the Indian Ocean in recent years, and the agreement they were reported to have made with Mauritius for servicing facilities for Russian fishing trawlers. I needed to check whether these facilities were being used also by their naval ships, whose increase in numbers was causing some anxiety for security of our British trade routes in the Indian Ocean and the littoral states. In the evening we were all invited by the Carters to supper and the Port Louis Theatre to see the Gala Night of *Oklahoma* which we thoroughly enjoyed.

The next day we flew on to Mahe, the main island of the Seychelles, where I think we were the first to land on the brand new runway, which the UK had built for them and which HRH Princess Margaret was due to open officially in a few days' time. We were met by the Governor, Bruce Greatbach, a big man who matched his name! and he took us to settle in at his residence, Command House, at the capital, Victoria. It was a large house with a big coco de mer palm tree bearing a large fruit with a two-lobed nut, and there was a huge cement *tombeau* in an otherwise not very exciting garden. It had a wooden balcony all the way round the first floor of the house and I remember Bruce Greatbach wondering about which room to put Princess Margaret in when she came without other guests being able to look in on her from the main balcony to which all the rooms had access!

After the PSO and I had a general discussion session with Greatbatch and the Deputy Governor, I went to call on the Chief Minister of the Islands (James Mancham) with whom I had a long and interesting meeting. He was an impressive youngish man, enthusiastic and with a good sense of humour, and I was very sorry to hear several years later that he had been ousted while out of the country, at the Prime Minister's Conference I think, and that someone else had taken over. At that time he certainly seemed in full charge of Seychelles affairs. He appreciated the value of the RN Survey ships which dropped in on the Seychelles from time to time and said he would like them more often. He then went on to say: 'We love the Royal Navy. They enjoy themselves here, and every time they come the population gets a little whiter, which is good!' Later we were all taken on a tour of the northern part of the island before attending a cocktail party at Government House. The next morning the Captains of the two RN survey ships visiting at the time (HMS *Beagle* and *Badger*) came to call and I was able to tell them what the Chief Minister had said!

After that Bruce Greatbatch took us on another long tour to the other side of the island where most of the lovely beaches are. He drove us up over the mountains, where incidentally Archbishop Makarios had been interned for several years earlier after being banished from Cyprus, and then we went on down to the west coast. On the way he explained to us his plans for developing the Seychelles tourist industry and he then showed us his chosen site for a hotel in every bay – but sensibly limited initially to only one in each bay to prevent overcrowding. This took nearly all day as there was a maximum 15 m.p.h. speed limit on the island with all the narrow roads! The day ended with a dinner party that evening at Command House and an early night as we were leaving for Singapore early the next morning. It had been an interesting and enjoyable visit, and on the way back to Singapore we diverted slightly to fly over the Cocos Islands where at Diego Garcia the US had a useful base with a good runway. We didn't land there but flew round to have a good look at it before going on to land at Changi in Singapore on 22 August quite late in the evening after ten days away.

SINGAPORE (23 AUGUST–1 NOVEMBER 1971)

On return to Singapore for our last two months there was much to do. There were a number of visitors including the new US of State for Air (Mr Antony Lambton), the US of State Army (Mr G. Johnson Smith), the New Zealand CGS (Maj. Gen. R. J. Webb), and the Royal College of Defence Studies (RCDS). We had a cocktail party for the latter which the American C-in-C Pacific (Admiral McCain) and his wife (and Mrs Willis) also attended as they were staying the night with us at Command House.

I paid a last visit to the Royal New Zealand Infantry Regiment (RNZIR) and to the Royal Australian Regiment at Selong Garrison, and I flew up several times to Kuala Lumpur to finalise arrangements in connection with the integrated Jungle Training with the Malaysia General Tan Sri Ibrahim. Captain D. R. Reffell RN (the Chief Staff Officer Plans and Policy COMFEF, and later Admiral and Governor of Gibraltar) called to update me on the Navy movements, and the new ANZUK Force Commander (Rear Admiral D. C. Wells of Australia) came to 'case the joint' and to meet up with some of his future staff. The Air Force in the meantime was busy handing over RAF Tengah to the Singapore Air Force and had a big Handover Ceremony on 15 September. On Saturday 18th there was a Final Parade of The Queen's Colour and a Reception to mark the 31st Anniversary of the Battle of Britain. Another ceremony at that time was when the New Zealand CDS (General Bill Thornton) came to present Colours to the 1st Battalion RNZ Infantry Regiment at Dieppe Barracks. Betty Rowlands from London then came to stay with us for a week and also Norman and Eileen Pertwee from Frinton for the long weekend. Other visitors at that time were General Sir Antony Read (QMG) and AM Bob Hodges (by then AMP) so we arranged a big dinner party at Command House to which Lee Kuan Yew and his wife also came. On the Sunday we took Betty, the Pertwees and the Hodges on our usual lunch party on *Uriah Heep* which they much enjoyed.

The next day Val and I flew up to Bangkok for a quick visit to Thailand before I attended the SEATO Military Advisers' Conference (MA35C). We had a couple of days in hand, so we flew on up to

Chiangmai for a day there and after staying the night at the super Runconose Hotel, we flew to Nan near the Laos border, where I was given a briefing on their problems with Communist infiltration. On the way back to Bangkok we then called in at Ayudhya, the ancient Siam capital, and had a look round the ruins and many resplendent old temples there. Back in Bangkok we stayed at the Erewan Hotel where we met up again with the other SEATO Military Advisers and their wives, and there was the usual very hospitable dinner and reception parties for all concerned, including in my case also Reg Hibbert, Brian O'Rorke and his wife Elisabeth, and Richard Sanderson my ADC who had come on this trip with me. The conference went on for two days but we had time to have a good look round Bangkok and go on the delightful early morning boat trip to the floating market when it was fascinating seeing the Thais all along the river bank jumping into the river to wash themselves, their hair and even their teeth in the muddy water!

On 2 October we flew back to Singapore in time for the RN farewell party and the arrival that weekend of Denis Spotswood (the new CAS) and his wife Ann for whom we had a lunch party before dining with them and the Maynards at Fairy Point. After that, during our last month in Singapore, there was a farewell lunch or dinner party practically every day as people were beginning to be posted back to UK or were sending their wives home in advance. We, of course, had many of these farewell parties at Command House, for most of the senior Army, Navy and Air Force officers, the British High Commissioners and various Singapore ministers, officials and friends that we had made out there. We also had two final launch picnic parties on *Uriah Heep*, whose crew had looked after us so well on many Sundays. I also had two final golf matches between my C-in-C's team and our Malaysian and Singapore golfing friends. They both included lunch and later cocktails at Command House which was fun. I remember in particular the Singapore match of eight pairs in which Dr Goh (the Minister for Defence) and Dr Yeo (the Speaker) were playing against Pat Howard-Dobson and me. It ended in an exciting draw with the last putt, on the last green, in the last match! Val and I also went to many farewell dinners with the three Service Commanders, and other senior officers, as well as Reg and Anne Hibbert and the ANZUK High Commissioners Sam Falle, Norman Parkinson and J. R. Rowland. We were also dined out by a number of Singaporeans – Chief Justice Wee, the Defence Minister Dr Goh, the Speaker Dr Yeo, Tan Chin Tuan, Runme Shaw and others, before the final big farewell

Lee Kuan Yew presents me with a silver salver

dinner on 16 October which Lee Kuan Yew and his wife gave for us at the Istana. At this dinner there were more than eighty people including Mr Sheares (the President) and his wife and all the Singapore Cabinet Ministers and senior officers of their Armed Forces, as well as the ANZUK High Commissioners, my Chief of Staff (General Pat Howard-Dobson) and three Service Commanders and most of the new ANZUK Force Commanders, plus all their wives. It was quite an occasion. In his farewell speech, Lee Kuan Yew paid high tribute to the British Far East Command for helping to bring stability and security to the area, particularly during the years of confrontation with Indonesia, and for helping the Singapore and Malaysian Armed Forces to expand so that together with the smaller but significant ANZUK Force they could continue to look after their own security after the British Far East Command closed down on 1 November. He then presented me with a splendid silver salver suitably engraved to 'The last Commander-in-Chief Far East Command', with both the Singapore and Far East Command Crests on it. This, he said, was to remind Val and me of what he hoped had been a happy time in Singapore.

In my reply thanking the PM for his wonderful farewell dinner and the silver salver, I said that, although the closure of Far East Command after so many years was the end of a chapter of British military history, it would also mark the beginning of a new and exciting chapter in Five Power Defence partnership in this theatre, in which a small integrated ANZUK force would be working alongside the expanding Singapore and Malaysian forces. This ANZUK force was now well established and I was confident it would continue to maintain the stability and security of the Singapore/Malaysia area. Finally, after saying how much Val and I had enjoyed our time in Singapore and wishing them all the best in the years ahead, I presented Lee Kuan Yew with a fine clock as a token of our esteem and to mark the historic occasion of the closure of Far East Command.

The following week I flew with Val up to Kuala Lumpur to make my farewell call on the Malaysian PM, Tun Razak, when we exchanged gifts to mark the historic occasion of the closing down of Far East Command. I also had a further meeting with General Ibrahim, the Chief of their Armed Forces Staff, and we stayed at Carcosa when the HC Sir John Johnston and his wife kindly gave a farewell dinner party for us.

By now, with only two weeks left, the ANZUK Force Steering Committee under General Pat had sorted out nearly all the main issues. The Integrated Air Defence System (IDS) involving all five nations had been operational since 1 September and the only issues still outstanding were a few minor ones of real estate, i.e. which buildings and installations were still to be handed over to Singapore and which retained for the ANZUK forces. On Jungle Warfare training, Malaysia insisted on retaining full control of the J. W. School at Ulu Tiram and had to be persuaded to accept a minimum number of ANZUK and Singapore trainees per year. This meant several more visits by me to see General Ibrahim in Kuala Lumpur and they eventually agreed to meet all the ANZUK Brigade training requirements and most of those needed for the visiting UK Battalions. So the matter was finally concluded satisfactorily at the eleventh hour with an exchange of letters confirming the arrangements on 30 October!

During the last week there were a few more farewell calls I had to make – to the President Mr Sheares at the Istana, to Dr Goh the Defence Minister and to the Australia, New Zealand and British High Commissioners. I also had a final Press Conference and a last visit to the ANZUK Force at their HQ at the Naval Base. On the last morning, Friday, 29

October, at the Phoenix Park HQ I addressed all the FEC Staff and had a final meeting with the Service Commanders and General Pat, followed by farewell drinks in the mess. Later, after changing into No. 1 uniforms the final closure of the Command was marked with due ceremony by a large and impressive farewell parade and fly-past of all Forces still under my Command including the Australians and New Zealanders. The three Single Service Commanders (Rear Admiral Troup, Major General Thomas and Air Vice-Marshal Maynard) all came on the saluting base with me, and after I had addressed the parade there followed the Beating of the Retreat after sunset and the haul down of the flags. The parade was then marched past by Brigadier Mike Walsh, the Commander of the 28th Commonwealth Brigade and the new ANZUK Army Commander, with bands playing and flags flying. It was certainly a very nostalgic and memorable occasion.

Finally, two days later on Sunday 31 October, the Far East Fleet staged a magnificent steam-past of sixteen ships with a fly-past of 26 Buccaneers and Sea Vixens, and 24 helicopters from HMS *Eagle*, whilst I took the Salute from the RFA *Stromness* in the Singapore Straits accompanied by

With Major General Thomas, Army Commander at Farewell Parade of FE Command

Taking Salute at final sail-past of FE Fleet

Rear Admiral Troup and Rear Admiral Wells. Afterwards I was taken in a helicopter to land on the Guided Missile Destroyer *Glamorgan* to have lunch with Rear Admiral D. Williams (later Governor of Gibraltar) who had led the steam-past of ships which were mostly heading back to the UK.

These last two farewell ceremonies by Far East Command were attended and much appreciated by Dr Goh as acting Prime Minister in the absence of Mr Lee Kuan Yew abroad.

The Far East Command was about 91,000 strong by the end of Confrontation but had already reduced to about 43,000 when I took over in May 1970. By the time I left on 1 November 1971, the overall strength had reduced to 4,500 only, of whom many were also due to return to UK shortly. The remaining rear parties then had the task of finally closing the Command and handing over the rest of the installations to either the Singapore Government or to the ANZUK force by the end of December 1971.

During my eighteen months as C-in-C, I travelled some 145,000 miles (the equivalent of nearly six times around the world) and visited twenty-five countries and territories. Some of these visits might appear to be largely 'swanning' but I believe they served an important purpose and were of great value. I was sometimes surprised to find that, in countries outside the Five Power Defence arrangements, a number of Ministers and officials were only vaguely aware of what our post-1971 presence in the Far East would be. I hope I managed to enlighten them and that this was a help to our representatives in the countries concerned.

We also had a fairly large number of contingency and other plans covering my area of responsibility, for which it was important for me to maintain close contact with the British representatives and High Commissioners. In fact, I only had to mount one of these contingency plans (Plan Alpine) which involved the evacuation of British nationals from East Pakistan in March 1971 when some 220 individuals were evacuated by RAF and a few civil aircraft. The Command's assistance had also been required in November 1970 when a tidal wave and cyclone struck the coastal region of East Pakistan causing severe damage over an area of about 3,000 square miles. For this I had to mount a relief operation (called Burlap) in which units of all three services under my command took part over about four weeks. Another similar relief operation (called Epigram) was mounted in January 1971 at the request of the Malaysia Government, when exceptionally heavy rainfall caused widespread flooding and damage in West Malaysia. These operations were only relatively small in nature but had to be launched with little or no notice and some knowledge of the areas was invaluable.

During all the final farewells Val and Colour Sgt. Parry had been busy packing everything up at Command House and arranged to send most of our heavy luggage back with Transport Command, including our car, so that it would be waiting for us on our arrival.

After saying a sad goodbye to all the staff at Command House, we set off on 1 November for Changi where we were seen off by the HC (Sam Falle) and Pat Howard-Dobson in the Comet for our farewell visit to Hong Kong, the US C-in-C Pacific, Australia and New Zealand before returning to UK by sea in RHMS *Britanis*.

At Hong Kong we were met by Air Cdre. and Mrs Godwin with whom Val did some shopping, and we then joined CBF (General Sir Richard Ward) and his wife at Flagstaff House where they had a dinner party for us. The next morning, while Val and Elisabeth O'Rorke (I still had my PSO and ADC with me) did more shopping, I called on Commodore Hong Kong at HMS *Tamar* and the Acting Governor (Sir Hugh Norman-Walker). We then took off and had lunch in the Comet before landing about five hours later at Andersen Air Force Base (Guam). After a night there and an early round of golf for me with US Col. Dunlap (instead of breakfast!) we flew on another four hours to Wake Island, where we only stayed for refuelling before a further six hours flying. We had dinner in the Comet and landed after dark at Hickam (Honolulu). We were met by Col. McClanahan and put up overnight in the comfortable Fort de Russy Beach Cottage. Incidentally on the way we had crossed the International Date Line so had gained an extra day which I reckoned we could enjoy in Honolulu! In the morning I made my farewell calls on the Chief of Staff (General Corcoran), the new C-in-C Pacific Fleet (Admiral Bernard Clarey) who had taken over from our friend Admiral Jack McCain, and the C-in-C Pacific Air Force (Gen. L. D. Clay) who kindly took us to lunch. In the afternoon we were free to enjoy the swimming before an excellent dinner hosted by General Corcoran.

After leaving Honolulu it was a six-hour flight to Pago Pago in Samoa, where we stayed again at the Inter-Continental Hotel, before going on to Nandi (Fiji). We had lost our day again by crossing the Date Line in reverse so we only stayed there for refuelling before another five and a half hour flight to Sydney with dinner again on the Comet. We stayed in Sydney at the Gazebo Hotel and spent the Sunday there when we went to see the RHMS *Britanis* which was in harbour to check up on our cabin and our embarkation arrangements for 11 November from New Zealand. We then flew to Canberra for a couple of days and were met and looked after very well as usual by the Defence Adviser (Slab Wilson) and his wife, who held a farewell dinner for us. The next morning I did my farewell calls on the Defence Minister (Hon. David Fairbairn) and the Defence Secretary (Sir Arthur Tange) and had lunch with Admiral Smith and the Chiefs of Staff. There was another farewell dinner party for us that evening and we left in the Comet the next morning for New Zealand. Landing at Wellington we were met by the new New Zealand CDS (Lt. Gen. Webb) and later taken to Government House where we had a good game of croquet before dinner and stayed the night with the Governor General and Lady Porritt. Our last day in New Zealand for me was taken up by a final press conference, then discussions with the NZ Chiefs of Staff, the Minister of Defence (Mr D. S. Thompson) and the British HC (Sir Arthur Galsworthy). There was then a farewell dinner that evening for Val and me hosted by CDS and with them CAS Ian Morrison and his wife Dinnie. The next day, 12 November, Brian O'Rorke (my PSO) and Elisabeth his wife and Richard Sanderson (ADC) left for UK in the Comet while Val and I embarked on RHMS *Britanis*.

RETURN TO UK

After all the hectic farewells ending my command in the Far East I had elected to have a restful journey home by sea via the Pacific and Panama Canal. Unfortunately the only luxury suite, to which we were entitled, had been previously booked but we were given two inter-connected cabins with one as a sitting room, and this worked very well as Val and I spent quite a lot of time at sea sorting out and sticking in the hundreds of photos we had of our time in the Far East. We had a short visit ashore in Tahiti, where we enjoyed a swim in the sea but we spent a lot of time on deck lying and relaxing in the sun, except when we were passing through the Panama Canal which I followed closely and found very interesting with all the lake area incorporated as part of it. Not long after passing through the canal there was a slight drama when the ship's engines packed up and we were left quietly drifting in the Caribbean Sea for several hours! Eventually the ship got going again and went on peacefully to reach Lisbon where we had a day walking around sightseeing. From there it was not long before we eventually disembarked at Southampton on Friday 10 December.

That was the end of a fascinating and rewarding final RAF appointment which both Val and I agreed was the best in my Service career.

12

BACK IN UK PRIOR TO RETIREMENT FROM RAF

10 DECEMBER 1971–11 MARCH 1972

From Southampton we went straight back to Heather Hill, which the Lewises had now vacated and where our heavy luggage and car were delivered the next day which was ideal. Bob also came to stay that weekend and we enjoyed being back at home. Val had quickly arranged to pick up Rusty, our dog, from the Pringles, who had kindly looked after him while we were abroad. They loved having him and looked after him so well I had been worried that Rusty might want to stay with them, and I was relieved to find that he was after all happy to come back to us in the country.

On the Monday my first job was to call on Peter Hill-Norton (CDS) and Lord Carrington (Minister of Defence) as well as a number of other people in Whitehall. They had all had my lengthy End of Tour Report, so there was not much more to say, and I was free to start my terminal leave after a final audience with The Queen, who was most interested to hear about the closing down of the Far East Command and what was left behind with the ANZUK forces in Singapore and Malaysia.

Bruce came back from Germany the next weekend but unfortunately couldn't stay for Christmas, though Bob was with us and we got going again with our golf and bridge with the Smiths and the Holders. Otherwise it was a fairly quiet Christmas at home, and we got busy with our local architect (Mr Newsome) with a view to extending the house and building on a new wing with a comfortable suite on the ground floor. I also arranged to do a DIY resettlement course at Aldershot nearby for four weeks in January 1972 which was good fun. This was known as the 'plumbing course' but was mostly brick laying, carpentry and decorating. For the wallpapering and plastering we worked in pairs and were told to pick our 'mate'. There were about twenty people on the course, mostly retired Army officers and a few servicewomen including, I think, the ex-head of the Army Nursing Service who immediately came and asked if she could be my 'mate'. I was delighted, of course, as she was always cheerful and charming, and a big strong woman. Unfortunately she was also inclined to be a bit heavy handed with her sawing and was at times rather clumsy so that when we were doing plastering she succeeded in pouring much of it down my sleeve! We got on very well, however, and had a lot of fun.

It was the height of the squash rackets season then and, as I had always taken a keen interest in the game, when they heard I was back in UK I was invited to take over from Philip Le Gros as the President of the SRA. He had been Chairman and their President for many years and felt it was time to give up, so I agreed to take over from him. It was an interesting time in the development of the game with the new gallery court at Wembley which our patron the Duke of Edinburgh came to open, and Jonah Barrington, at that time the World Champion, played an exhibition. Much work was also being done to develop the portable all-glass court which would enable more people to watch the Championship matches. I did my best to persuade the BBC to televise and popularise the game, but it was difficult and not easy on TV to see the ball during the rallies. Many experiments with the ball were carried out and I am glad anyway that the TV coverage is now very much better and I think it has helped to get more people playing this very good game.

In January Hugh Johnstone, my cousin-in-law, came for a weekend and also Gus and Brenda Walker for golf and bridge. I was dined out officially on 18 January at Admiralty House by my colleagues on the Air Force Board which was a happy end to my Service career. As I was still on my terminal leave, Val and I decided in February to take the car to Europe and go skiing for six weeks, to make up for missing our annual skiing holiday while we were in Singapore and to visit some of the ski resorts we hadn't been to before. On the way we called in for a night with Hugh and Dany – and their big black and white spotted dog – at Mons in Belgium where they were staying while posted to NATO in Brussels. From there we drove to Mönchengladbach and stayed a night with AM Micky Martin (C-in-C RAF Germany) and his wife and then another night in Ulm before reaching St Anton in Austria where we had booked in at the Rosanna Stuble. In St Anton we had an excellent fortnight's skiing and also visited Ishgyl one day and Lech and Zurs two other days. I remember there was a lot of snow there, as I had to buy some snow chains before we were allowed to drive over the Arlberg Pass. After that we drove to Brand, still in Austria, where we had a day's skiing and then met up with a man called Von Bethman Holweg, an ex-Olympian ice skater I believe, whom we had met recently at our next door neighbour's house at The Sands and who was the inventor of what was rather rudely called the 'bidet' which was a seat on skiis which was low on the ground and easily negotiated through wooded areas. We didn't try it, but I was told it was quite popular with older skiers and enabled them to enjoy being out in the mountains long after they had to give up proper skiing. I am surprised it hasn't caught on more. After Brand we drove on to the Hotel Alpenhof in Andermatt, run by Eve who was well known to many British skiers who had been going there for years, and particularly the Navy Ski Association who ran their package tours from there. Bob, who was on holiday, joined us for the week at Andermatt and we did a lot of skiing together and met up by chance with the father of Richard Sanderson (my ex ADC) who was also enjoying a skiing holiday there. Bob went into one of the ski races called 'The White Rabbit' I think, and did very well winning it. He then had to go back to work but we went on to Engelberg, which I remember was Dan Maskell's (the tennis player and Wimbledon commentator) favourite ski resort. We went there because there was a fairly new very steep run called the Titlis which I was told we simply must do. Unfortunately it snowed solidly the first two days we were there, so it wasn't until the last two days that we plucked up the courage to go down (or rather struggle down!) the steep Titlis gully. It was a challenge and worth it – particularly when we saw a couple of very good Japanese skiers going down it with a series of stops and kick turns!

From Engelberg we drove on to Adelboden where Val had been in 1936 before the war with Joan Bearder and some other friends. They had stayed at the Hotel Adler and Val was interested to see it looking just the same. It was there that all the girls fell for their ski instructor as usual, and Val and I had surprisingly met up with him again many years later in 1947 at Manchester, Vermont. He was still just as good looking, Val said! We had two good days skiing in Adelboden up at the Haanenmoos but then decided to move on to Gstaad as we were already into the second week of March with snow getting a bit thin and Gstaad was relatively low-lying. For the first time we found that we couldn't get a room in any of the hotels in Gstaad. Before going on elsewhere, however,

I thought we might take the opportunity in Gstaad to call on an old Air Force friend, G/C Tubby Vielle, whom I had known some twenty years earlier in No. 3 Group at RAF Upwood and who had now retired to a chalet on the outskirts of Gstaad. Luckily I had my address book with me so we drove round and knocked on their door at Chalet Bergblick much to their great surprise. They seemed delighted to see us, however, and despite our initial refusal, they insisted on us staying with them as their spare room was all ready, etc. So we were very lucky and in the end stayed for two nights, when we thoroughly enjoyed talking about old Bomber Command days and RAF friends and how he was now, having always been very keen on the stock market, making a good living on the telephone to London buying and selling shares. Val and I did go skiing for one day but the snow was not very good and the Vielles did not come with us.

After that nice surprise visit, we headed north to Berne and Basle. On the way we had a last little bit of skiing for an hour in the morning at Schoenried and another hour in the afternoon at Saanenmoser, before leaving our skis to be sent on by train to wherever we told them later we would be going next year. In Berne we tried to get in touch with an old friend, Greta Saar, but without success, so went on to Basle where we stayed the night in a hotel before driving to Bonn where we had planned to stay with Reg and Ann Hibbert. He had been my Political Adviser in Singapore and was now head of Chancellery with Sir Nicholson Henderson, our Ambassador in Germany. After a night with the Hibberts in Bonn, we drove on up to RAF Laarbruck to see Bruce, who was stationed there in a Canberra squadron. We stopped the night at the small Goldener Alpfel hotel nearby but left the next day to return to Heather Hill on 16 March after six weeks away. It had been a great holiday and good to catch up with our skiing and to see a number of new to us skiing resorts which we had heard so much about but never been to. The day after we got back Bob came for the weekend and we had some golf. Brenda Walker came too for golf with Val, and Red and Sylvia Merson from Australia came to stay for the weekend. Red loved chopping wood and was an expert at splitting logs so I kept him busy doing some for me!

On 11 March I finally retired from the RAF when I also ceased to be an ADC to The Queen. I was offered a couple of non-executive directorships in the aircraft industry but there was nothing that took my fancy and I decided to have a ‘gap year’ anyway. My salary as an Air Chief

Marshal had been approximately £21,000 and my pension after nearly thirty-eight years service was £7,000 p.a., only a third in those days. However, in the early 1970s that was not bad and I used to do quite a lot of business with shares on the Stock Market which was helpful. The pension also, I am glad to say, was index-linked, so I felt reasonably well off without doing another job.

At Heather Hill we had just under six acres of land, mostly woodland, but I enjoyed doing a lot of clearing work, and Val and I did a lot of redecorating, painting and wallpapering in the house. I also enjoyed building a woodshed out of all the packing cases from our heavy luggage. So I had enough, with plenty of golf, to keep me nicely busy. I also had to take up my Wimbledon Committee duties again. As I was reasonably free the Chairman (Herman David) put me on a number of sub-committees including the important Ground Sub-Committee, which I was particularly interested in with some of the new developments being planned. At the same time I was persuaded by Della-Porta to start playing tennis again and to join his weekly group of players. There were usually eight of us oldies in our sixties whom he organized to play doubles every Tuesday afternoon, and we then went on to have a cup of tea and play a couple of rubbers of bridge. It was great fun and good not only in keeping us playing tennis regularly, but also for our bridge as Della was a first class player and happy to give us advice whenever wanted.

Around this time also we started what Val called 'Operation House Building' when we added 49 per cent (the maximum allowed) to the house. We loved the position and the view over the treetops to the Hindhead-Liphook range of hills, so had decided to make Heather Hill our permanent home and to build on a complete new wing and suite for ourselves at ground level so that in our old age we could stagger around without going upstairs, which could be left to the young and grandchildren when they came. At the same time we widened the main sitting room and the dining room to look over a new patio and lawn – before that heather and bracken came right up to a small path round the back of the house. Luckily we had a good architect, Ron Newsome, and building contractor so all went very smoothly and well. However, living in while all the building was going on was not easy and we went off most weekends to stay with friends – to Joan and Johnny H-B at Sadlers, in Lymington, when we played golf with the Wadleys, to the Pertwees at Frinton and to the Balmes and the Boxers also at Lymington when the latter took us sailing on their super yacht. Another weekend we went to stay with Norman and Mary Melhuish at Penshurst in Kent and when we got back to all the dust and mess with the builders I remember Val said she could not stand it, so we jumped back in the car and drove off down to Cornwall for another week! By Easter weekend the alterations to the main part of the house had been done and we were able to have people to stay including Viv Crone and Joan Bearder, as well of course as Bob, and we had plenty of golf and bridge with them and the Holders and the Smiths. It was good also that Bob had his friend Christopher Smith from St Andrews University nearby to play golf with. His parents, Joan and David Smith, had so very kindly looked after him for some of his holidays while we were away in Singapore. Other visitors to stay as soon as the house alterations were finished were Brenda and Gus Walker, and Hugh Johnstone who was visiting the War Office and helped me with cutting down some big trees. John and Cécile Grandy, Andrew and Agnes Humphrey and the Broadhursts also each came for a day in the country and a walk in the woods. We then paid a visit for a couple of days to Beaulieu in Hampshire to stay with AM Sir John Whitley and his wife Alison who had a lovely house there looking down to the river where they kept their boat moored.

In April and May, as well as my regular visits to Wimbledon to play tennis, there were a number of committee and sub-committee meetings there for me to attend. There was also the AGM in London as well as the club dinner. At home, Val and I spent a lot of our time tidying the garden and bush-whacking all the overgrown heather and brambles down the hill. It was hard work but very satisfying. Another old friend I ran into at that time who was living nearby was Charles de Boinville who had been up at Wadham College, Oxford with me in the 1930s and we started to see quite a lot of him and his wife.

On 14 May the Wimbledon grass courts were due to open and Bruce and the Pertwees came to stay the weekend, and Norman and I played in the usual opening American Tournament on the Sunday before the club cocktail party. We did not do particularly well but it was great to play on grass again. After that I played in the Admirals/Generals/Air Marshals annual golf match and also for the old boys against the IDC (now renamed RCDS). Those matches were always good fun as one met up with many old friends. As I was away so much at that time with our Triumph car we bought a new little Mini Clubman for Val to use for shopping and to go for her golf at Hankley Common and her painting at Bramley.

Over mid-June weekend the Ladies Wightman Cup was held at the All England Club Court 1. The Club Chairman, Herman David, and Mavis kindly invited us to the dinner the night before, so we stayed with Gus and Brenda Walker in their flat nearby at Roehampton and took them with us to watch the tennis on the Saturday and Sunday. The United States with Chris Evert and Patty Hogan were, I am afraid, too strong for our Virginia Wade and Joyce Williams and they won by 5 matches to 2. There was, however, some good tennis and an excellent dinner at the Dorchester in the evening!

The next week was Ascot week and we were lucky enough to be invited again by the Broadhursts for lunch and the races there, with several other Air Force friends.

It was now the Wimbledon Championships time again and it was good to be back having missed the last two years while we were in Singapore. There had been a few changes in 1971 with the number of seeds reverting to the old figure of 8 instead of 16 the previous three years; also the tie-break was introduced for the first time though not in the final set at Wimbledon. This had all gone fairly smoothly, but in 1972 commercial interests intervened when professionals under contract to Lamar Hunt (WCT Organisation) were banned by the International Lawn Tennis Federation from official ILTF tournaments. This meant that Newcombe, the holder, and some of the other best players including Laver, Rosewall and Ashe were not allowed to play. This was very disappointing – not least for John Newcombe who was unable to defend his title. However, ironically, the Men's Final in 1972 between Stan Smith and Ilie Nastase was the best final most of us had ever seen. It was a match of tremendous quality and the result uncertain until the last ball was hit for Stan Smith to win 7-5 in the 5th set. Incidentally the final had been put off to the Sunday because of rain all Saturday, so Billie-Jean King, who won the Ladies Singles for the fourth time beating the previous year's holder Evonne Goolagong in straight sets, was the sole Champion at the LTA ball. I can't remember who danced with her to open the ball!

Val and I drove to Wimbledon every day as we had friends in our seats and to lunch or tea. It was a great way to be able to return hospitality and entertain friends, and as a member of the Committee I attended with Val all the various cocktail parties and dinners including the LTA Ball. It was all very enjoyable. Incidentally, after the Championships were over and a day's rest for everybody, Herman had started a very memorable custom of inviting the secretaries and one or two members of the

Committee to play on the Centre Court before it was put to bed, re-seeded and so on ready for the next year. I was usually lucky to be able to do this and it was fabulous to walk out on to the Centre Court to play. Dan Maskell, the Club professional and BBC television commentator, usually umpired or ball-boyed for us, to add to the fun.

The week after Wimbledon Val and I went down to Sway in the New Forest to stay a couple of days with the Kyles when we played golf with them at Brockenhurst, and also with the Wadleys. When we got home Rex Sterry came down on the Saturday and he and I went to Charterhouse for OC Day. The rest of the summer we spent mostly at home with plenty of golf and bridge locally, as well as sorting out the house and the garden. However, we did have another weekend at Frinton-on-Sea with the Pertwees, a couple of days with the Melhuishes at Penshurst who took us to the opera at Glyndbourne, and a weekend at Lymington with Joan and Johnny H-B when we went sailing with the Boxers and Whitleys.

I kept in touch with the RAF as much as I could through some of the senior officers I knew who were still serving. I also attended the annual Air Marshals Club lunch at the RAF Club when the CAS always briefed

Order of the Bath Ceremony with parade of GCBs (the Old Crocks' Race)

members on the latest developments in the Service. Val and I also went as usual to the Battle of Britain Service at Westminster Abbey. In October also there was the Order of the Bath Service at Westminster Abbey which was attended by The Queen and Prince Charles (the Grand Master) and the Princess Alice Duchess of Gloucester. This only took place every three or four years when the half dozen or so new GCBs were installed in the Henry VII (Bath) Chapel, and all existing GCBs in their gowns and full dress regalia paraded through the Abbey bowing to The Queen as they passed. This was my first what was nick-named 'the Old Crocks' Race' and it was fun meeting again all the Three Service senior officers past and present. I also took Val to the opening of the new RAF Museum at the old RAF Hendon.

The squash rackets season was starting to get going and I had several meetings with Peter Woods, the Secretary, and Sir Denis Truscott, Chairman, on the Agenda for the SRA Annual General Meeting which I chaired in London at the end of October. I was invited by Gus Walker, the Chairman of the International Sportsmen's Club, to speak at the dinner being given at the Café Royal in honour of Jonah Barrington who was the World Squash Champion. Soon after that in December we had the Benson and Hedges Amateur Squash Championships. There was a last minute problem over the venue for it, as the Lansdowne Club withdrew their facilities because of a threatened demonstration by the anti-apartheid movement against the South African side touring England at that time. We had to change at very short notice to the newly opened Lambton Squash Club in Westbourne Grove. The winner was Cam Nancarrow of Australia and my old squash and skiing friend David Vaughan won the Veterans.

Prior to this, as far as I can remember, the South African touring team were well received and had a successful tour beating Scotland and Wales, but losing to Great Britain after winning the 1st Test at Cheltenham SRC and losing the 2nd and 3rd Tests at Queen's and the New Croydon SRC.

1973

Our favourite time for skiing was the second week of January so we arranged to go to Zermatt then with Joan and Johnny H-B and David and Sue Balme. We flew to Zurich and then went by train to Zermatt where Johnny had arranged for us to take over a small châlet. This was not a great success as with the three bedrooms there was only one bathroom and loo, and one of the bedrooms rather small and poky. We tossed up for choice of rooms and the Balmes were unlucky and decided to leave after a week which was a pity. We had some excellent skiing and enjoyed going out to different restaurants for meals. Neither of the boys came with us that year; Bruce was still running the RAF skiing and took the team to Livigno in Italy and Bob went with friends to Saas Fee I believe. They were both now based in England – Bob with Cooper Brothers in London and Bruce near Huntingdon looking after Air Cadet Training – so they came to us at Heather Hill most weekends and usually joined me in golf against David and Christopher Smith which was fun. Others who came to us for weekends were Betty Rowlands, Joan Bearder and Gus Holden. Chantal (Hugh and Dany's elder daughter) came to us for ten days in April over Easter when we took her to the Yvonne Arnaud theatre in Guildford and to a point-to-point with Sir Michael and Enid Walker. This was followed soon after for me by the All England Club AGM at the Café Royal and the Club dinner at the Senior Army and Navy Club (known as 'the Senior'). As usual, on the second weekend of May we had the opening of the grass courts season at Wimbledon when Norman and Eileen came to stay and attend the cocktail party in the Club after he and I had played again in the American Tournament.

In June we had another golfing weekend in Suffolk staying with Viv Crone at Barton Mills and went to Christopher Melhuish's wedding near Cambridge. After that Val and I went for a week's holiday to Ireland. We took our car on the night ferry from Swansea to Cork and called first for a couple of days with the Paddy Bandons (the abandoned Earl!) and visited my cousin Jocelyn Burnett to collect a lot of silver inscribed with the Burnett crest, which her husband Fassett had left in his will for the male Burnetts of the family. We then drove on to the west coast where we were lent the use of their country cottage by the Claytons at Bantry Bay. It made an ideal base from which to tour round the lovely countryside, and we fitted in rounds of golf at the Glengariff and Killarney Clubs. Soon after our return home I had an EGM of the Squash Rackets Association in London and Bing and Brenda Cross came to stay with us for the annual Admirals/Generals/Air Marshals golf match at the Royal Berkshire Club at the weekend.

It was then Wimbledon time again starting with the IC dinner dance at the Royal Gardens Hotel on the Saturday evening before. If the 1972 Championships had its problems with a few top players not being allowed to play, 1973 was far far worse when with a very few exceptions all the top class players boycotted the Championships. The problem was that Nikki Pilic, a very popular competitor with the other players, had unfortunately refused to play Davis Cup for his country, Yugoslavia, and had been suspended by his National Association. This meant him being banned from playing in official ILTF tournaments but, as I understand it, he was already taking part in the Italian Championships so the Italians defied the ILTF and allowed him to continue. Similarly his entry for the French championships had already been accepted so the French allowed him to play in Paris. When it came to Wimbledon our Committee felt that someone must uphold the ILTF, the Governing Body of the game, and Pilic's entry was accordingly refused. The newly formed Association of Tennis Professionals (ATP) felt that their members should no longer be answerable to national associations in this way and they sought to secure an injunction in the High Court to force the AELTC to accept Pilic's entry for Wimbledon. Both parties agreed to abide by the Court's decision. The High Court finally ruled against the injunction, but nevertheless the ATP Board instructed all their members to boycott Wimbledon and eighty-one men withdrew their entries for the Championships. There were three, however, who did not, including happily our Roger Taylor and Ilie Nastase who were then unfortunately fined $5,000 by the ATP. Two other top players who entered were Jan Kodes of Czechoslovakia, the 1970 French champion, and Alex Metreveli, the Russian No. 1, and then there was for the first time the teenager Björn Borg with his following of frenzied teenyboppers. The British public were also in full and enthusiastic support and the attendances in 1973 were larger than ever. Altogether it was a very successful Championships and a triumph for Wimbledon, though a great worry for the Chairman, Herman David, while it lasted. Nastase, the favourite, was unexpectedly beaten in the 4th round by the young American Inter-Collegiate Champion Alex Mayer who in turn lost to Metreveli in the semi-final. I remember watching the Nastase v Mayer four-set match on Court 2 from the members' stand there, which is low down close to the court, so one gets a very good idea of the speed of the game. There was some brilliant tennis and Mayer's win was all the more remarkable because he had hurt the thumb of his right hand which was heavily bound up and he had a streaming cold which didn't become obvious until later at his interview with the press which I also attended.

In the other semi-final Roger Taylor was defeated 7-5 in the fifth set of a very tough match by Jan Kodes, who went on to win the final relatively easily against Metreveli. In the Ladies Singles, Billie-Jean King won the title for the fifth time beating Evonne Goolagong in the semi-final and Chris Evert in the final.

A couple of days after the Championships were over we had our usual game with the Chairman on the Centre Court, and the following day I played in the Club match on grass against the Lords and Commons team. At the weekend Rex Sterry came to stay a night and we went again together to Charterhouse for OC Day. It was then Val's turn for a lot of ladies golf at Hankley Common though we went to lunch and tennis one day with Alan and Dorothy Brown near Henley and for the last weekend of July to the Pertwees at Frinton. August was all at home with a number of visitors including Joan Bearder for a weekend, the Broadhursts and Michael Walker as well as Bruce and Bob on holiday part of the time.

In September, however, we took the car over to France on the hovercraft from Folkestone to Boulogne and drove to Le Touquet for the IC tennis and golf match. We stayed with the rest of our team at the Westminster Hotel, which interestingly was situated alongside Whitley Road which had been named in honour of our friend AM Sir John Whitley who had stopped there on his way back to England when escaping as a prisoner of war after being shot down over Germany. The programme at Le Touquet involved a round of golf in the morning, in which Val also played, and then tennis doubles in the afternoon at which Jean Borotra, Marcel Bernard and Bobby Addessalam also took part. This went on for two days and was followed by a cocktail party given by the British one evening, and on another evening a dinner party by the French at a local restaurant further out in the countryside. Some of us usually ended up each evening at the Casino, so it was a fairly exhausting weekend but very good fun. I'm afraid the French won the tennis but we did manage to halve the golf with the help of Val winning the vital last single!

After that Val and I took a few more days' holiday and drove on out to the west coast of Britanny. We went via Rouen and Caen and stopped a night at Deauville, which I had known of old, and on to Brest where I had received a very hot reception of flak in May 1941, when I bombed the German battleships *Scharnhorst* and *Gneisenau*, which were in the dry docks there being repaired. From there we headed south down the coast to Quimper and Benodet where my mother had often taken Douglas and me on our summer holidays from school. Val and I enjoyed a couple of days there in a very good hotel right on the beach. After fifty-one years

Benodet had, not surprisingly, changed quite a lot but for me it brought back many happy memories. I remember there were two rather older French sisters of about eighteen or twenty who had invited Douglas and me round to play tennis on their private court. They seemed to like playing with us though we were some six or eight years younger and it was more fun for us than on the hotel court, usually by ourselves. The name of the prettier one was Ginette, I remember! They also very kindly took us round to some of the other beaches in the area. While at Benodet, Val and I also drove on down the coast to Concarneau which was a well known sardine fishing centre and it was interesting to see it when all the boats came in. After that we set off for home, stopping for a quick swim in the sea at Dinard and a look over Mont Saint Michel near St Malo. We then drove up to Cherbourg and caught the ferry back to Southampton.

We got back home just in time for Gaynor Smith's wedding to Tim Farmer and also for the annual Battle of Britain Service at Westminster Abbey after which we had drinks with the Air Force Board and then lunch with Gus and Brenda Walker at the RAF Club with several other Air Force friends. In October we were off again on holiday for two weeks in Scotland. We drove up, with one night's stop in the Lake District, to Tarland near Ballater to stay at Alastrean House and join Paul and Elisabeth Holder. Alastrean House was a superb Scottish mansion which had been left to the RAF – and later all three Services – for R&R (Rest and Recuperation) and for holidays by Lady McRobert who had lost three sons in the RAF during the War. It was run, when we went there, by a retired Group Captain at a very reasonable rate and at a high officers' standard, so was excellent value. Val and I played bridge most evenings with the Holders and golf every day on either the 9-hole course at the bottom of the garden, or on other golf courses in the neighbourhood. We also did a bit of sightseeing in the area near Balmoral and Crathes Castle which used to belong to some distant relatives of the Burnett family including an Admiral and a General Burnett. Unfortunately, while we were there we had trouble with our car and had to take it into Aberdeen for a couple of days for repair, so we had to amend our return plan via Skye and the west coast and had to come more or less straight back south again, which was a pity. However, we did have a lovely two weeks in Scotland.

Back home for me there were a number of squash and tennis meetings to keep me busy, and the Kyles came for a weekend of golf as did Joan and Johnny H-B the following weekend. Bruce and Bob plus girlfriend then came the weekend after, and Hugh Johnstone the one after that. On my way to London for the Squash Rackets AGM I called in, as I did on several other occasions, on one of my favourite older cousins, Helen (Evans) Luard and her husband Trant, an ex-Marine Colonel who was 100 and still going strong! I also went up for the Oxford and Cambridge squash match at the RAC which Cambridge won 4-1. Val and I also went to the final of the Amateur Squash Championships at the New Croydon Club when Mohibullah Khan beat Zaman, both players from Pakistan.

Over Christmas Bob went skiing to Courcheval with friends but Bruce came to us as well as Gus Holden and Joan Bearder so we had plenty of golf and bridge with the Smiths, including a New Year's Eve dinner party for twelve of our local bridge players which became a regular event each year with five of us taking it in turns to hold the party.

1974

At the All England LTC, Tony Cooper, the Assistant Secretary, was wanting to retire and I was co-opted on to a sub-committee with Herman David and Rex Sterry to select a successor. We had several interviews with possible candidates and chose Chris Gorringe, and this was endorsed later by the full Committee. On looking back I think this was one of the best decisions the Committee ever made, as he went from strength to strength to become Secretary only a few years later and then Chief Executive. He was an outstanding success and over the next thirty-two years played a large part in maintaining the Championship's reputation for being the best run tennis tournament in the world. Tony Cooper had done very well and side-stepped at the Club to start the Wimbledon Museum of which he later became curator after its opening in 1977.

Early in the New Year we had a lot of snow in Surrey and I enjoyed a bit of skiing down our hill and through the woods to the fire-break, but it was hard work climbing up again! Bruce went with the RAF ski team to Obertauern in Austria and Bob came back from Courcheval for a weekend at home. The Pertwees then came for a night and went off with us the following day for our skiing holiday at Sauze d'Oulx in Italy. To get there we flew to Turin and the Balmes, together with their daughter Fenella, joined up with us at the small hotel right on the nursery slopes where I had booked us all in. The skiing was not particularly challenging at Sauze d'Oulx but there were a number of interesting runs through the woods in which Fenella, who was a very good qualified 1st Class skier, led the way. Norman often went skiing on his own with her as he was practising for his 1st Class test, which he went on two weeks later to take successfully at Murren, I think. We had hoped to join up also with Joan and Johnny H-B who had booked in at Sauze d'Oulx with other friends, but we failed to connect with them for a day or two by which time Johnny had had an accident and was confined to bed until he could arrange to be flown home.

Anyway, Val and I thoroughly enjoyed the holiday and got back in time for a few days at home, before driving up to Sheffield for the Open Squash Championships at the Abbeydale Sports Club. Geoffrey Thompson and his wife Pat very kindly had us to stay the night. The next day the Final was between Jonah Barrington and Alauddin, after beating the two best Australians Geoff Hunt and Hiscoe in the semi-finals, and I was pleased to present the trophy to Jonah who played exceptionally well and won surprisingly easily for his sixth Open title.

After that we had a fairly quiet few weeks with plenty of golf and bridge in the evenings, though we went to a rather special wedding anniversary lunch party given by our friends Harry and Venetia Hogan in their son-in-law and daughter's, Peter and Sarah Stevens, house near Alton in Hampshire. There were many of our Air Force friends there and it was great fun.

Part III

Second Career in the Tennis World as Chairman of the AELTC Wimbledon 1974–84

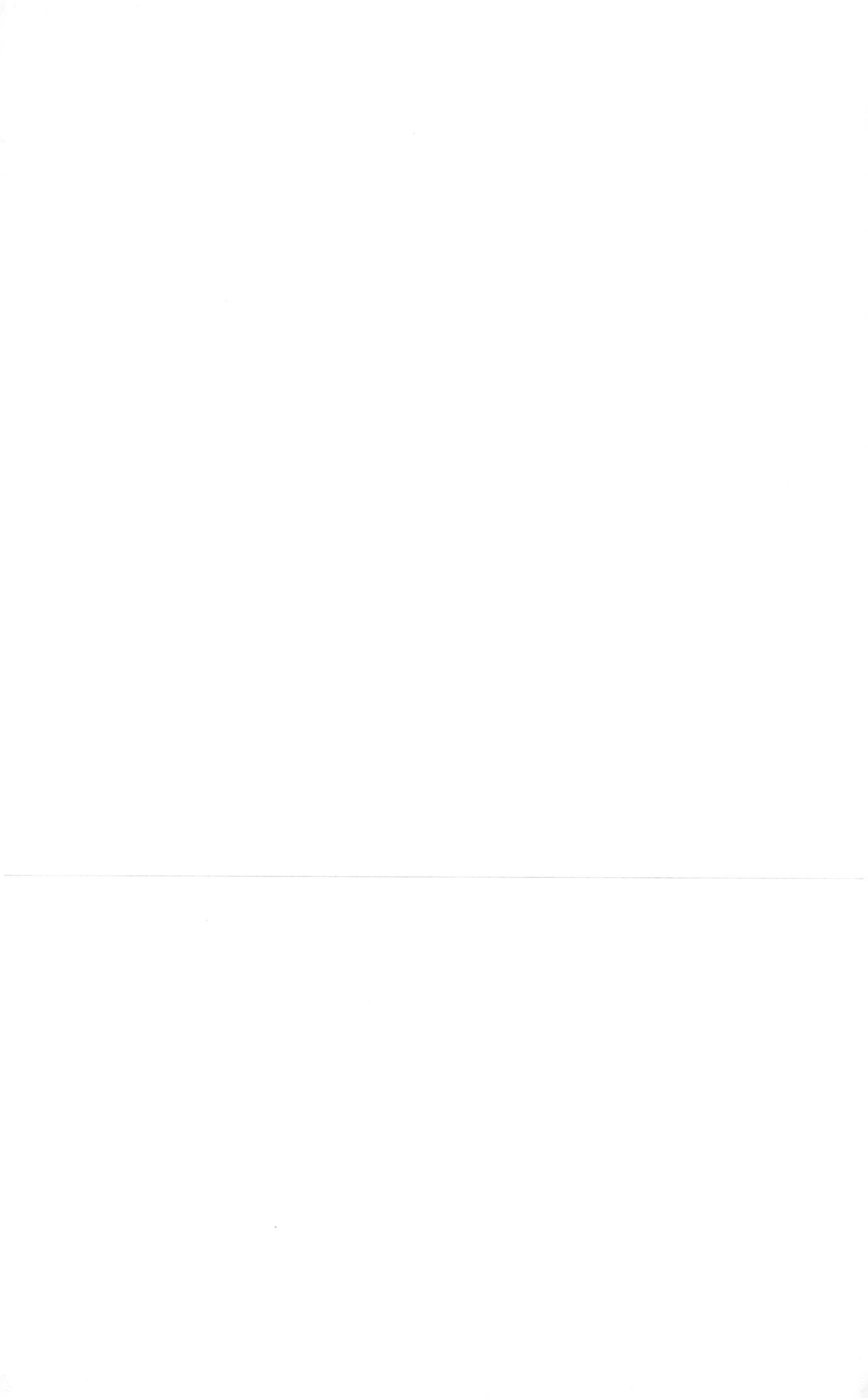

13

THE SEVENTIES

1974

Early in 1974 Mavis David was not well and had to go into hospital for a few weeks but worse still, when he was about to leave to fetch her home, Herman himself had a mini stroke, I think, and when he got to the hospital to collect Mavis he saw the doctor who insisted on keeping him in. Sadly he died there a few days later on 25 February. As All England Club Chairman for sixteen years and the man responsible very largely for tennis going 'open' there was of course much publicity and many messages of sympathy from all over the world, and his funeral was held on 4 March at Wimbledon. Soon after that there was a Club committee meeting with the Vice-Chairman Rex Sterry at which it was decided to recommend me at the Club AGM next month to take over as Chairman. This then took place on 17 April when I was duly elected Chairman and this was followed by an interview with the press. It was undoubtedly a great honour and privilege to reach the top of the tennis tree at Wimbledon, and I could only promise to give my full time to the job and do my best to maintain the high standard set by my predecessor. Herman, who lived nearby in Wimbledon, had found that it took him about three days a week at the Club and at the start, though about an hour away at Farnham, I found it much the same plus quite a lot of work telephoning and drafting letters at home. Major Mills (David), the Club Secretary, and Mrs Stopka (Enid), my Private Secretary, who had both been with the Club for many years, were extremely helpful as they knew the form running the Championships. I had, of course, to consult the members of the Committee pretty regularly and I found it very different being Club Chairman from being a C-in-C.

Soon after that there was the annual Club Dinner for the first time at the old 'Senior' Army and Navy Club which had been taken over by the

Institute of Directors. Early in May Val and I were invited to the Football pre-Cup Final Lunch at the Wembley Stadium. I can't remember the final result now but the match went on for ages with over-time and was very exciting. That evening we went to the SRA Ball at Hurlingham.

The grass courts at Wimbledon were then beckoning with the Opening American tournament followed by the Club cocktail party, for which the Pertwees came to stay the weekend with us as usual. Then, as the new AELTC Chairman, I was invited with Val to the finals of the Guildford Tournament and the next weekend to Bournemouth for the Hard Court Championships. A couple of weeks later we went to Paris to represent the Club at the last four days of the French Championships. We stayed at Herman David's favourite hotel, Hotel St James et d'Albany, but Philippe Chatrier, the French Chairman, looked after us very hospitably (with seats at the tennis in the front row of the Tribune) and special lunches at Stade Roland Garros and dinners at various renowned restaurants in Paris together with many of the other overseas tennis representatives. Philippe was always a great admirer and very pro-Wimbledon and on one occasion after an IC lunch with the four French Musketeers (Borotra, Cochet, Lacoste and Brugnon) at a small restaurant a couple of miles down the road, when the cars weren't ready to take us back to Stade Roland Garros I heard him rather crossly reprimanding poor Benny Berthet and saying, 'That wouldn't happen at Wimbledon!'

Björn Borg, the young teenager, won the men's singles in Paris for the first time. He was a great favourite also with the French and I remember watching one of his matches earlier on when he wasn't doing too well. I was sitting in the front row next to Benny Berthet who kept calling him on, shouting, '*Allez Borg! Allez Borg!*' Paris was the first of the Grand Slam Championships that year and there was as usual a big attendance of past champions and tennis administrators there, and it was interesting to meet up with them again to discuss tennis matters both during the tennis and in the evenings. I remember one day, for example, sitting next to Lacoste when we had a long discussion about the pressure in tennis balls with a view to perhaps speeding up some of the rallies on slow red clay courts at Stade Roland Garros. He was in favour of increasing the pressure in the balls they used.

Val and I stayed to watch the Finals and went to their excellent Championships' dinner in a lovely restaurant in the Bois de Boulogne, before flying back to England after our first of many delightful visits to the French Championships. After Paris came the London Queen's Club tournament on grass for men which Val and I went to watch, and I found there was quite a lot to do at Wimbledon the week before our Championships. I had always followed the tennis results world-wide so was particularly interested in attending the seeding sub-committee, chaired by our Referee Mike Gibson, and also the draw to see what good early round matches there might be.

As it was to be my first year as Chairman I felt that, rather than drive up early every morning from Farnham and back fairly late every evening, it would be better for us to stay somewhere nearer the Club. Luckily Bruce had a girlfriend, Veronica Fanshaw, who had a small house in Wimbledon village and was happy to rent it to us for the two weeks and make a bit of money on the side while she moved in with her parents who also lived quite close. This was fine and very convenient – only five minutes away – and we moved into it before going to the IC dinner and dance in London on the Saturday and the Hurlingham reception and garden party on the Sunday before the Championships started. This began for me in the office checking with the Secretary, Major David Mills, that everything was going according to plan. He and Tony Cooper had been doing the job for some years, so all was well. I then checked the Royal Box seating plan which I usually cleared the day before with my private secretary, Enid Stopka, who had to clear it in the morning with the Palace if, as on many occasions, there were any members of the Royal Family attending. Then on the first two days every year there was a small reception party, on the Monday for the stewards, and Tuesday for the press and media. These were held in a marquee in the garden of the Lodge near the west side entrance to the Club. After lunch then with our private guests, Val and I had to be at the main entrance to the Royal Box to welcome HRH The Duke of Kent (our President) and the Duchess of Kent. They always arrived very promptly so as to be in their seats when the players walked on the Centre Court at 'precisely 2 o'clock' as was our custom. Other guests to the Royal Box we either met before that on their arrival or at tea-time later.

We have always been very fortunate at Wimbledon with the interest shown by the Royal family ever since the days of King George V and Queen Mary and this, it is said, is reflected in our Club colours of royal purple and green grass. The Royals have certainly always added a bit of glamour to the Championships and in more recent years, not only the

Duke and Duchess of Kent but also Princess Margaret, the Duke and Duchess of Gloucester, Prince and Princess Michael of Kent and Princess Alexandra as well as some of the younger members of their families have been regular attenders several days of the fortnight and they really seem to enjoy it. Her Majesty The Queen and Princess Anne have also been several years, but I think prefer their horses and racing, and probably feel anyway that Wimbledon gets more than its fair share of Royal visits with all the Kent family. The Duke of Kent had taken over as President in 1969 from his mother Princess Marina when she died. She had been an avid supporter and used to come to the Championships almost every day, and the Duke himself still comes at least six days including the two Finals days when he and his wife, the Duchess of Kent, used always to present the Singles trophies on the Centre Court. The Duke is certainly an excellent President, always most helpful, and he invariably waits to the bitter end to present the Doubles trophies from the Royal Box.

For invitations to the Royal Box, I continued my predecessor's policy of inviting VIPs from all walks of life. This included not only all members of the Royal Family, the leading sports players and officials, but also the Prime Minister, the Law Lords, Archbishops and senior members of the Stock Exchange and the Law Society, and of the three Services who provide the Service Stewards at the Championships. Then there were also the various Ambassadors or High Commissioners and overseas representatives of countries whose players did well and earned a place on the Centre Court. We also enjoyed inviting our past Champions and quarter-finalists (known as the last 8 players) and their wives, many of whom happily come back every year.

As Chairman I had two large official lunches in the Members' Enclosure in the first week and three in the second week, and the LTA President (Cecil Betts in 1974/75) usually had three or four as well. Some evenings after about 7 o'clock there were a number of cocktail parties including that of the Veterans LTC, the Club Secretary's party and the Club Championship cocktail party, which Val and I went to when we could depending on the state of play in the Royal Box. There was never a dull moment! The Kent family always all came to my official lunch in the Members' Enclosure on the Finals day and Princess Margaret and the Gloucesters often a day or two before and they usually stayed for a drink on the balcony in the evenings. This then became the normal procedure every year during the ten years of my Chairmanship. At tea-time they usually invited a couple of other Royal Box guests to join them for a

The Royal Box

change and this left me free for a while to talk to some of the other guests.

Incidentally, starting from the days when the Duke's mother, Princess Marina, was the President, she and the Kent family always seemed to love both the lemon and the chocolate cakes which the caterers produced at tea, so we usually used to put one in the boot of the Royals' car at the end of the Championships! Princess Marina also started the custom of having sweets in the front row of the Royal Box and passing them round to the first two rows.

At the tennis with the Duke and Duchess of Kent in the front row of the Royal Box with me and several of their guests, Val was usually just behind at the end of the second row with the Duke's Private Secretary Lt. Cdr. Richard Buckley (later Sir Richard) so that if any of the Royal ladies wanted to go out she could get out easily to go and look after them. This often happened and on one occasion later in the second week when Princess Margaret had lunch with us and had knocked back a couple of gin and tonics first, she left the Centre Court after the first set and when Val showed her where the Royal loo was she said, 'What I would really like is another gin and tonic!' Later she took it to drink on the balcony and expressed surprise when she saw some of the veterans playing and said, 'Good Lord, what are those old things doing here?' When Val explained it was the over-45 doubles event and that Drobny and Budge Patty were two of them on court, she said, 'Oh yes, of course! I recognize

Drobny now.' And then she added, 'But they are having fun, aren't they?' Quite right too – as it should be.

After watching the tennis for a couple of hours or more, tea was taken on the balcony or in the Club dining room behind the Royal Box, and sometimes afterwards I used to persuade the Royals to go over to Court 1 for a while as the public there always appreciated seeing them too. After 6 o'clock the bar of the Royal Box was open for the guests to take a break before watching more tennis, which went on always to about 8.00 p.m. or later, and this was a good opportunity for some of our tennis friends from overseas in the International Box to be invited over to join the Committee for a drink on the balcony.

After about 8.30 p.m. when nearly everyone had gone from the Royal Box, Val and I were able to have supper in the Club dining room and I usually asked one or two of the Committee who had been working late to join us with their wives. This made for a peaceful end to a busy day and sometimes I called in on our way for a few minutes to the Referee's office, where they were still working hard on the order of play for the next day.

It was a great relief after the boycott of 1973 for us to have a full entry for the Championships as usual in 1974. Ken Rosewall at the age of thirty-eight got to the Final for the fourth time after beating successively Roscoe Tanner, John Newcombe and Stan Smith, but then surprisingly lost in three straight sets to the exuberant twenty-one-year-old Jimmy Connors. The Ladies' Singles was won by a young up and coming nineteen-year-old Chris Evert for her first time and without losing a set. Her opponent in the Final was Olga Morozova, a Russian lady also for the first time in a Wimbledon final, who had beaten Billie-Jean King on the way as well as Virginia Wade in the semi-finals. The Men's Doubles was also remarkable in that Newcombe and Roche won it for their fifth time.

On the morning of the Ladies' Final that year of 1974, the Committee had invited Kitty Godfree to join them to celebrate the 50th Anniversary of her winning the Ladies' Singles Championships (when incidentally her prize was, I think, just a £5 voucher!). She was then Kitty McKane and she beat Helen Wills 6-4 in the final set. On behalf of the Club I presented her with a small clock to mark the occasion and congratulated her on winning the Mixed also in 1926 with Leslie Godfree. Leslie, with Mrs Shepherd-Barron, had lost to Kitty and J. B. Gilbert in the 1924 Final but had obviously decided 'if he couldn't beat her he would join her' so they got married and won the Mixed together two years later as Mr & Mrs Godfree! At the Champions' Ball at Grosvenor House on the

Saturday evening, when I was sitting next to Chris Evert, who I understood at that time was engaged to Jimmy Connors, I suggested that when married she and Jimmy should enter the Mixed Doubles next year to try to equal Leslie and Kitty Godfree's 1928 record of being the only married couple ever to win the event at Wimbledon. She was rather intrigued by the thought and told Jimmy straight away at the dining table that they should definitely do it next year. Unfortunately it never happened as their engagement was broken off not long afterwards! Their engagement had, of course, had much publicity and, when later it was finally off, Chris Evert was reported in the press as saying, 'When I do get married I want my husband and me to do it on our own – and not have a lot of outside people looking on!'

On the whole 1974 had been a very enjoyable and successful first year for me as Chairman. Attendances were going up and reached a Wimbledon record of some 33,900 that year. To avoid overcrowding we started having to close the gates when the daily numbers exceeded 30,000 though we opened up again after 5.00 p.m. when some people had gone home after tea. These late arrivals often did rather well as there was still some three hours play left and they were sometimes lucky enough to get seat tickets for the Centre Court which had been left by some of those leaving early. Profits from the Championships were also up to some £87,500 which all went to the LTA for British tennis. Compared with the profits of millions today, this doesn't seem very good but in those days in the 1970s it was not bad from a two-week tennis tournament without sponsorship or advertisements all round the courts like at most other big tournaments. At Wimbledon we had always opposed this and preferred to maintain more of a garden party ambience.

After the Championships were over, a couple of days later, I had the Chairman's usual game on the Centre Court with several of the committee and another day I played in our Club match against the Lords and Commons. We also had a large thank-you party one evening for all the Club staff and groundsmen up at the Dog and Fox in Wimbledon village.

At the Club, preparations for the next year's Championships began almost immediately after the last one had been completed. This started with the re-seeding of the Centre Court and Court 1, unless they were required for a Davis or Wightman Cup match, as they had the most wear and tear of play during the fortnight – both with some fifty matches. After that, apart from regular mowing, servicing and watering when necessary, they are put to bed with TLC (tender loving care) until the weekend before the next year's Championships when four lightweight lady members are usually selected to play on them to run them in gently! The year's works services and building programme, based on all suggestions for improvement, is then decided on by the Committee. This invariably included something for everyone, for example modernisation of the changing rooms and restaurant facilities for the players, increased seating on Courts 1, 2 and 6 and a new toilet block for the public, an enlarged restaurant for Debenture Holders, more modern studios for the press and for TV interviewers, and for the Royal Box a refurbished lady's loo and an extended dining room and balcony so that all seventy-six invitees could be seated for tea at the same time if necessary.

Val and I were then back to normal for a couple of weeks at Heather Hill with our golf, gardening and bridge before going up to Frinton for our usual few days with the Pertwees for tennis and braving the North Sea! We came back south in time for the RAF Tennis Championships and the Inter-Services in which I again played for the RAF in the Veterans Doubles event. The following weekend we were at Wimbledon again supporting the Oxford and Cambridge Prentice Cup team in the match against Harvard and Yale after which, on behalf of the All England Club, I hosted a dinner party for both teams at Hurlingham.

On August Bank Holiday Val and I enjoyed playing in the Hankley Common Golf Holiday Foursomes before then flying off to New York for the second week of the 1974 American Tennis Championships. We followed Herman David's custom of staying at the delightful River Club from where we were kindly taken out daily to the tennis – then at Forest Hills still. The VIP Enclosure was in a marquee on one side of the two grass courts in the main stadium. Jimmy Connors was the winner of the Men's Singles, beating Rosewall again, and Billie-Jean King won the Ladies' in a 7-5 final against Goolagong. Much to my surprise, for the presentation afterwards a smart brand new car was driven on to the court in front of the VIP Enclosure as an extra prize evidently for the Champion. While we were in New York Stan Malless, the USTA President, and his wife Janie invited many of us to a dinner party at the top of one of the skyscraper buildings with a wonderful view of the Manhattan sky-line. Another evening the American IC held a dinner for all the overseas tennis representatives, while Janie very kindly took Val and several of the wives out to the theatre and a night club so they got home later than the men! It was all very enjoyable with many new and old tennis friends.

Incidentally, it was while Val and I were staying at the River Club and enjoying breakfast in comfort in our room every morning, that the NBC was trying to get me for a breakfast meeting and interview. Much to Mark McCormack of IMG's amusement, apparently I turned them down saying breakfast was something I shared in bed with my wife and was not an experience I wished to share with NBC!

After the American Championships were all over, Val and I were driven out the next day to Easthampton on Long Island to stay a couple of days with Larry Baker (an ex-USTA President and frequent visitor to Wimbledon). His son, who was a very strong swimmer, persuaded Val and me to go in the sea one day when there was a *very* big surf, the danger flags were out and one man further down the beach had already had to be rescued and the lifeguards were down the beach helping him. Larry Jnr however went in and seemed quite OK, so Val and I felt we had better have a go and unwisely went in too. We were both immediately dumped by a huge wave and didn't stay long, which was just as well as not long afterwards we saw young Larry struggling to get in from quite far out and shouting he might need some help! Luckily he didn't as there was no way I could have helped and the lifeguards were quite a long way down the beach.

The next day Larry Jnr was driving us, together with Sally, his attractive girlfriend, back to the airport where Val and I were due to catch a flight up to Canada when unfortunately the car broke down. There was nothing we could do about it and no cars seemed to want to stop so we sent the pretty girl a few hundred yards up the road by herself. It was no time then before a big car stopped! and she was able to persuade the driver to take Val and me and our luggage straight to the airport – leaving the two of them behind to get further help. With only minutes to spare, Val and I just made the flight to Toronto where we were met by our friends Bill and Hope Pigott and taken off to stay with them at Ancaster for four or five most enjoyable days of golf and meeting many other old friends of my Hamilton/RAF Mount Hope days. We finally flew back to England around mid-September after an excellent two weeks away.

The last weekend of the month I played in the AELTC match against the Lugano Tennis Club and Val came with me when some of us took them all to dinner and the theatre in London. I also continued with my Tuesday tennis and bridge at the AELTC with Della, and we went to Deeside for a couple of days to watch the Ladies' Wightman Club match v the USA. We were glad to see GB win 6-1 this time with our team of Virginia Wade, Sue Barker, Glynis Coles and Lesley Charles. On return to Heather Hill we picked up Romaine (Hugh and Dany's younger daughter) from school to spend a week with us before Hugh and Dany came for a night and took her away to France.

October was on the whole a very busy month for me with the All England Club and Squash Rackets Association (SRA) meetings, including the SRA AGM and the Frank Strawson Memorial Squash Match. Unfortunately the Chairman of the SRA Council Sir Denis Truscot had decided to retire after some ten years in the appointment, but we were lucky to get Bill Addison to take over from him. There had been a considerable expansion in the game with many new clubs and courts and with club affiliation fees to the SRA being based on the number of courts. This was helpful to SRA funds for developing the game in different ways, including more championships, league competitions and international tours. The affiliation fees had in fact already had to be raised at the end of the previous year to improve the viability of the SRA which had been in deficit by some £5,000. Court affiliation fees then became a bone of contention with the newly formed Court Owners Association leading to many long discussions and meetings, but it enabled the SRA to slightly more than break even the next year. In the meantime work was progressing well on the new Squash Centre at Wembley with its fourteen courts and a Championship Court with a glass back wall and spectator accommodation for about five hundred, plus space for full TV presentation.

At Wimbledon all was going ahead with the works programme so, as our 30th wedding anniversary was due on 4 November, Val and I decided to fly down to Agadir in Morocco for a change and a week's holiday on our own, which was lovely.

In the meantime, the Wembley Squash Centre was completed and I had invited HRH Prince Philip, The Duke of Edinburgh, the Patron of the SRA to come down to open it officially. This he kindly did on 26 November and after lunch in the restaurant there we all went to watch Jonah Barrington give an exhibition in the Championship Court. This was followed a few days later by the Oxford v Cambridge squash match at the RAC Club in London which I went to and which Oxford managed to win 3-2. The next squash match of interest was at Hurlingham between the SRA and the Women's SRA (WSRA) when the women received a handicap of 1 'hand' and 2 points, but still lost 4-1, I'm afraid.

This reminded me of matches I played in the 1930s against Susan Noel and Margot Lumb, successive Lady Champions. I can't now remember the handicap I had to give them but I remember well if I tried playing the more delicate drop shots I started losing but by switching from side to side and keeping them at the back of the court I could normally win. I was told it had something to do with ladies' hips! Another interesting event in this context was in the late 1920s when Susan Noel and Amr Bey, both world champions, were asked to play each other. This took place at the Cumberland LTC, Hampstead. Susan said she would be delighted if Amr would promise to go all out and say what handicap he would give her. A slightly embarrassed Amr said that on those conditions he would try to give her eight points and put her in to serve first. He got her out and she got in again, but never won a point!

In early December, Val and I were invited out to Australia by Commercial Union for the Masters Tennis Tournament at the Kooyong Club just outside Melbourne. We stopped off for a night on the way at Singapore when we stayed at the famous Raffles Hotel and met up briefly with some old friends. In Melbourne we had been booked in to a small hotel with a swimming pool, which was super as there were several other overseas tennis representatives also staying there, including Hockey and Mary Harcourt-Woods and Walter and Ellen Elcock from the USA. We were all taken out to Kooyong every day for the tennis and looked after very hospitably by our Australian tennis friends including the Frasers and Tobins.

The first day I was roped in for a press interview as the new AELTC Chairman by Bud Collins, the American commentator, and also in connection with my last visit to Australia in 1938 with our Long Distance Record Flight which many Australians still seemed to be interested in. I hadn't been to Kooyong before so was interested to see their very nice Club with its twenty-six (I think) excellent grass courts and the main stadium with three courts. The tennis was superb with Nastase beating Newcombe in three straight sets in the semi-final but then losing to Vilas in five hard fought sets which could have gone either way. Incidentally, Nastase had seen me sitting in the front row watching and, when changing ends, he kept coming up to me and saying, 'Why haven't I been made a member of Wimbledon?' and 'When are you going to make me a member?' My reply was, 'When you have won Wimbledon, but win this match first!' If he had concentrated a bit more he probably would have done!

One of the days we were in Melbourne we joined Hockey and Mary Woods in a drive into the country and visited a local copper mine which we found most interesting. Then, when the tennis was all over, we contacted an old LRDU friend A/Cdre Nick Gething and his wife Mardi who lived at Kangaroo Ground a few miles south-east of Melbourne, and Nick came in to take us out to lunch at their house 'Gardenhill' with its magnificent views across a lake to hills in the distance. It was certainly lovely country all round there and great to see them both again after over thirty years.

After that Val and I flew to Sydney for a couple of days where we stayed at the Wentworth Hotel but called in to see Sylvia and Red Merson and managed to fit in a quick visit to Bondi Beach for Val to enjoy a swim in the sea.

From Sydney we flew home getting back just in time for the end of year All England Club Committee lunch for all the staff. The British Amateur Squash Championships were also on at the Wembley Centre for the first time and we went to the Final when Mohibullah Khan beat his fellow Pakistani, Zaman.

It was then nearly Christmas time and we looked forward to having Bruce and Bob home for about a week when we also had plenty of golf and bridge with David and Joan Smith and the Holders.

I had felt for some time that our AELTC Committee was getting too old with several members well into their seventies and I had managed to persuade several of them to retire to make way for some younger members. Lord Ritchie (Ken) agreed and started the ball rolling in 1974, followed by Eric Peters in 1975 and Eric Simond in 1976. Bob Tinkler also decided to retire in 1976. Those four were all made Vice-Presidents and were replaced on the committee by Lord Belstead, Buzzer Hadingham, Peter Jackson and Mike Hann. In 1977 the Marquis of Zetland also retired and was replaced by Judge Barry Carter. The members had also been hankering after changes and, although they welcomed those that I had made, pressed me to restrict the time members should serve on the Committee to say five years to give other members more of a chance to get on to it. I would not agree to do this, as they clearly didn't understand the importance of continuity in the job or the amount of work to be done or time given to all the various sub-committees. New members of the Committee had no idea of this either until they got on to the Committee themselves. Anyway, I then felt satisfied that I had a good well balanced Committee, with Ted Avory, Rex Sterry and Bimby Holt as my experienced main supporters, and I didn't want any further changes for a while.

1975

The New Year started fairly quietly with just my regular visits to the office at the All England Club and one full committee meeting in London. I also had a meeting of the SRA Council and went to the Wembley Squash Centre for a GB match v Pakistan. Val and I then joined Norman Pertwee's skiing party at Méribel where we stayed at Lorna Cooper-Key's lovely châlet 'La Gelinotte'. The others in the party were David and Sue Balme, Ronald and Elizabeth McGregor, the Gabriels and the Hartnell-Beavises. We were lucky with the weather and had a wonderful two weeks' skiing taking it in turn to ski with different couples. In fact it was such a success we repeated it with Norman every year for the next fifteen! There were only one or two changes occasionally with some new couples such as Gerard and Ralphia Noel or the Turners instead of the Gabriels or the Balmes after the latter had bought their flat up the valley at Motteret.

The day after getting home I went to the Final of the British Open Squash at Wembley which had been particularly interesting with previous winners Barrington and Hunt being beaten in the quarter finals by Zaman and Alauddin who went on to the final. There Zaman, despite a painful abscess on a wisdom tooth, played a brilliant match defeating Alauddin surprisingly easily in three straight games. This was followed some ten days later, on a lower key, by the annual Inter-Services Squash which was played for the first time, as far as I can remember, outside London at the unusually remote venue of the RN Engineering College Manadon, Plymouth. The Army succeeded in winning, thus upsetting the run of eight consecutive wins by the RAF.

Bruce and Bob came most weekends around this time, together with either Gus Holden or Joan Bearder, and Viv Crone from Mildenhall came for a few days during the week for golf with Val. Rupert and Venetia Hogan also came to stay one night which was fun.

As Chairman of the AELTC, I found myself being invited to speak at various lunches and dinners about the Championships at Wimbledon and there were two in March which I remember – a dinner at St George's Hill Tennis Club and a lunch at the Baltic Exchange in London whose Chairman was an old squash friend Tommy Turnbull. There were other lunches to which I was invited, for example, by the Chairman of Lloyds, Sir Henry Mance (who had been the small boy who had lost a leg and been coached by my mother to get a scholarship to Charterhouse!) and in turn by each of the Chairmen of the Stock Exchange, the Law Society and Barclay's Bank. Most of these invitations I realise stemmed from their invitations to the Royal Box, including a private dinner for Val and me with the Bishop of London and Jane Ellison when Princess Margaret was also dining with them.

Towards the end of March my brother Douglas came to stay for a few days and over Easter, when Bruce and Bob had gone skiing, we had a fairly quiet weekend with bridge in the evenings with the Holders and the Smiths. Hugh and Dany had now been posted to London and were living near Twickenham where we went to lunch with them one day. Andrée came over from Grasse to stay with them and came on to stay a few days with us at Heather Hill until Hugh and Dany came down to collect her.

In March 1975 the Club Committee had been considering various ways of making better use of the Centre Court stadium out of season with some other event such as boxing or a concert, including possibly with a sliding roof. None of these alternatives were considered sufficiently profitable or worth while compared with the risk to the grass turf and the extra work involved for the staff, but we did decide to look at detailed plans for a sliding roof for the Championships. After contacting Sir Frank Taylor, a member of the All England Club and Chairman of his construction business Taylor Woodrow, he and his experts produced a plan and a quote but they couldn't assure us that the plastic roof would not flap in a strong wind. Unfortunately this was often the case when there were rain storms over Wimbledon. For this reason and also because we felt that just one covered court out of eighteen that we need to complete the Championships was not really the answer, and might be considered to favour just the few Centre Court top players, the Committee decided against it at that time. Later with the enormous increase in world-wide TV coverage, improved technology for the sliding roof cover and the use of a large Centre Court TV screen on the outside of Court 1 so that the public can watch happily under their umbrellas from the so-called Henman Hill, I am glad to say that the Committee have now decided to go ahead with a new sliding roof which should be ready by 2009.

April was a busy time at the AELTC with a number of other meetings as well as the AGM at the Café Royal and the Club Dinner. I also attended an Air Marshals' Club lunch when we were updated by the CAS on the latest RAF developments and there was too Rex Sterry's light-hearted Public School Lawn Tennis Club annual dinner which was always good fun. Val and I also had a very interesting invitation to the Royal Academy dinner at Burlington House one evening, and the next weekend we went to the large lunch at Wembley prior to the Football Cup Final and then to the SRA Ball that evening at the Hurlingham Club.

In May 1975 Val and I went to Bournemouth for the Hard Court Championships. On the way we stopped at Lymington for a couple of nights with the Balmes and a game of golf with the Kyles. At Bournemouth we stayed at the Roundhouse Hotel with some of the LTA reps and went to watch the finals. Soon after we got back I had a meeting at the Club about the plans for the new Wimbledon Museum with Tom Todd, a member who was generously making available to us his considerable private collection of tennis memorabilia on permanent loan, to help start the Museum off. Mr Wade, a well known museum architect whom we had specially selected, was also present and showed us his planned layout for the proposed museum. The next day I had to have a quick meeting in London with Peter Woods, the SRA Secretary, and then a Wimbledon committee meeting that evening.

Two days later Val and I were off to Hamburg where we had been invited very kindly for three days at their expense to attend the 1975 German Championships. They had not been quite sure about my travel arrangements and Ted Avory was rung up by Dr Kleinscroth, an Honorary Member of our IC and an old friend of his and Pat Hughes, to ask whether I would 'expect to go first class'. Ted in his usual inimitable way said, 'Of course, as an Air Chief Marshal he is always accustomed to travel first class!' In due course two first class air tickets had arrived for us and we flew there in great comfort. On arrival we were met and taken off to the Hotel Vier Jahreszeiten. After settling in there we went out to the tennis to meet Dr Kleinscroth and the various German LTA officials running their Championships, and to watch some of the tennis.

The next morning before going out to the tennis again we had the chance to look round Hamburg a bit, and I was reminded of the hot reception I had had during World War II when bombing the marshalling yards there in 1942. I had to limp home in my old Whitley bomber badly damaged and carrying a large lump of flak which had ended up in my cockpit! We were amazed at the remarkable way the city had built up again since it was flattened later in the war by a large bombing raid which had created some of the worst fire storms which swept through the city. Our hotel was virtually opposite the fairly large lake in the centre of the city, which during the war they had completely covered with barges to hide the water and prevent its use as an aid to target identification from the air. The rest of the day we stayed watching the tennis where we were well looked after by 'Happy' Gorneman and his wife Renate from Lübeck where he ran a chocolate factory. We got on very well with them and invited them to Wimbledon later that year and they sent us a large box of chocolates every year for the next two or three years for Christmas! At the tennis, we watched in particular our Roger Taylor but regrettably he lost in the semi-final, I think, to Eddie Dibbs of the USA, the eventual winner. On the Sunday before the final Val and I were taken to lunch by Gottfried Von Cramm, the outstanding pre-war German player who got to the Wimbledon final three years in a row, 1935, '36 and '37 when he was beaten by Fred Perry (twice) and Don Budge. It was fascinating talking to him and hearing his views on all the pre-war players.

Altogether we greatly enjoyed our three days in Hamburg and were very grateful to Heinrich Kleinscroth and the German LTA for inviting us. We then flew back home for a night before going to stay at Roehampton with Gus and Brenda Walker for the Order of the Bath Ceremony at Westminster Abbey attended as usual by The Queen. The following weekend we had the opening of the grass courts and cocktail party at Wimbledon. The Pertwees came to stay with us at Heather Hill again to take part.

Early in June we had decided to have a large buffet lunch party at Heather Hill for about thirty of the AELTC and Championship Committee and their wives. Luckily the weather was fine and we were able to be outside mostly on the patio and to take it in turns to play boules on the lawn which added to the fun. I then had several days of tennis enjoying the grass courts at Wimbledon before flying with Val to Paris for the last four days of the French Championships. This time Philippe Chatrier had arranged for us to stay at a very small pension called the Résidence du Bois in Rue Chalgrin near the Arc de Triomphe. It had a small garden at the back where we usually had breakfast when it was fine. The Sedgmans and the Tobins from Australia were also staying there as well as Bimby and Daphne Holt from the All England Club, so it was super. Incidentally, the Résidence had previously been an official brothel and Val fell in love with it because the loo paper was scented!

We always went back there for the next eight years that we went to Stade Roland Garros for the French Championships. As usual their arrangements, with the help of Régine, Philippe's personal assistant, were excellent and Philippe was as hospitable as always with his dinners or theatre or evening cruise along the Seine with all his VIP visitors. The latter was delightful, cruising along quietly past Nôtre Dame Cathedral while we were having drinks or dinner. I remember in particular one lovely summer evening cruising along the Seine in one of the Bateaux Mouches, when Val and I were sitting next to Carmen Tobin who was highly amused and giggling away at seeing a lot of young Parisians lying about on the grass banks busy courting and making love in the open!

After the French Championships we flew home for a week, though I spent most of the time at the All England Club checking on all the pre-Wimbledon arrangements and works services and attending the Seeding Committee and the draw. Veronica's little house was not available this time, so we had booked in to the Gloucester Hotel which had been refurbished and where we had arranged special terms for the Wimbledon players and officials. Val and I moved in there over the weekend and went again to the IC Ball and the Hurlingham garden party. Everything then went as usual though we had started having a William Hill betting tent. The idea was to save people who liked to have a bet going in and out of the grounds during the Championships and walking up the hill to Wimbledon village, which they used to do. However, it encouraged too much betting and possibly even players defaulting, or throwing a set, and we decided it was a mistake not to be repeated another year.

The other new thing that year was the introduction of marquees for which we let out some of the hard courts to some of the bigger companies for entertainment purposes. We started this first year through the Bagenal Harvey organization, the Club's PR consultants, with just one large hospitality marquee for Commercial Union who ran the end of year Grand Prix Masters Tournament. This proved very popular and we ended up several years later with about forty of these hospitality tents. By this time, Mark McCormack of IMG had joined in the act. It was up to the firms to have their marquee put up and to provide all the catering, TV sets and other things for their guests and all we had to do was to provide them with the space and a small extra allocation of Centre Court seat tickets. The companies involved were usually already Debenture Holders and had some tickets anyway. Altogether this project brought in thousands of pounds to add to our Championship profits for the eventual benefit of British tennis.

A slightly controversial matter which arose every year during the Championships was coloured clothing. At Wimbledon we have always insisted on 'predominantly white clothing' for the players. Apart from a small amount of coloured trimming, we feel that this is more in keeping with our garden party atmosphere, which we like to retain, and is on the whole much nicer for the spectators as it doesn't show the unpleasant perspiration marks to the same extent. The players on the other hand were being offered large sums of money to wear different companies' coloured clothing and were naturally keen to get the extra money. There was also much pressure from the clothing manufacturers to show off their latest designs, as well as over the permissible size of their logos. The coloured clothing issue came to a head this year when a delegation of Colin Drysdale, President of the Players Association, John Newcombe and Arthur Ashe came to see me and Bimby Holt during the Championships, asking us to change our rule saying that it meant literally thousands of pounds to some of the players. I'm afraid our answer was 'no'. We were sure that there was no way our Committee would agree. It just wouldn't be Wimbledon, in the same way as if we accepted advertisements all round the courts like other tournaments. The only advertisements we allow are for companies who provide items on court for use during the Championships, for example Slazengers. However, the arguments still go on, though I was interested a year or two later on a hot day in Paris at the French Championships when Ilie Nastase came up to me and said, 'You were so right about insisting on predominantly white clothing. It doesn't show the horrible sweat marks!'

In those days at the Championships ladies often wore hats and Rex Sterry, who was in charge of the Royal Box, had the sometimes rather embarrassing job, if necessary, of being the official 'hat' remover when too large! Like Mavis David before her, Val always made her own elegant small hats which were much admired and saved me a lot of money. I remember her telling me that when sitting one year in our Members' seats a man nearby asked the lady in front of him in a large brimmed hat if she would mind removing it. Unfortunately she declined, so after a further period of frustration and not being able to see properly, the man whipped the hat off. The lady was of course furious and leant back to grab the man's tie and nearly throttled him before they were parted! Rex was too tactful for this to happen in the Royal Box but I did warn him!

I was fairly busy again with Royal Visitors most days. The tennis, as always, was superb with Arthur Ashe coming through to the Final and beating Jimmy Connors, the defending champion, in four sets. It was a fascinating match with Ashe changing his normally hard hitting style, slowing the game up and denying his opponent any pace. He won the first two sets easily and when one of the spectators, influenced no doubt by the betting tent, called out, 'Come on Jimmy!', Jimbo shouted back, 'I'm trying for Christ's sake!' – as he always did. He managed to fight back to win the third set 7-5 but Ashe got home 6-4 in the fourth. It had been a remarkable tactical victory. In the Ladies' Singles Billie-Jean King won a close semi-final against the holder Chris Evert, and then had a fairly easy win against Evonne Goolagong (the 1971 Champion and now Mrs Cawley) to become Lady Champion for her sixth time. The other interesting result was in the Ladies Doubles when two Japanese, Kiyomura and Sawamatsu, won the first Wimbledon title for Japan.

After that the All England Club was back to normal with our works programme for improvement for next year. There was my usual game on the Centre Court and the Lords and Commons match at the Club, and the party for the ground staff and other workers at the Dog and Fox in Wimbledon village. Val and I then drove the next weekend to Frinton-on-Sea to stay with the Pertwees, who took us for the usual swim before breakfast in the sea and then a couple of sets of tennis, before watching the finals of their tennis tournament. On the way back home we called in for a couple of nights with Dulcie and Michael Thompson and had some tennis on David and Caroline Thompson's new court.

In July I also had to have an EGM of the SRA and, on its conclusion, I announced my decision to retire from being the President. I was finding that with the increasing popularity and expansion of the game of squash I couldn't give it the attention it deserved, as my priority was inevitably Wimbledon and tennis. I had previously sounded out my old Carthusian friend, Major-General Roderick Fyler, who had played squash for the Army in the Inter-Services competition and also for Kent, to see if he would take over from me as President at the end of October. This Roddy was pleased to do and the SRA Committee happily agreed.

The first weekend in August Val and I were invited to the Lords Test Match one day and then we went to the RAF Tennis finals followed by the Inter-Services, in which I played again in the Veterans Doubles. At the end of the month we went to my Singapore ADC Richard Sanderson's wedding to Sarah whose parents lived not far away from us.

It was then the IC weekend again at Le Touquet for our tennis and golf match with the French. As ever, that was most enjoyable and afterwards, instead of going on to Britanny as last year, we drove south to stay a week at Grasse with Douglas and Andrée. From there we drove on to my favourite holiday resort Alassio on the Italian Riviera and then to Lugano in Switzerland where we met up with other members of the All England Club for our match against the Tennis Club Lido. This was always a friendly mixed match with ladies playing as well. Bimby and Daphne Holt, Chris and Jenny Gorringe and Roger and Susan Ambrose were amongst our party and I played with Bimby in the Men's Doubles event. It was all very good fun with a lot of matches over the two days and we were very hospitably looked after and entertained by Chico and his Club members. After that Val and I drove slightly north to Ascona near Locarno where Greta and Rudy Saar were living. She was Richard Tauber's beautiful operetta singing partner when in London, and was quite a friend of my brother Douglas and used to come to Traddles occasionally when Val and I got to know her. We dined with them in Ascona and they very kindly put us up in a super hotel, Monte Venta, overlooking Lake Maggiore. After a couple of days there we drove back to England, stopping just once again en route after an excellent three weeks away. It had meant, however, us missing going to New York this year for the 1975 US Championships.

At home we were then back to our normal routine of golf, gardening, bridge in the evenings, my visits to Wimbledon and regular visits at the weekends of Bruce, Bob and Joan Bearder. At the end of October, I had my last Squash Rackets Association meeting with the AGM in London, when I finally retired and they kindly made me a Life Vice-President. The next day I had Roddy Fyler to lunch at the All England Club to finally hand over to him as the new Squash Rackets President.

The next major tennis event for Val and me to go to was the Dewar Cup in that wonderful arena of the Albert Hall in London. Not long after that we went to Frinton where Eric Bland, the President of their Tennis Club, had invited me to the annual dinner to talk to them about Wimbledon. All went well and we stayed the night with the Pertwees. On the way back we stopped a night with Bruce in the new little house he had bought near Huntingdon so that he could live out while he was based at RAF Wyton.

The Grand Prix Masters in December 1975 was at Stockholm where Val and I were invited by Commercial Union. It was held in the

Königshalle covered court and was won by Nastase, rather surprisingly, having in the first round of the Round Robin been disqualified against Ashe but then getting through to the final and beating Borg, the favourite. It was, as always, an interesting few days and enabled all the senior representatives of international tennis to get together and discuss their problems. We flew back home in time for a big lunch party given by Buzzer Hadingham, the Slazenger Chairman, and our pre-Christmas lunch for the All England Club staff. We then had Christmas at home again with the boys and Gus Holden and golf and bridge with the Smiths and Holders.

1976

Val and I drove out at the end of January to Méribel and La Gelinotte to join Norman Pertwee's ski party again. We travelled on the night ferry from Southampton to Le Havre, leaving there about 7.30 a.m. and aiming to get to Méribel about 6.00 p.m. All went well, according to plan, until I decided to fill up with petrol before getting up into the mountains and stupidly filled the tank by mistake with diesel! That was that and we had to get towed in to the nearest village where we could stay overnight and get the car fuel pipes cleaned out the next morning, so I had to ring Norman at La Gelinotte and tell him we wouldn't be there until midday the next day. After this bad start, however, we had a lovely holiday with excellent snow and plenty of sun. One day I had stopped temporarily on the ski slopes waiting for Val when someone pulled up beside me, and to my surprise it was HRH The Duke of Kent who apparently often went to Méribel where he stayed and skied with Sir Edward Tomkins, our ex-Ambassador in Paris, who had a châlet close to La Gelinotte. Val caught up with us shortly on the slopes but had difficulty curtseying to the Duke on her skis! After we got back to England we were glad to have both Bruce and Bob home most weekends and there was a lot going on at Wimbledon for me.

A hardy annual for discussion before the main tennis season started was the matter of prize money. The USTA had been persuaded by Billie-Jean King and the WTA in 1974 to agree to equal prize money for the women despite opposition from their men, who claimed that it was an 'inequality against them as they played longer matches and considered they were the primary box office attraction for all major tournaments'. The WTA, however, had won the day in America and were putting pressure on the other Grand Slams to follow suit. The Director of the WTA (Jerry Diamond) came to see me at the All England Club and we had several meetings to discuss details. At that time, in line with the other Grand Slams, we were giving ladies approximately 60 per cent. We thought this about right and fair as they were on court for only the best of three sets, compared with five for the men, and their standard of play in depth was relatively poor so that the women's early rounds were not very exciting for spectators. Billie-Jean had told me that the women would play five sets if necessary, but I said that was probably the last thing we would want unless the standard of play in depth improved considerably. As a reason for equal prize money, people often quote the fact that in 1973 Billie-Jean King beat Bobby Riggs, the 1939 world champion, but they tend to forget that he was then fifty-five years old (twenty-six years older than her) and had anyway only the year before beaten Margaret Court, the Ladies' No. 1 in the world, despite being so much older. The fact that at Wimbledon applications for tickets for the first Tuesday, so called Ladies Day, was very much smaller than for the first Monday when the men started, was a fairly clear indication to us of what the public preferred to watch. We did, however, accept that the standard of play for the Ladies' last eight was now much better and provided some excellent matches, so our Championship committee agreed to compromise by raising the ladies' prize money at the top level to 90 per cent. Considering they were on court and providing entertainment for the spectators for far less time than the men, we felt that this was more than fair. The French have been more or less in line with us at Wimbledon, but the Australians later went on to equal prize money, mainly I believe to encourage more of the top women players to travel all that way to Melbourne which some of them had been reluctant to do. Total prize money has of course increased enormously over the years and at Wimbledon every year the proportion given to the ladies is closely assessed. As their standard of play in depth has improved we have gradually increased their prize money. We have, however, borne in mind the principle of equal pay for equal work, in other words the time on court entertaining the public and contributing to the commercial success of the tournament. There is also the fact that by playing only the best-of-three set matches, more of the leading women players have felt able to enter the doubles events than the men, thereby winning more prize money altogether than their men opposite numbers. Anyway, the gap has gradually narrowed. In 2006 at Stade Roland Garros the French accepted equal prize money at the very top for their Men's and Ladies' champions and at Wimbledon Mauresmo, the Ladies' winner, received 95 per cent of Federer's £655,000. In recent years, with the influx of many attractive and hard-hitting young Russian and European women players, there has apparently been a change of heart. For 2007 the present Wimbledon Committee have finally accepted equal prize money for women, even in the early rounds. That is, perhaps, another Grand Slam victory for Billie-Jean King! Hopefully now she will no longer call me a 'male chauvinist pig' as she did in the 1980s!

For the 1976 Championships, we had two key personnel changes, Fred Hoyles had taken over as referee from Mike Gibson, and Bob Twynam who had been our excellent head groundsman for many years had decided to retire and had handed over to Jack Yardley. The latter's first surprise job was when, in May, the Centre Court was broken into at the North End and vandalized by intruders. They had daubed part of the North Stand and scoreboard with red paint and dug a hole and emptied a pot of red paint in the very centre of the court, leaving a trail of paint across the court as they left. We never discovered who they were, but they weren't very clever if they had really meant to ruin the court because the main damage in the centre of the court did not matter too much as it would mostly be covered by the tennis net. Luckily too, with nearly eight weeks before the Championships were due to start, Jack and his groundstaff were able to repair the damage so that it was hardly noticeable. After that, however, we decided to step up the police security for the grounds for a longer period before the Championships. Another security matter of this kind was when a certain strongly anti-apartheid MP threatened to dig up the court where one of the top South African players was scheduled to play on the first day. Fortunately we heard about this in advance and I spoke to Denis Howell, the Minister for Sport, who said he would speak to him and explain that Wimbledon had always insisted there should be no politics in the sport and that this was an individual sport with players playing primarily for themselves and not particularly representing their country. Denis Howell apparently did this, as the MP decided to call it off.

There were occasionally other security problems in connection with the Royal Box during the Championships when, at the time of the IRA bombings in London, we received threats of a bomb under the Royal Box. The first time, the police came to me asking whether they should evacuate the Centre Court. They had searched the area but couldn't find anything suspicious and thought it must be one of many hoax messages they received. They could usually tell from the type of warning message and where it came from but they said the decision whether to evacuate was mine and up to me. After further discussion we decided that it must be a hoax, but in future I insisted that the police should come up with a definite recommendation as they were in the best position to assess the evidence from the message. Luckily all the three or four threats that we had were in fact hoaxes, but it was very worrying and we introduced more sniffer dogs and thorough searches of the grounds every day before and after play. We also prepared an emergency evacuation plan for the Centre Court just in case.

In May 1976 Val and I went again to the Football Cup Final at Wembley, then to Eastbourne for a Davis Cup match, before the opening of the grass courts tournament and annual Members' cocktail party at the All England Club. At the end of the month we had an enjoyable visit to Rome for the last week of the Italian Championships.

Adriano Panatta beat Guillermo Vilas in four sets in the final with the help of the typical partisan Italian crowd, when they occasionally threw pebbles on to Vilas' side of the court to put him off!

After Rome, Val and I took a week's holiday, going by train to Naples where we hired a car and called in at different places down the coast. We got a room in a very pretty little hotel overlooking the sea at Capo la Gala which we made our base for several interesting visits to Pompeii, Sorrento, Amalfi and the island of Capri, none of which Val had been to before. We then flew back to England for a few days before going off again to the French Championships for the last four days. We stayed again at the Résidence du Bois where we were delighted to meet up with the Tobins and Sedgmans, and Philippe Chatrier looked after us all as well as usual. The tennis at Stade Roland Garros was splendid in spite of the very hot weather on those dusty hard courts. Panatta followed his Italian victory by winning the French Men's Singles and Sue Barker won the Ladies, the first British winner for ten years since Ann (Haydon) Jones.

When we returned to England there were a number of meetings to discuss and approve detailed plans for the Wimbledon Museum and its official opening the following year. Honor Godfrey and Ann Gould were the two principal researchers and they and Tony Cooper, our ex-Assistant Secretary who was to be the Curator with Valerie Warren as his Assistant Curator, were progressing well.

The Committee was also having to decide on many special arrangements for our Centenary Championships in 1977. These included the design of the Centenary Spode Plate and the Silver Medals for all past Champions which Garrards of Upper Regent Street were going to produce for us – also the Silver Salver to mark The Queen's Jubilee and the Centenary of the Championships, one of which was to be presented to each of the 1977 Singles Champions. We also needed to consider the preparation of the *100 Years of Wimbledon* book, which we authorized Lance Tingay, the lawn tennis writer of the *Daily Telegraph*, to produce. There was also the week before the Championships the Seeding Committee and the draw which I liked to attend.

My American friends Uppy and Ginny Moorhead had arrived in London early for the Championships and they came to lunch with me at Wimbledon one day, when I had a game of tennis on grass for him, with Buzzer Hadingham and Gus Holden, on Court 4. On the Saturday too I had a game on Court 3 with Jean Borotra. He still loved to play on grass at Wimbledon. He now served underhand to give him time to get up to the net to volley! Ted Frith and Gus also made up the four and this became a regular event every year for a while during the weekend before Wimbledon.

Tennis with Borotra, Gus Holden and Ted Frith

The 1976 Championships then went ahead, starting with the IC Ball on the Saturday, and Hurlingham Garden Party on Sunday with several special exhibition games for a few of the players who wanted to practise on grass. In the Men's Singles of the Championships Nastase reached the final for the second time but Borg, who had beaten Vilas and Tanner and not lost a set throughout, became the Champion for his first time and was the first Swede to win a Wimbledon crown. In the Ladies' Singles all eight of the top seeds, including Sue Barker, reached the quarter-finals and the four top seeds (Evert, Cawley, Wade and Navratilova) the semi-finals, but Chrissie Evert beat Mrs Evonne (Goolagong) Cawley 8-6 in the final set of a great final, which went on for two hours in the boiling sun and could have gone either way.

Altogether it was a brilliant Championships with all the doubles matches also going to the final set and the weather back to its old Wimbledon 'holiday time'! All the usual members of the Royal Family came and the total attendances of the public increased, as did the Championships' profits for the benefit of British tennis.

After the Championships were over we got busy on the preparations for our Centenary year. There was also a weekend in August when we held the Davis Cup match against Italy on Court 1. Although we were defeated, the Lloyd brothers won an exciting doubles which kept the match very much alive until the third day. On a lower scale, I also had the Inter-Services matches to attend to at the Club, and Val and I had two good weekends – one at Frinton again with the Pertwees and a golfing weekend with Gus and Brenda Walker up at Brancaster.

We also had a good day at Lords for the cricket Test Match against India, before setting off for New York and the American 1976 Tennis Championships. Here again we checked in at the River Club but were taken off for the middle weekend by Uppy and Ginny Moorhead to their home at Rumson, New Jersey for a bit of tennis and golf ourselves. The Moorheads were also staying at the River Club so drove us out every day to the tennis at the West Side Tennis Club, including one evening for one of the late night sessions which the USTA had introduced in 1975. Most other evenings we seemed to have dinners organized by Stan Malless, the USTA President, or the Tuckers, the West Side TC President and his wife Lillian, or for me with the US International Tennis Club. At the tennis, Connors won through to the final and beat Borg in four sets, whilst Chris Evert playing incredibly well won rather easily in two sets this time against Evonne Cawley.

On return to UK we found that our great Canadian friends (Bill and Hope Pigott) were visiting London and we persuaded them to come and stay with us a few days at Heather Hill, which was great as we had been to them so often. We had tried before, without success, to get them to come over for the Wimbledon Championships but it was good to have them now anyway. Other visitors to the All England Club, who it was good to see again, were Chiko and members of the Lugano Tennis Club who had come over for their annual match against us.

In October and November I was able, between meetings at the Club, to fit in my weekly game of tennis and bridge at the All England Club with Della Porta's group which helped to keep me fit. Val and I went to watch the Wightman Cup match at the Crystal Palace but this time the Americans were too strong for us again. We also went one day to the Benson and Hedges Tennis Championships at the Empire Pool, Wembley where nearly all the top men players were taking part.

In December then it was the time for the Grand Prix Masters, and Val and I were invited by Mr Dunlop of Commerical Union to go to Houston in Texas where it was being held. This we were delighted to do, travelling first class on them, but we decided to break the journey at Key West near Miami for a night. Unfortunately Val's suitcase went missing and never arrived so she had to wear my spare pyjamas until we could do some shopping. Eventually, when we got to Houston, Laurie Pignon, one of our lawn tennis writers, expressed regret but said he was disappointed as he thought Val would be arriving with no clothes on! The suitcase in fact was never found, so Val had to do quite a lot of shopping in Houston, mostly covered fortunately by our insurance policies. The other near drama was at the hotel we were all staying in, where there was a serious fire alarm late one evening and we all had to rush downstairs in our dressing gowns or whatever we had on and with any valuables we could collect on the way. Fortunately after an hour or so, and much concern, we were cleared to return to our rooms. At the Grand Prix Tennis in 1976, where we were hospitably looked after by Gordon Dunlop and his wife, the tennis was on a 'round robin' basis and I thought was rather disappointing with Orantes eventually winning the final against Fibak. The doubles was I felt better, which I think Ramirez and Gottfried won.

Flying back afterwards, Val and I decided to go via Miami hoping possibly to find her suitcase in the lost luggage! However, in vain. We then flew on to stay a few days at the Balmoral Beach Hotel in Nassau.

There we managed to contact Fiona who had been skiing one year with us in Méribel. She was now working for the well-known millionaire A. J. P. Taylor from Canada, who made his name during the war building naval frigates and who owned the estate at Lyford Cay on the north-west tip of Nassau. Fiona was his secretary and part-time carer for his wife, and lived in one of the small cottages on his land and had her sister and granddaughter staying at the time. While we were in Nassau we hired a car so we drove out to see her, and she had arranged for us to call in to meet the Taylors and have lunch with them before going for a swim in the sea from their private beachhouse. It was a very enjoyable day and so nice to see Fiona again and talk to AJP about his invaluable wartime contribution to shipping.

We then flew back overnight for a week at Heather Hill before Christmas there with Bruce and Bob, Gus Holden and Joan Bearder.

1977

In January it was good to get back on a covered court at Wimbledon for my usual tennis. All was going well with the special Centenary arrangements for the Championships as well as the many works service improvements including the replacing of the Centre Court standing room with seats, so that at the end of the month Val and I went off for our annual two weeks' skiing at Méribel with the Pertwees and Joan and Johnny H-B in the super châlet La Gelinotte. Again I remember we were lucky with the snow and the weather and we had lunch out on the balcony in the sun nearly every day, and we had some marvellous skiing and a good party round the log fire in the evenings.

When we got home, it was back to our regular routine of meetings and tennis for me at Wimbledon, and golf and gardening with Val at weekends with bridge often in the evenings.

In the meantime, HM The Queen had accepted the invitation to come to lunch and the Ladies Wimbledon final, and Sir Philip Moore, her private secretary, came to see me in March at the All England Club to discuss details of security and other arrangements for her visit. In April then there was the WCT tennis in Earls Court and the Lord Mayor's banquet at the Mansion House for Val and me, plus a Championships Committee meeting and the All England Club Dinner.

An Official Wimbledon Centenary Film was produced by TransWorld International UK (TWI) in May and another by the BBC which was shown on television the week before the Championships. Lance Tingay's *100 years of Wimbledon* book was also ready for sale in May, as were the special Centenary Magazine, silver medals and Spode plates, which all added to the publicity and interest shown at the opening of the Wimbledon Museum by HRH The Duke of Kent, the All England Club President, on 19 May. The nucleus of the museum was the private collection of Tom Todd, supplemented by the purchase of more material and donations from the All England Club, the LTA and numerous other individuals. Apart from all the trophies, memorabilia, tennis rackets, clothing and so on recording the development of the game over the years, a rather lovely touch was a model of the old men's locker room with the original decorative blue and white china basins which we bought from the school that had taken over the old All England Club at Worple Road. There was also a recording of an old match taking place and a viewing platform overlooking the Centre Court as well as a splendid library of tennis books, magazines and programmes, which we named after Lord Ritchie, a long standing member of the Club Committee. The whole was designed by Robin Wade Design Associates recording the history of the game and was a great success, which I think inspired the USTA to renovate their Tennis Hall of Fame at Newport, Rhode Island and brought many thousands of visitors to Wimbledon throughout the year to make it a profitable going concern. Nearly thirty years later, like all museums, it was running out of space and an even bigger and better Wimbledon Museum had to be built and was opened again by the Duke of Kent in April 2006.

The following weekend there was the annual grass court opening Members' tournament and cocktail party at the All England Club when Norman and Eileen Pertwee came to stay with us. A couple of weeks later Val and I flew off to Paris again for the last three days of the French Championships at Stade Roland Garros. We stayed at our delightful Résidence du Bois and met up again with our Australian friends there – the Sedgmans and the Tobins. Philippe Chatrier's hospitality, with the help of Régine, was as excellent as ever so it was good fun as usual, but the tennis was slightly disappointing, I thought, though Vilas won the Men's Singles and Mima Jausovec the Ladies'. We flew back to England the day after the finals for a couple of busy weeks at Wimbledon leading up to the Centenary Championships. While at the Club I managed to get in a game of tennis myself each week as well as my annual game on the Saturday with Jean Borotra together with Gus Holden and Ted Frith making up the four. This was followed by the IC dinner dance at the Kensington Royal Garden Hotel and the IC lunch and garden party on the Sunday at Hurlingham.

David Mills, the Club Secretary, who had previously stayed in one of the ground floor rooms in the Lodge at the Somerset Road entrance to the Club during the Championships, had moved into a house in Barnes near enough for him to do the Championships from there. After installing a new bathroom the garden lodge was made into quite a good little one-room flat for Val and me to stay in during the Championships. It was most convenient and saved us a lot of commuting to and fro. Whilst I was Chairman we always stayed there in future for the Championships. However, there was a snag. It seemed to have become known that we stayed there for the two weeks, and someone took advantage of this and burgled our house at Heather Hill. Two men were in the car, and at the top of our drive asked the milkman on his rounds if that was where the Burnetts lived. The milkman said 'yes' but suddenly realized we were away, so sensibly made a note of the car number and on completing his round about an hour later reported to the police, who came round to find the house had been broken into. It was reported to us at Wimbledon and the next morning we hurried down to see the damage. The police had boarded up the window the men had broken and made it reasonably secure until we could get it repaired. Luckily not too much had been taken – only silver and Val's favourite clock, but it was maddening. The police traced the car to south-east London and brought the driver down later to Farnham Police Station for an identification parade with half a dozen other men. Unfortunately they all had dark glasses on so the milkman couldn't be certain as the driver hadn't glasses on when he originally saw him. He explained this to the police but incredibly, they said, they were not allowed to ask them to remove their dark glasses and the men got away with it! How stupid can we be! The police thought they had got their man when they had discovered in the boot of his car a walking stick with a silver knob on top and the initial 'B' – and it surprised them when I told them it was not mine.

The first day of the Centenary Championships then started with an official lunch with the Duke and Duchess of Kent for all past Singles Champions in the Members' Enclosure followed by a Parade on the Centre Court when each one, except for Jimmy Connors who discourteously chose instead to practise on one of the outside courts with Ilie Nastase, was presented by HRH The Duke of Kent with a Centenary

Past Wimbledon Champions lining up for presentation of Centenary silver medal

silver medal. The medal portrayed a man and a lady player on each side in 1877 and 1977 tennis dress. The medal also rather conveniently fitted into the base of a silver ash tray so that it could be useful as well as ornamental.

Other special arrangements to mark the Centenary were additional floral decorations around the grounds and the further extension of the main tea lawn to cater for the large crowds expected. All competitors were to be presented with a Championships pen/pencil set, and a silver salver to mark The Queen's Silver Jubilee and the Championships' Centenary was to be presented to each of the Singles Champions in addition to their other trophies. There was also to be a Government Reception at the Banqueting House, Whitehall for all the players and officials from overseas. It had also been agreed that the whole of the daily gate money on the day of The Queen's visit would be donated to The Queen's Silver Jubilee Fund. Another change to the normal programme was that instead of the LTA ball at the end of the Championships, when the two Champions danced together to open it, the LTA were to have their ball at the London Hilton Hotel on the middle Saturday, so as to attract more of the players, and the final event was to be the Champions' dinner at the Savoy Hotel when the two Champions would say a few words and, as the Chairman of the Championships Committee, I was expected to wind up the proceedings. This became the pattern of events in future years also.

The Queen and Duke of Edinburgh arriving at the Members' Enclosure for lunch with the Committee

The tennis throughout the fortnight was, I think, exceptionally exciting with many surprises and with the young eighteen-year-old John McEnroe, a qualifier, fighting his way through to the semi-final before losing in four sets to Jimmy Connors. In the other semi-final Björn Borg beat Vitas Gerulaitis 8-6 in the final set of one of the best matches many of us had ever seen, before going on to win a superbly fought final 6-4 in the fifth set against Connors for his second Wimbledon Championship in a row. In the Ladies' Singles we had two English players in the semi-finals – Virginia Wade and Sue Barker. Sue should have won then against Betty Stove from Holland, who had surprisingly beaten Navratilova earlier, but she unfortunately lost 6-4 in the final set to let Betty through to the Ladies' Final. Virginia, however, was on top form and saw off Chris Evert in three sets to reach the final, which she then won against Betty Stove in front of The Queen to become Lady Champion – the first British champion since Ann Jones in 1969. The Queen and the Duke of Edinburgh had arrived earlier at the Members' Enclosure for lunch with the Committee before watching from the Royal Box. The crowd on the Centre Court were ecstatic and burst into song of 'Rule

The Queen in the Royal Box in Centenary year

Picture by Arthur Cole

All Past Singles Champions at Wimbledon for lunch with the Duke and Duchess of Kent in 1977

Britannia' and 'Land of Hope and Glory', while I accompanied The Queen and The Duke of Edinburgh down to the Centre Court to present the Trophies. It was a marvellous ending to The Queen's visit and a wonderful surprise present for her in her Silver Jubilee Year.

Another interesting special event was a Centenary Invitation Doubles, which included approximately twenty past Singles or Doubles Champions and other top players, making sixteen pairs in four groups playing on a round-robin basis. It was won by Sven Davidson and Torben Ulrich who beat Vic Seixas and Rex Hartwig in the final, and Frank Sedgman and Bob Howe won the play-off for third place. All the games with past Champions were a great draw for the crowds who were glad to see them back. Altogether it had been a wonderful Centenary Championships which brought back many many memories of all the great Champions and tennis players over the years.

After the Centenary Championships were over, I had my usual game on the Centre Court and then Val and I went a week later for a long weekend with the Pertwees at Frinton for our annual swimming and tennis activities. After that we went to the RAF Review by The Queen at RAF Finningley in Yorkshire when we stayed a couple of days with the Thompsons at Holbeach. Back at Wimbledon at the beginning of August there was the RAF Tennis finals and the Inter-Services competition which as usual we went to. The rest of the month, apart from a few days with Sir Alan and Pam Boxer in Lymington, we were mostly at home, with Bruce and Bob a couple of the weekends, until the beginning of September when Val and I went for our annual IC Tennis and Golf weekend against the French in Le Touquet, and then on to Fontainebleau and Versailles. There Philippe Chatrier had arranged a big dinner in the Palais de Versailles for the four French Musketeers (Borotra, Cochet, Lacoste and Brugnon) to celebrate the 50th anniversary of their winning the Davis Cup. About a hundred people were there including all the Musketeer families and all the other well-known French tennis players such as Boussus, Marcel Bernard, Pierre Darmon and Destremeau. It was a great occasion. Philippe and Henri Cochet were the main speakers on their memories of those fifty years but they couldn't stop Jean Borotra also getting up to say his few words! Val and I had been invited to represent Wimbledon at their celebration and, at the dinner, Philippe asked me also to say a few words which he said he would translate into French for me. I had rather suspected I might be called upon and had prepared a little speech in my best French, which I had more or less memorized so was able to speak without any notes in French much to their surprise, particularly Philippe's who said to Val he had no idea I could speak a word of French as I never had to him over the many years we had known each other!

The next day Philippe escorted me with the four French Musketeers to the Elysée Palace where the French President Giscard d'Estaing welcomed us all to a glass or two of champagne, and later Val and I were invited to lunch by Toto Brugnon at Maximes. It was all hugely enjoyable and interesting.

We were then back to normal at home until the end of September when we had our Canadian friends Bill and Hope Pigott for a long weekend at Heather Hill before Val and I flew off to Ibiza for a ten-day summer holiday. We had managed to rent a flat in San Antonio next to Joan and Johnny H-B's which was very convenient with a shared balcony where we had breakfast together every day. After that we went for a swim in the sea and our picnic lunch on one of the many lovely beaches, followed by dinner out at the Yacht Club or different restaurants in San Antonio. A lovely holiday as always.

Soon after getting home there was the Maureen Connolly Trophy match at Torquay in Devon, between the under 21 British and American girls. As always Nancy Jeffet was in charge of the USA team so Val and I drove down to Torquay to see her and support our girls, though I am afraid they didn't win. Two weeks later the Benson and Hedges indoor tennis at Wembley was on, including most of the world top players such as Borg, Nastase and Connors, and we watched the semi-finals. Apart from those two tennis events, I was kept busy with an ITF meeting with Philippe Chatrier at Queen's Club, official lunches with the Baltic Exchange, Lloyds Shipping and with Lord Orr-Ewing at the House of Lords to 'talk Wimbledon', and the LT Writers Association dinner at the Hurlingham Club. I was also invited to a lunch in London by Sir Denis Hamilton and Marmaduke Hussey of *The Times* Newspapers Ltd. In December I had another meeting with Jerry Diamond on women's prize money and later with the press to explain our up-to-date position. One evening also with the Club Media Sub-Committee I went to a meeting followed by a dinner with BBC Radio.

Soon after that it was Christmas which we had at home with Bruce, Bob and Gus Holden with plenty of golf and bridge with them, the Holders and the Smiths. It was all good fun as ever. Val and I also went to the New Year's Eve dinner dance party at the All England Club which was a new event that year and was a great success.

1978

Early in 1978, Val and I flew to New York for the Masters Tennis at the Madison Square Gardens Stadium which had now become its regular home. We stayed at the Plaza Hotel on Central Park South with most of the other international tennis officials whom it was good to meet up with at the beginning of the tennis season. As expected the tennis was superb but Jimmy Connors started off faster than anyone, beating Borg in the final and getting away with the winner's purse of $100,000.

After flying home I got in a bit of tennis myself in the Club's Covered Courts during the next few weeks, before Val and I headed off to Geneva and our annual skiing holiday at Méribel in France. We were with most of our regular Pertwee party but with RAF friends Mike and Moyra Le Bas this time, which was good fun both on and off the slopes. On return to the UK we were back to our tennis, golf and bridge routine and I had a very pleasant invitation to dine with the RN Board, when it was good to meet up again with many of my old Admiral friends whom I had known in the Services, such as Peter Hill-Norton, Terry Lewin and Derek Empson from Singapore days, Gordon Tait from Inter-Services skiing and Jim Eberle from Navy tennis.

Other highlights around that time were a weekend with the Whitleys at Lymington and a GB King's Cup match at the Farnborough Recreation Centre, and the England v Ireland rugger match at Twickenham. There was also a meeting and dinner at the BBC/TV Centre for the Club Media Sub-Committee, a RAF 60th Anniversary Service at Westminster Abbey and the Open Squash final at Wembley which Val and I attended. I had several lunches in London – with Lloyds and Colgates (who were now the sponsors of the Masters Tennis) and with the Chairman of Barclays Bank (our Wimbledon bankers) who very kindly arranged for Val and me to be looked after and provided with a car when we were going to be in South Africa later in the year for the South African Tennis Championships. The Club annual dinner was then held this year at the Hyde Park Hotel and I was invited to an excellent dinner in the City at Inner Temple by Sir John Pennycuick. The last weekend of April we went to stay with Joan and Johnny Hartnell-Beavis at Lymington and we attended Fenella Balme's wedding with all our friends down there. Val and I also went to another wedding at Fulmer for Tara, the younger daughter of my old friend Charles Simpson, who married Mike Stotesbury, a member of the All England Club.

Towards the end of May there was the usual All England Club opening of the grass courts tournament and cocktail party, for which the Pertwees stayed with us again. There was also the Guildford LTC tournament which Peter Jackson, a member of the All England committee, now ran and who had invited me to present the prizes on the final Saturday. One day I also attended the four-yearly Order of the Bath Service, with The Queen present, at Westminster Abbey when I joined the 'Old Crocks' Race' with many of my old Service friends! For the May Bank Holiday weekend, Bob and Joan Bearder came to stay at Heather Hill and we enjoyed a game of golf every day including the Family Foursomes competition.

Val and I were then off to Paris for the second week of the French Championships staying as usual at the Résidence du Bois. Philippe Chatrier's hospitality was again marvellous and the tennis on the whole pretty exciting. Björn Borg, after beating Adriano Panatta two weeks earlier at the Italian Championships, beat Vilas at the Stade Roland Garros to become the French Champion for his third time. The Lady Champion was, a little surprisingly to me, the improving Virginia Ruzici who got everything back on the slow courts to frustrate all the other lady players.

Back at home we were busy getting ready for the Championships at Wimbledon, interrupted only by the RAF Peregrines Tennis Jubilee Dinner at RAF Halton and the cricket test match against Pakistan at Lord's. I then had my annual doubles game with Borotra as usual on the Saturday before the IC dinner dance and garden party reception at Hurlingham on the Sunday.

For the Championships, the Committee were keen to improve relations with the players and had appointed Ted Tinling to a new job as Player Liaison Officer. He was ideal for the job as he was an established figure on the tennis circuit as both player and official. For many years he had done 'call boy' duty at Wimbledon, responsible for escorting players on to court for their matches. He was also, of course, well known as the designer of women's tennis dresses and the Gussy Moran's frilly pants episode many years earlier! He therefore knew most of the players well and arranged for me the day before the Championships started to address a meeting of all the players. Also during the Championships whenever there was a rain delay he took me, and various members of the Committee, round to introduce us to the players in their restaurant. It was all good PR and, I hope, helpful to the players.

The Championships then started quietly compared with the drama and excitement of the Centenary year, though there was a close call for the Champion Borg in the first match on Centre Court when the big hitting Victor Amaya took him to 6-3 in the final set. After that the weather was appalling, particularly during the first week when there was no play at all on the Thursday. By the Friday night we were about a hundred matches awry and the Order of Play Committee decided to start play two hours earlier than usual. This led to problems for the ground staff who always mowed, rolled and marked the courts every day before play, and they threatened to go on strike. I refused to accept this and said they would all be sacked; when asked what will happen then, I said rather rashly that if necessary I was sure the members would volunteer to do the courts themselves! This seemed to take them by surprise and the threatened strike was thankfully called off.

Anyway with the extra two hours a day the Referee was able to catch up with the programme and, in the end, we were lucky to complete all the finals just a few minutes before the rain set in again. During the fortnight, however, there had been some wonderful matches with Björn Borg the eventual winner 6-2, 6-2, 6-3 in a performance of the most devastatingly brilliant tennis which many of us had ever seen on the Centre Court against his great rival Jimmy Connors. In doing so, he equalled Fred Perry's record of winning Wimbledon three years in succession. Fred was the first to congratulate him afterwards and said to the press, 'You would have to go a hell of a long way and wait years to see anything like that again.' In the Ladies' final, Martina Navratilova of Czechoslovakia won in a close 7-5 final set against Chris Evert who had beaten Virginia Wade, last year's Champion, in the semi-finals. Sadly for her the Czech Government would not allow her parents out of the country to come to Wimbledon to watch and they had to go up to near their border with Germany to watch the final on television. However Martina was, I think, pleased to find that her prize money had gone up to 90 per cent of that of the Men's Champion at Wimbledon for the first time. In the Men's Doubles the new young partnership of Peter Fleming and John McEnroe were beaten in three quick sets by the experienced pair of Bob Hewitt and Frew McMillan, previous winners in 1967 and 1972, and the Women's Doubles was won by Wendy Turnbull and Mrs Reid in three close sets.

After the Championships Val and I went for our usual summer weekend with the Pertwees at Frinton-on-Sea; then back via the Royal Worlington Golf Club and a night with Viv Crone, before going to support the RAF in the Inter-Services matches at Wimbledon. Our next move was to fly to Toronto where we had been invited by Sydney Hermant, an old friend from my Mt. Hope days and the President of the Canadian IC, to attend the Canadian Championships. We stayed in a hotel in Toronto and were taken to the tennis the last two days. I am not sure now who the Singles winners were but I think it was Eddie Dibbs and Regina Marsikova, with Tom Okker and Fibak taking the Men's Doubles. After the finals, we were collected by our Canadian friends Bill and Hope Pigott and taken for a couple of nights to their home at Ancaster near Hamilton, where we met up with a number of other old Hamilton friends. On the Monday we returned to Toronto for a game of tennis at the Toronto Queen's Club and a dinner when I was Guest of Honour and made an Honorary Member of the Canadian IC. The next day Val and I hired a car and drove up to the lakes near Muskoka where Bill and Hope lent us their lakeside cottage for a week and where we enjoyed the cooler weather. It was away from any other houses and had its own landing stage from where we were able to dive in the lake and have a daily 'skinny dip' which they all apparently did up there! We drove around the countryside some of the days, but it was lovely and peaceful being there on our own for a while before heading south again and flying to New York for the US Open.

In New York we had booked in to the River Club as usual where the Moorheads were also staying, and Uppy drove us out to the tennis every day. This was now at Flushing Meadows instead of Forest Hills. The USTA under Slew Hester had broken away from their long-term relationship with the West Side Tennis Club on Long Island after their 1977 Championships. I am not sure of all the reasons but the players were not happy with the courts there. Grass courts in America are difficult to maintain and get cut up easily by the players, so after many complaints from players they had replaced the main stadium grass courts at Forest Hills with the grey 'Har True' clay courts in around 1975. These were much slower and suited the clay court experts such as Manuel Orantes of Spain, who won that year, and Chris Evert who they felt was unbeatable on the slow surface and had then won the Ladies' Singles several years in a row. Forest Hills was also short of car parking space and the only other way to get there was by train and then quite a walk, and also quite a walk from the Club House facilities to the Courts, which was by no means ideal. The USTA had conveniently just negotiated a new and very lucrative TV contract, so decided to construct a new $6 million Tennis Centre on the site of the 1964 World Fair at Flushing Meadow. This project involved the re-building of the city-owned Armstrong Stadium which they remarkably completed within the twelve months before the 1978 Championships. It also had the advantage of being able to use the car park of the nearby Shay Baseball Stadium. The only snag was that it was not far from the end of the runway at La Guardia Airport, so that aircraft taking off were frequently very low over the stadium. The old Armstrong Stadium was cleverly divided into two, with one half built up to provide seating for 20,000 people for their main court and the other half converted into their No. 1 court stadium. All the courts in the grounds were hard and made of a new faster surface called Deco Turf which the USTA have used ever since and which are usually referred to as cement courts.

The first weekend of their Championships was American Labour Day and the Moorheads took us down to Rumson to stay with them. Whilst there, Uppy arranged some tennis for me at the Seabright Club with Larry Krieger, Secretary of their IC, and their new Chairman Paul Lambert and when introducing me to his friends always mentioned that we had originally met in 1933 in the Harvard-Yale v Oxford-Cambridge Prentice Cup match. They always asked me who won, so it was great to be able to say, 'I did!' Val and I also had a couple of games of golf with Uppy at his Tequesta Club, and it all made a very enjoyable break from nearly always watching rather than playing tennis. Back in New York there were the usual USTA and US/IC dinners which were always good fun, and one morning Uppy and I had a game of tennis on the River Club indoor court against Judge Bob Kelleher (ex USTA President) and Donald Dell. Otherwise we went with the Moorheads every day to Flushing Meadow where again we met up with Slew Hester and some of our other American friends such as Hockey Woods, the Mallesses, Bill Clothier and the Delatours as well as most of the other International Tennis representatives, during the lunch interval.

The tennis went more or less according to plan and the seeding, with the added excitement, I remember, of the young sixteen-year-old Pam Shriver fighting her way through to the final using one of the first large Prince rackets. There unfortunately she succumbed to a brilliant Chris Evert who became the Lady Champion for the fourth year in succession. In the Men's Singles Jimmy Connors, playing superbly on the fast Deco Turf court, won for the third time surprisingly easily against Björn Borg in three sets.

When the tennis was all over Val and I flew back to the UK and after a bit of a rest at home, we flew out to Ibiza for our summer holiday in the flat next to the Hartnell-Beavises. The Whitleys and the Harvey-Millers came with us this year too and so we hired a couple of cars and all joined up every day for our picnic lunch and swim at one of the many lovely sandy beaches.

We got back in time to attend a Davis Cup match at the Crystal Palace, have Hugh Johnstone for the weekend and various Club and Wimbledon Committee of Management meetings. A particularly important one at that time involved the decision to accept a change in the method of re-turfing badly worn areas (for example the base lines) on the grass courts. This had always been done from the mature grass on the sides of the court which was then replaced from our small turf nursery. The job was thus having to be done twice. ICI now offered to provide a much larger turf nursery at their Fernhurst research centre in Sussex where they could have enough mature turf for us to use straight on the courts. They took deep samples of the soil at Wimbledon and reproduced the exact growing conditions, so we thought this was a good idea and Jack Yardley, our Head Groundsman at the time, looked forward in two or three years' time to doing the turf replacement job direct. Unfortunately this did not work out very well in the end.

In November there was the excitement of the Wightman Cup in London at the Albert Hall in which the British team of Virginia Wade, Sue Barker, Michelle Tyler, Anne Hobbs and Sue Mappin won by four matches to three against the United States team of Chris Evert, Tracy Austin, Pam Shriver and Billie-Jean King. It was a great match which, rather against the usual form, went to the final set of the last doubles match and ended in a standing ovation in the Albert Hall well deserved by both teams. Two weeks later there was the annual Benson and Hedges Indoor Championships at Wembley featuring most of the world's top men's players including Borg, Connors, Nastase, Panatta, Gerulaitis, Ashe and our Mark Cox. Val and I managed to go to some of these matches but couldn't get to all of them.

The last week of the month we flew to South Africa where Val and I were invited for their Championships in Johannesburg, but we had a week's holiday first at the Beverley Hills hotel by the sea at Umhlanga Rocks near Durban. Whilst we were there, the sea was a bit rough for swimming but it was lovely walking along the sea front watching the waves breaking on the rocks. Also we had been lent a car by the SA

Tennis Association so enjoyed driving around to see some more of the country, including calling in to see some ex-RAF friends near Pietermaritzburg. In Durban also we had a bit of a walk around the main golf course, which I was interested to see, before meeting an old friend of mine from Wadham College, Norman Knight, who was also the brother of our great friend Joan Bearder, for dinner. After this splendid week's introduction to South Africa we flew from Durban to Johannesburg where we were met by Margaret and Blen Franklin, the South African Tennis President who took us off to the Sunnyside Park Hotel where we stayed five days to attend the tennis. There was a SA/IC dinner one evening and we went out to lunch with all the Franklin family at their house in the country on the Sunday. We had met Blen several years at Wimbledon but it was good to meet him again with his family and in his own environment, where he looked after us so hospitably. After the Men's final, which Heinz Gunthardt of Switzerland won, I was invited to present him with the Championship trophy which I gladly did. The next day Val and I flew to Port Elizabeth on the east coast and spent several days relaxing at the Beacon Island Hotel at Plettenburg Bay. We also called in to see an old RAF tennis friend, Group Captain Young, and his wife who were living there. Heading further south we drove to the small airport of George and flew down from there to Cape Town, where we were booked in for a week at the President Hotel on Beach Road overlooking the sea and a good sandy beach. Whilst there we were kindly taken out for a long drive in the country by the Chairman of the South African Barclay's Bank and his wife to see the well-known wine district and have lunch there. He also arranged for us to be lent a car while we were in the Cape, so we were able to get around a bit including visiting an old girlfriend of mine, Joy Cox, now Pickering and married and living in the country about an hour out of town. Val and I also, of course, went to the top of Table Mountain one day as well as right down to the southernmost part of the Cape, and I made a point of visiting their tennis facilities and their renowned rugby stadium. Finally after a wonderful two weeks in South Africa we flew back over-night to England in time for the All England Club AGM at the Café Royal and the Staff Christmas lunch party.

At Heather Hill, Bruce came for ten days over Christmas – also Gus and Joan Bearder – and we had a lot of golf with them and David Smith.

1979

Early in 1979 Val and I set off for New York to attend the Colgate Masters Tennis, now held in the Madison Square Gardens stadium. This time they kindly put us up in style in the Colgate suite at the Waldorf Towers which was super. There was some excellent tennis again, as expected, with Borg beating McEnroe 7-6 in the final set and Gerulaitis beating Connors in the semi-finals, though Borg won the final very convincingly in straight sets. The next morning I remember it was snowing hard but we got away just in time before New York became completely snowbound.

After a couple of weeks at home, Val and I flew out to Geneva for our annual skiing holiday at Méribel with the Pertwee party. It was very good fun as usual although, according to my diary, the weather was not too good for skiing with rather a lot of cloud, fog and sleet and only four sunny days which was a pity. When we got home again Bruce and Bob both came for the weekend and I was back to normal with meetings at the Club and my tennis and bridge there every Tuesday. Val unfortunately was caught for doing her turn of Jury Service for several days in Guildford, but enjoyed having Betty Rowlands, Viv Crone and Joan Bearder to stay three of the weekends. Bob and his new girlfriend Val also came to stay one weekend which was great and the first time we had met her. One day we also went down to Chichester for their squash finals and another day to the Open Squash final at Wembley. In May Val and I also went again to the Football Cup Final at Wembley and I kept in touch with the RAF at the Air Marshal's Lunch when the CAS briefed us all on the latest developments.

The grass court season was now upon us and we had the usual American tournament at the Club followed by the annual cocktail party, and the Pertwees joined us again for that weekend.

Our next move early in June was to fly to Paris for the French Championships again. We got to our Résidence du Bois in time to attend the World Champions Dinner, which Philippe Chatrier as President of the ILTF organized at the super Pre Catalan restaurant in the Bois du Boulogne. The rest of the programme in Paris and at Stade Roland Garros was very enjoyable as usual and it was interesting to see the various improvements Philippe was making each year including the statues of the Four Musketeers. The tennis on the slow red clay courts was excellent with Borg as the Men's Champion again and Chris Evert (now married to our British player John Lloyd) the winner of the Ladies'. We were back in England in time for the opening of the enlarged Debenture Holders Lounge and the four new grass courts on the north side of the Centre Court. There was also the Première of the 'Players' film in London starring Ali McGraw which we went to, and at the Club the usual last minute completion and tidying up of the works services improvements for the Championships. Val and I also moved into the small flat at the Club cottage for the two weeks and I had my usual four at tennis with Jean Borotra, Gus and Buzzer on Court 3 on the Saturday prior to the IC dinner dance at the Kensington Gardens Hotel, and the IC garden party and overseas reception at Hurlingham on the Sunday.

It was then all the normal procedure as the 1979 Championships got going with the Champion Borg on the Centre Court in the presence of our president, the Duke of Kent, and the Duchess. There were the meetings with the umpires and stewards and the media and as the tournament progressed the various official lunches and drinks parties. Like Borg the previous year, the Ladies' Champion Martina Navratilova had a fright in her opening match, losing the first set before winning comfortably in the end. Martina may have been a bit nervous to start with as her mother, at the special invitation of the All England Club, had been allowed out by the Czech Government to watch her this year and was in the players' friends box seeing her play for the first time in four years. Fortunately for her, though, she came through to beat Chris Evert (Lloyd) in the final. It was Shakespeare who once said, 'Uneasy lies the head that wears the crown' – but not Björn Borg's! He went through the draw pretty easily including Connors in three sets in the semi-finals and then beat Tanner in five sets in one of the best finals for years to make it four years for him in a row. In the Men's Doubles John McEnroe and Peter Fleming won for the first of many times, whilst Billie-Jean King and Martina Navratilova won the Women's Doubles. Sadly, on the second Friday, Elizabeth (Bunny) Ryan, one of the greatest Ladies' Doubles Champions of all times, who jointly held with Billie-Jean the record of nineteen Wimbledon titles, died whilst at the All England Club. At least she did not know that her treasured record was to be beaten the next day by Billie-Jean with her twenty Wimbledon titles. After the finals it all ended as usual with the Champions' Dinner at the Savoy.

My brother Douglas had been staying with friends in London and came with Val and me a couple of days to Wimbledon before spending several days with us at Heather Hill afterwards. There was my usual game on the Centre Court with some of the Committee on the Monday before a meeting to discuss improvements for the next year. Plans were approved to extend the stands on Court 2 to provide an extra 370 seats, making over 2,000 there in all. Another major development, which started straight away, was the raising of the Centre Court roof by three feet which provided another 1,100 odd seats. This would help to make up for the loss of seats due to stringent new fire precautions, with widening of the Centre Court gangways and two new staircases on the east and west sides of the court. This was quite a major project with the roof having been there for over sixty years and I remember later hurrying back from the US Open to make certain all was going well and the Centre Court not collapsing! With the growing popularity of Wimbledon, of course, more and more seats were required and, as an example of the pressure for them, I always remember the story of the empty seat on the Centre Court when after a while the man behind asked the lady in the next seat whether her husband was coming as it was wasting a valuable seat. The lady replied, 'No – he has unfortunately died.' The man then said how sorry he was but could she not have brought a friend? The lady's reply was again, ' No – they've all gone to the funeral!'

After that we were busy at home with the Hogans one weekend, when we had Bill and Jean Hobson for lunch, and Joan Bearder for another weekend. We also went for our annual visit to the Pertwees at Frinton, and the Thompsons at Holbeach on the way back. We called in for a night to see Bruce in his new little house at Wistow which he had bought so as to live out while at RAF Wyton. At the end of the month there was a farewell party at the Club for David Mills who was retiring after doing so much for the Club and the Championships for about sixteen years as the Assistant Secretary and then the Secretary, in the days before we brought in a Championship Director, a Financial Director and Marketing Director as well to help. Fortunately I had a good replacement to hand in Chris Gorringe, the Assistant Secretary for the last six years.

It was then time again for the Inter-Services tennis at the Club and several weekends of tennis with Bruce and golf with Bob. We also had a lovely weekend of golf with Cyril and Margot Boyes, old friends of Val, who came to stay at Heather Hill. Towards the end of September we were then due for our annual summer holiday in Ibiza with the H-Bs which was great as always.

Soon after we got home we flew to Spain again to Barcelona where we had been invited by Pablo Lorenz, the President of the Spanish Tennis

Association to attend the week of the Spanish Championships. We stayed at a good hotel nearby, where Philippe Chatrier and Heinz Grimm of Switzerland were also staying, so we had a very enjoyable time there. With Heinz I had a game of tennis against a couple of the Spanish IC players one morning, but Val and I spent most of the time watching the tennis at the Real Club and being entertained by Pablo and Jésus Serra the President of the Club.

We then had a week at Heather Hill before Val and I flew out, over the Pole, to Tokyo where I was due to open a Wimbledon Trade Fair being organized by Mamiya of Dentsu Incorporated at the Seibo Department Store. Bimby Holt, the Vice-Chairman and Daphne, and Chris Gorringe, now the AELTC Secretary, came with us – the latter carefully guarding the Wimbledon trophies which are not normally allowed out of the country but were due to be on display in Japan – and we all stayed at the huge Takanawa Prince Hotel. After a day of meetings with some of the interested Japanese sports companies for me, and shopping for Val, we held the Opening Ceremony for the Trade Fair which was attended by the British Ambassador, Sir Michael Wilford, who had stayed with us in 1971 in Singapore. This was followed by a press

Val and I at the opening of Wimbledon LT Museum in Tokyo with British Ambassador Sir Mike and Lady Wilford and Borg

conference and reception. We also went up to the top floor of the department store to meet some of their young players and watch the Wimbledon Champion Björn Borg give a brief exhibition on the roof-top court. He was fortunately playing in the Seiko tournament and was able to come and help us.

Tennis in Japan was growing rapidly and there was a great demand for anything to do with Wimbledon, including tennis clothing with our 'W' logo on it. We got income from royalties in Japan which increased enormously with the help of Mark McCormack and his International Management Group. Hence the idea of the Trade Fair to boost this marketing.

On the Saturday we were driven out by Mamiya to see some of the country and Mt. Fuji and there was a Japanese IC dinner. On Sunday we went to the Japanese Open Tennis finals and their Federation dinner, and the next day I had further meetings with the Japanese tennis firms and we went to a Seiko reception in the evening.

Val and I then flew down to Los Angeles and then to West Palm Beach in Florida to support our Wightman Cup team in their match against the USA at the Wellington Country Club. For this we stayed with our friends Uppy and Ginny Moorhead who had a house not far away at Tequesta. We went with them each day for the tennis where we met up with many other friends which was fun, but the match was very disappointing. Although we had Virginia Wade, Sue Barker, Anne Hobbs and Jo Durie, we lost all seven matches against Chris Evert, Tracy Austin, Kathy Jordan and Rosie Casals. When that was over, we flew back to the UK after two interesting weeks away and it was good to get back to our usual routine with tennis, bridge and golf, meetings at the Club and the boys home most weekends.

During the last two Wimbledons I had received lots of letters saying, 'Why can't we have all British commentators?' The general public in England were proud of Wimbledon and our traditions, and wished to keep it all British. This was really up to the BBC who were, however, strongly in favour of keeping to Jack Kramer of the USA, in partnership with our inimitable Dan Maskell. I had tried in vain to persuade Slim Wilkinson, the BBC/TV Executive, to make a change but for two years he had refused. Our committee felt that the public's point of view was important to us and I thought John Barrett, who had been our main commentator on Court 1 for several years, would be ideal. At the dinner that month with the BBC I pressed Alasdair Milne, the Managing

Director of BBC Television, on the matter, virtually threatening not to sign the new contract with the BBC which was due for renewal unless they went further to meet the All England Club views. This did the trick and for next year they did appoint John Barrett instead of Jack Kramer and this worked out very well. However, Jack and a lot of the players felt that Wimbledon was discriminating against him because of his part as ATP's Executive Director in supporting the players' boycott of Wimbledon in 1973. I now had many letters, such as from Arthur Ashe, John Newcombe, Cliff Drysdale and others, saying we were being unfair to Kramer in that it was definitely the players, not he, who had insisted on the big boycott. I have found it difficult to persuade them that this was not the reason for the change and that it was at the request of the British public – but you can't win! However, John Barrett has done us very well and is only just retiring after more than thirty years in the job.

14

THE EIGHTIES

1980

In 1980 I was extremely sorry to lose my Private Secretary (Enid Stopka) at the All England Club who retired on grounds of ill health. She had been one of the first to join the staff of the All England Club in 1946 and served in many different capacities, including handling the ballot and allocation of tickets and taking the minutes of all the many Committee and Sub-Committee meetings. She had also made herself invaluable with the hundreds of invitations to the Royal Box and with her many contacts with the Royal Household, the Embassies, overseas tennis officials, ex-Champions, players and others. She was extremely popular also with all the members and helped to organize many of the Club parties or functions, and was thrilled when she was deservedly made an Honorary Member in 1977. Fortunately I was lucky to get a very good successor in Paula McMillan who took over very quickly and well.

At Wimbledon all was going well with the raising of the Centre Court roof gradually inch by inch, and other changes, so Val and I went off happily on the Southampton-Le Havre overnight ferry and drove down to Méribel for our annual skiing holiday. Actually this time we went first for a couple of days to stay with the Balmes who had bought their own flat at Méribel-Mottaret just a few miles up the valley. We then moved in to La Gelinotte to join up with the Pertwees, Hartnell-Beavises, McGrigors and a new couple, Bill and Nan Fea. As usual it was all great fun. Bruce, who was on holiday also at that time in Courcheval skied over one day to ski with us at Méribel, and Val and I skied over to Courcheval another day to ski with him over there.

Soon after driving home, I was sad to hear of the death of an old school friend, Roddy Fyler, who had been a Major-General in the Army and had taken over from me about five years earlier as President of the Squash

Rackets Association. The Patron of the SRA, Prince Philip the Duke of Edinburgh, asked me to represent him at the Memorial Service at Beaconsfield which I gladly did as I was going to it anyway with Val to support Anthea, Roddy's wife, whom we knew well. I also maintained my connections with the services when I was invited to lunch at the House of Lords by General Lord Bourne who had been the Commandant when I was at the IDC and also my opposite number as President of the Army Tennis. Val and I also went to dinner one evening with the new Chief of the Air Staff, Mike Beetham, and his wife Pattie.

A major excitement, however, was in March when Bruce, having announced his engagement in January to his latest very attractive girlfriend, Chryssie, came to Heather Hill for the weekend when they arranged to have their bans read in our local church in Seale. At the end of the month then, Val and I drove up to Boston in Lincolnshire to meet George and Joan Baxter, our future in-laws. We stayed the weekend with the Thompsons at Holbeach Hurn not far away which was very convenient. We then had three normal weeks at home, with the All England Club Dinner at the Institute of Directors in London and much for me to do at Wimbledon before we drove north again to Boston for Bruce and Chryssie's wedding on 26 April. Val and I stayed with the Thompsons again for it and Bob who was best man, stayed with David and Caroline Thompson also nearby at Holbeach. The wedding was super with Chryssie looking lovely, and the Baxters gave an excellent reception and lunch party afterwards at the Woodhall Spa Golf Hotel.

Not long after getting back home there was the All England Club opening of the grass courts and annual cocktail party, with the Pertwees staying and also Bruce and Chryssie back from their honeymoon. The summer tennis season having already started Val and I were off again soon to La Résidence du Bois in Paris for the French Championships which we always greatly enjoyed and which Borg and Chris Evert-Lloyd both won again. Then there was The Queen's Tournament, the important warm-up on grass before the Championships at Wimbledon. All was now ready at the Club with its raised Centre Court roof and other major improvements to the north and east stands. The ball then literally started with the IC dinner dance and Hurlingham garden party before the battles on court began on Monday 23 June.

Unfortunately rain bedevilled play most of the first week and, although we were able to use the four new courts on the north side of the Centre Court for the first time, this year we were forced to start play earlier at

Bruce and Chryssie's wedding

12.00 p.m. every day. An interesting innovation this year was the introduction of the 'magic eye' (Cyclops) on the Centre and No. 1 Courts to help with the service line decisions. This proved to be a great success in cutting out players' arguments with linesmen and umpires, and was adopted by many other Championships except those on clay, where the ball usually leaves a mark which the umpire can get down from his chair to check.

In the Ladies' Singles all the top seeds got through to the last eight including the fourteen-year-old Andrea Jaeger from the USA, who beat Virginia Wade, the Centenary Year Champion, on the way. She then lost to Chris (Evert) Lloyd who in turn beat Martina Navratilova, last year's Champion, to reach the final for the sixth time. She too, however, then lost to Evonne (Goolagong) Cawley, the Champion of nine years earlier who had seen off Tracy Austin in a very close semi-final match before winning the final in a second set tie-break. This was the first time a Wimbledon final had been won in a tie-break and the first by a married 'mum' since Mrs Lambert Chambers in 1913! From the Seeding Committee's point of view it had been the perfect Ladies' semi-final with the four top seeds reaching their appointed places.

In the Men's Singles Borg went through fairly comfortably against Gottfried, and John McEnroe beat Jimmy Connors in the other semi-final in a hard fought contest of four sets between two pugnacious opponents. McEnroe was at his argumentative worst at times, and the Referee had to be sent for when he was given an official warning before he went on to get his revenge on Connors who had beaten him in the semi-final in 1977. When he and Borg walked on to the Centre Court two days later the crowd actually booed McEnroe to show their disapproval of his frequent bad behaviour. This must have impressed him as throughout the long final he behaved impeccably.

The final started with McEnroe winning the first set, then Borg the next two before leading 5-4 and 40-15 with two Championship points in the fourth set. These were both saved with brilliant shots by McEnroe who won six points in a row to draw level and enter the tie-break with a somewhat shaken Champion. The tie-break itself was the best and most exciting any of us had seen. It lasted more than twenty minutes, with both players in turn producing unbelievable passing shots and volleys. Borg had five match points and McEnroe seven set points before the latter scrambled through by 18 points to 16 to level the match at two sets all. After this set-back we all felt Borg might react badly but both players continued to play incredibly well and hung on to their services until at 6-7 McEnroe faced his eighth match point and Borg became Champion again for the fifth year in a row. The final had arguably been the best ever and had lasted nearly four hours with all of us, including the Duke and Duchess of Kent, riveted to our seats throughout. The standing ovation for both players, including McEnroe as he had behaved well and put up such a great fight, went on for a long time and during the Cup presentation on court, I was told later that over 63 million watched the final on NBC Television which was on 'live' at breakfast time in New York.

Other interesting results at Wimbledon in 1980 were the Australians McNamara and McNamee winning the Men's Doubles after beating McEnroe and Fleming, the holders, in the semi-finals and Lutz and Stan Smith in an excellent four-set final. It was also good to see J.R. and Tracy Austin, brother and sister, win the Mixed Doubles for the first time. In line with the other Grand Slam tournaments, prize money at Wimbledon had gone up again and was now more than £294,000.

After the Championships I had my usual game on the Centre Court with Chris Gorringe and members of the Club committee. There were several Club meetings to confirm the arrangements for further alterations to the north stand of the Centre Court and the virtual re-building of the No. 1 Court south stand. This was to provide an extra 700 seats in the north stand and 550 in the Court 1 south stand plus a larger players' restaurant, lounge and writing room as well as new offices for the Referee, umpires and ball boys.

Val and I then had our regular weekend up at Frinton with the Pertwees and a night stop again with Bruce on the way back near Huntingdon. Back at home I was able to get in my weekly tennis at Wimbledon where Val and I also went again to the Inter-Services tennis, before a very enjoyable weekend with Norman and Mary Melhuish at Penshurst in Kent. They took us on a very interesting visit to look round Chartwell, Churchill's old house.

By the end of August we were due to fly to New York for the US Open Tennis. We had booked in at our favourite River Club where we were met again by Uppy and Ginny Moorhead and had dinner with Helen MacPherson, who wanted to show me her late husband (Arthur's) many gold tennis trophies which he had won in Russia long before World War II and which she did not know what to do with as she was moving into a smaller apartment. I suggested she should give them to the US Hall of Fame at Newport, Rhode Island, but said that we would be delighted otherwise to have them in the Wimbledon Museum where I was sure they would be given a place of honour. Arthur MacPherson had, of course, been a very well known American Doubles player with Watson Washburn for many years around the 1920s. Helen preferred the latter idea, so I invited her over to the Championships the next year when she could bring them over and present them to the Wimbledon Museum, which she did.

After a couple of days at the tennis at Flushing Meadow, the Moorheads took us off for the weekend to Rumson where we played some tennis with Larry Krieger and Paul Lambert, the President of Seabright Tennis club, on their excellent grass courts. We then went back to the River Club in New York for the rest of the US Championships at Flushing Meadow, with their great hospitality including dinners every night with the US/IC, the USTA, Hockey and Mary Woods, Hunter and Eugénie Delatour, the Mallesses and the Tuckers. At one of the lunch intervals I was invited to a meeting of the US Wingfield Club which they had formed some years earlier in honour of Major Henry Clopton-Wingfield, the English founder of the lawn tennis game, and I was elected an Honorary Member. In the tennis, the Men's Singles was won by McEnroe in an excellent match 6-4 in the final set against Borg who never seemed to quite make it in America. Chris (Evert) Lloyd won the Ladies for the fifth time, beating Hana Mandlikova, also in the final set. In the Doubles, McEnroe and Fleming won the Men's again as did Billie-Jean King and Martina Navratilova the Women's.

It had been a very enjoyable ten days in the USA and we flew back to the UK in time for the visit of the Lugano Lido Club to Wimbledon when we joined in taking them all to dinner and the theatre in London. Later that month we flew again to Ibiza for a lovely break of sunshine and bathing in the Mediterranean with Joan and Johnny H-B, the Whitleys and other friends from Lymington. On returning home I had a number of club meetings at Wimbledon and the Veterans LTC and LT Writers Association dinners in London. There was also the Wightman Cup match at the Albert Hall which Val and I went to, including the dinner afterwards at the Kensington Hilton though there was not much to celebrate as the US with Chris Evert, Kathy Jordan and Andrea Jaeger defeated our Virginia Wade, Sue Barker and Anne Hobbs rather easily by 6 matches to 1. However, one of the mornings I was able to enjoy having Hunter Delatour and Jo Carrico, the new USTA Chairman, who were over to support their Wightman cup team, to lunch and a game of tennis at Wimbledon with me and Ted Frith.

The rest of the year, November and December, was back to normal at home but with my weekly tennis at the Club and several other days there each week for meetings with Philippe Chatrier, Bucholz of the USA, Mark McCormack, Bagenal Harvey, and Knight Frank & Rutley. We had the Club AGM at the Café Royal mid-December and then for Christmas Joan Bearder, Johnny and Joan and Gus came to us at Heather Hill when we had a lot of golf and bridge.

1981

Early in the New Year there was the Masters Tennis again in New York – now taken over by Volvo – but we didn't go to it as I was very busy with one thing or another: a press conference, Ground Company Board meeting, Club and Committee of Management meetings. Val and I then later drove off for our annual skiing holiday in Méribel. It snowed the first few days, I remember, but it was then lovely and sunny for the remaining ten days we were there, with excellent skiing conditions. We were so lucky and with most of our usual gang at the super La Gelinotte châlet plus Paul and Mary Lambert, who Norman had persuaded to fly over from Seabright in America, it was great fun.

Soon after we got back Bruce and Chryssie came for the weekend as well as Bob for the next two. In the meantime, Val had got keen on her painting again and went to her weekly painting class, while I was back to my regular tennis and bridge at the All England Club plus numerous other meetings there. In particular in March we had the Wimbledon Ground Company AGM when amongst other things we decided on the next Debenture Issue, which is so vital for funding all the expensive works services improvements at the Club. Later there was also the Club AGM, the 'Topping Out' party for the new buildings on Court 1 and the Club dinner. Val and I also went to the lunch and Cup Final at Wembley again in May, before the Members' tournament and opening of the grass court season at the All England Club.

After that we flew off again to Paris for the French Championships at the Stade Roland Garros. We stayed as usual at our favourite La Résidence du Bois where Bimby and Daphne Holt joined us and where our Australian friends the Turpins and Sedgmans were also staying. It was good fun as always with Philippe Chatrier's wonderful hospitality when he took us all to the best restaurants for dinner every evening, including the Moulin Rouge, Maxime's, Maison Laffitte, the Lido and a place in the Latin Quarter. There was also the special dinner for the official reigning World Champions which Philippe had started in 1978. The international panel of judges were Don Budge, Lew Hoad and Fred Perry for the men, and Margaret Du Pont, Althea Gibson and Ann Jones for the women. They made their assessment at the end of each year based on results at the game's Grand Slams and other most important events, and the presentations were made each year in Paris during the French Championships. Borg had been voted the World Champion for the last three years but McEnroe was the number one choice for 1981 and after a very difficult choice over Tracy Austin, Chris (Evert) Lloyd was voted the Women's World Champion for her third time in four years. This did not, however, prevent Borg winning the Men's French Championships this year for his sixth time, nor Hana Mandlikova from beating Chris in the women's semi-finals before going on to win the final too. It only went to show how difficult the judges found it to choose between the top players that year.

On returning to England, there was the Queen's Club Tournament when we went to the finals before getting ready for our Championships with the many alterations to Court 1 and Court 2. Other changes were a new contract which Bimby and I had arranged with the Rolex Watch Company of Geneva to replace the twenty-two clocks around the grounds and up-date the entire digital time-keeping system, including duration of matches. Also for the first time there was a merchandising area or shop where products made under licence for the All England Club could be bought. This was a great success and added considerably to the Championship profits for the benefit of our LTA. There was another spectacular addition to this year's Wimbledon scene with the new official uniforms for the umpires and linesmen, which were presented to the Club by ICI Fibres. They were very smart in the official Club green for the blazers and pale green for the trousers and ladies' skirts. It was a pity, I thought, that some years later these were changed to blue and white instead of the traditional green although I understand there were considerable financial and other reasons for the change.

A few days before the Championships started this year our American friends Uppy and Ginny Moorhead came over on the *Queen Elizabeth* to stay at Shepperton near the Avorys and I had them to lunch at the Club and a game of tennis for Uppy on grass court 4 with Bimby and Ted Frith making up the four. We saw a lot of them during the Championships including one day in the Royal Box and they came to stay with us a couple of days afterwards when Uppy was thrilled when I invited him to join my Chairman's game on the Centre Court.

At the Championships that year the obvious top seeds for the Men's Singles were Borg, McEnroe, Lendl and Connors. Lendl went out in the first round to Fancutt of Australia, but the three others reached their allotted places in the semi-finals. Then Borg beat Connors in five sets whilst McEnroe beat Frawley of Australia in three closely fought sets when McEnroe's tantrums were apparently at their worst. I didn't see the match myself, as I was busy looking after some of the Royal visitors at that time, but I was told later that McEnroe should have been disqualified by the Referee. As it was, he had been lucky not to have been disqualified in his first round match against Tom Gullikson. However, he got away with it, and in the final he again behaved impeccably and in four close sets got his revenge on Borg for his defeat in last year's memorable final, thus becoming the Wimbledon Champion for the first time. He and Peter Fleming also won the Men's Doubles, for the second time. In the Ladies' Singles, the four top seeds were Chris (Evert) Lloyd, Hana Mandlikova, Tracy Austin and Martina Navratilova and, apart from Tracy who was beaten in the fourth round by Pam Shriver, all got through to the semi-finals. Lloyd then beat Shriver and Mandlikova won in three sets against Navratilova but lost in a disappointing match to Chris (Evert) Lloyd who after failing in three successive finals regained the title that she won in 1974 and 1976. Navratilova and Shriver won the Ladies' Doubles for their first time together, and Frew McMillan and Betty Stove won the Mixed Doubles for their second time against the Austin brother and sister winners of last year.

Unfortunately at the Champions Dinner at the Savoy Hotel in London, John McEnroe failed to turn up. He had been warned about it earlier by the senior committee member, Rex Sterry, when he had reached the final, though he apparently implied then that he would prefer to go out and celebrate with his chums. After he had won he was told about it again in the men's locker room by my Vice-Chairman Bimby Holt. I was unable to do so myself as I had the Duke of Kent and other Royals to look after at that time. John, however, pleaded exhaustion and said he just wanted to relax and celebrate with a few beers with his buddies. He suggested he might stop by later for a coffee and dessert but we felt that this would not be appropriate or do justice to the big occasion which was to honour both the Champions and was the main event concluding the Championships. We still hoped he would come and we waited for John at the dinner table for some time before starting, but expecting him possibly to turn up later. Unfortunately he didn't do so and when it came to the Champions' speeches Chris Evert-Lloyd, the Lady Champion, nobly spoke on behalf of both of them. This was the time McEnroe as the Champion would have been made an Honorary Member of the AELTC and presented with his Club tie, so he missed out on it and the Committee agreed later not to make him a member, anyway for the time being, in view of his discourteous behaviour.

Incidentally, in those days as Chairman of Wimbledon, I used to get many letters from headmasters of schools saying, 'For God's sake, do something about McEnroe's behaviour and his tantrums. All our young boys and girls are starting to copy him by abusing umpires and referees, and refusing to accept their decisions. This can't be allowed to go on.' This was really such a shame as John could perfectly well control himself, as he always did when playing Borg whom he greatly respected. He was such an incredibly good player we would have been only too delighted, if he behaved properly, to encourage the young to watch him and copy his stroke play, without the tantrums and often appalling behaviour.

When McEnroe realized later that it was for the first time in a hundred years that he as Champion was not being made an Honorary Member of the All England Club, it began to hit him, and his father even offered to fly over to apologise on his behalf if we would rescind that decision. Our Committee, however, didn't feel that was good enough unless John came to apologise himself, and he had to wait another two years until he won Wimbledon again in 1983, as he was beaten by Connors in 1982.

When Wimbledon was over Val and I went for our usual weekend with the Pertwees in Frinton. Vivy, Douglas' daughter, arrived from Australia and stayed with us for three weeks while she did a refresher course at the RAE Farnborough on Systems Assessments, in which she had a very good job in Melbourne with the Australian Defence Ministry helping to assess the F16 against the F11 aircraft, I believe. We enjoyed having her to stay and she managed to get a lift daily to and from Farnborough with an Australian neighbour of ours who was also then working at Farnborough which saved us lending her Val's car the whole time. It is interesting perhaps to note that her salary in Australia was more than that of our head man at Farnbrough at that time apparently.

At the Club we had our usual meetings to discuss improvement plans for the next year, and I was able to fit in my weekly tennis and bridge there. I also took Vivy to watch the Inter-Services Tennis to remind her of when her father, Douglas, used to run the Army Tennis.

Apart from a weekend then with Joan and Johnny H-B in Lymington we were mostly at home until Val and I flew to New York for the US Championships at Flushing Meadow. We stayed as usual at the River Club, going to the tennis every day with the Moorheads, but on the middle Labor Day weekend Val and I were taken to stay with Hockey and Mary Woods in New Jersey where Hockey had arranged a game of tennis for me with Larry Krieger and a couple of others. The programme during the Championships at Flushing Meadow was much the same and as always very enjoyable. In the Men's semi-finals McEnroe defeated Vilas in an excellent five-setter before winning the final again the next day in four sets against Borg. In the Ladies' Singles final Tracy Austin scraped home 7-6 in a final set tie-break which must have been heart-breaking for Martina Navratilova in her first final there. I was glad at Wimbledon we always insist on a final set being played out fully.

After returning home I had a very busy week of meetings at the Club and only one game of tennis myself before Val and I set off on our summer holiday with Douglas and Andrée at La Thébaïde in Grasse. We had a leisurely journey driving down there with two night stops, one at Beaune and the other at Méribel, our favourite ski resort, which I wanted to see in the summer with its golf course. The latter was rather disappointing as it was pouring with rain, the golf course flooded, and the village deserted. Most of the châlets and hotels were closed and we were only able to get a room for the night in a hotel crowded with all the workmen building new ski lifts. It was still raining in the morning and we were glad to move on, though Val had unfortunately left her new bedroom slippers under the bed. It is extraordinary the little things one remembers! On reaching Grasse we were greeted by a very heavy rainstorm and the main road down into the town from the mountains was a complete river. However, all was well later and the usual lovely sunny weather returned for the rest of our week with them. We then had another lovely week further along the coast at Le Lavandou in Bruce's large caravan which he kept there for holidays and occasional letting. It was in a large caravan complex high up above the town and only ten minutes in the car down to the sea. He had got a good secluded site away from the rest of the caravans so Val and I enjoyed a lovely quiet holiday there, going down for a swim in the sea in the mornings and to different restaurants for dinner in the evenings. We finally drove home, stopping for a night at our favourite place in Beaune, where we stocked up always with our full allowance of wine to take back into England.

The autumn was again a busy time for meetings at the Club regarding 'Promotions' and works service improvements of facilities including those in Aorangi Park for the public; but I soon got back to my regular four days a week at the Club and my weekly game of tennis, in the covered courts if necessary. There was also the IC match at the Club against the French IC which Val and I watched and then attended the reception and dinner afterwards with Abdesselam and Jean Borotra who always made a point of coming.

In November Val and I had an interesting invitation to dinner and the night at Windsor Castle with my ex-boss MRAF Sir John Grandy and his wife Cécile. He was now the Governor of the Castle and had an apartment there in the Norman Tower. The next morning they kindly showed us all round bits of the Castle which we hadn't seen before.

At the beginning of December Bruce and Chryssie presented us with our first grandchild which was exciting, and for Christmas Gus Holden and Joan and Johnny H-B came to stay as usual.

1982

The New Year started with our now regular New Year's Eve dinner and bridge party for twelve which we took in turn to host with the Smiths, Holders, Browns, Murrays and Norrises. Val and I went one year to the New Year's Eve dinner dance at the All England Club but on the whole we preferred our 'oldies' party with our local friends. We then drove up to RAF Bawtry in Yorkshire to stay with Bruce and Chryssie in their married quarter to meet our new grandson, Tom, for the weekend.

Not long after that we drove down again to Méribel for our annual skiing holiday with most of the regular Pertwee group, plus Gerard and Ralphia Noel whom we had met several times before at the Tennis Club at Frinton, and I had been able to help, I think, over the choice of the type of surface for their new private tennis court. They were both very good skiers – particularly Ralphia. We always had a good party in the evening round a blazing log fire and occasionally played games including bridge.

When we got home again there was much for me to do at Wimbledon but one day Val and I were invited down to Portsmouth to stay the night with Admiral Sir Jim Eberle, the Commander-in-Chief Fleet, and his wife who were having a number of people to dinner on HMS *Victory*, Nelson's old flag ship. Needless to say this was fascinating.

Towards the end of last year, 1981, Borg had been feeling the strain, I think of maintaining his top position in the game, and jibbed at signing the ATP commitment to a certain number of tournaments for 1982, fifteen I think, as well as the Grand Slams. If he didn't conform, the ATP said he would have to qualify for all tournaments first. This seemed a bit of a slap in the face for someone with his record and he had decided to quit. Philippe Chatrier and I, as well as many others including his long time coach Bergelin, tried in vain to make him change his mind. After much discussion, Philippe decided to call a Grand Slam meeting with the ATP at the beginning of April in Monte Carlo during the tournament there where Borg was going to be playing. Val and I, and Bimby and Daphne Holt, decided to go for a few days and stayed in the lovely Beach Hotel overlooking the harbour. We watched the tennis at the splendid Monte Carlo Country Club one of the days before Philippe's Grand Slam meeting when I put forward a compromise plan which would allow Borg, after his ten years on the circuit, a bit of a break and fewer tournaments initially. I was convinced I could persuade Borg to accept this compromise which was agreed by the ATP. Unfortunately when I saw Borg at the tennis he still refused and just said, 'No, I've made up my mind to quit the ATP circuit and, as you know, I am very stubborn!' So sadly that was that. There was no more we could do and Borg could not be persuaded to continue.

We got home for Easter weekend but then drove up to RAF Bawtry to stay the next weekend with Bruce and Chryssie for Tom's christening which went very well on a boiling hot afternoon.

The Bournemouth Hard Court Championships was then starting and Val and I drove down the next weekend and spent the night at the Royal Bath Hotel, before lunching with the LTA and watching the finals on Sunday. In the evening on our return we stopped off for dinner with Joan and Johnny H-B in Lymington and made plans for our summer holiday with them in Ibiza.

On weekdays I was back to normal at Wimbledon with my tennis and bridge every Tuesday. I also had the Club annual dinner at the IoD (Institute of Directors) one evening and a meeting with Mark McCormack and NBC/TV followed by dinner at Les Ambassadeurs another evening. Val and I then had another very pleasant weekend staying with the Whitleys when we met up with all our Lymington friends at the Yacht Club.

The grass court season was then starting at Wimbledon again with the opening members' tournament and cocktail party when Norman Pertwee came to stay again with us – but sadly without Eileen who had died a month earlier when Val and I had been to her Memorial Service at Frinton. It was a busy time for official lunches in London which I was invited to with Barclays Bank and Lloyds Insurance, and the Football Association at Wembley prior to the Cup Final. There was also the Order of the Bath ceremony at Westminster Abbey with The Queen and the 'old crocks race' for me. A week later Val and I were off to Paris again for the last few days of the French Championships at Stade Roland Garros, staying of course at our favourite Résidence du Bois. Bimby and Daphne came too and also Jim Cochrane, the new Chairman of our LTA and his wife, Margaret Mary. As ever, it was the usual enjoyable party with Philippe Chatrier as hospitable as always. At the World Champions dinner John McEnroe and Chris (Evert) Lloyd, the reigning Wimbledon Champions, were rated the official World Champions for the previous year 1981.

After getting back to the UK, the Queen's Club tournament was on and Val and I went one day to watch the semi-finals but there was a lot for me to do at the Club before our Championships. These started as usual with the IC reception and ball on the Saturday and the Hurlingham garden party on the Sunday. Ted Tinling (now our player's liaison officer) had also arranged a meeting again for me to welcome all the players to tell them about some of the changes and improved facilities, and to take the opportunity to talk to them about self control and general behaviour on court.

Fortunately we had decided for the first time to make the finals day the second Sunday as, although the Championships got off to a good start, rain was not long in coming and interrupted play throughout the fortnight. There were also rail and tube strikes which reduced attendances considerably. Nevertheless we were nobly supported by Royalty with some of the Kents or the Duchess of Gloucester almost every day and, in the end with the weather relenting slightly, all the main Championship events were completed on schedule, although the Men's Doubles final had to be reduced to the best of three sets. The match could not be put off until the Monday as McNamara and McNamee were due to fly back that Sunday evening to Australia for their Davis Cup match against Chile so, with the players' consent, we agreed to make it a best of three sets match, as there would not be time for more. The Australians won the match quickly 6-3, 6-2 defeating the holders Fleming and McEnroe. The latter had already had a long drawn out Men's Singles final which he lost in five sets to Jimmy Connors and understandably was not at his best in the Doubles, unfortunately. In the Ladies' Singles Martina Navratilova regained her title for the third time beating Chris (Evert) Lloyd in each of her finals. The one match which did have to be put off until the Monday was the Boys' Singles final which was interesting in that Pat Cash, a future Champion, was the winner and it was played on Court 1 with the public allowed in free to watch.

My game on the Centre Court with members of the committee was a day later; then we had the party for all the staff and our post Championship meetings to discuss plans for improvements for the next year. Bob then came for the weekend at Heather Hill before Val and I went for our usual summer visit to Norman Pertwee at Frinton for a few days. The Frinton tournament was on and Norman had a couple of the Harvard and Yale Prentice Cup players, who were playing in the tournament, to stay with him as well as us. They were both very pleasant lads and it gave us an extra interest in watching their progress in the tennis tournament, after we had had our swim in the sea and my tennis four with Norman in the mornings.

The next four weeks or so we were back at home but with much activity at Wimbledon including the Inter Services Tennis and the Prentice Cup. After that Val and I went for the weekend to Le Touquet for the IC tennis and golf match with the French and the following weekend flew to New York for the last few days of the US Open Championships. This was great as usual with all our American friends. We stayed again at the River Club and went to Flushing Meadow each day with Uppy and Ginny Moorhead and attended all the usual dinners. An extra this year was the Gala dinner dance at the Grand Hyatt Hotel at which I was being hosted by Jimmy van Allen and his wife Candy on behalf of the Newport Hall of Fame. Jimmy also very kindly arranged for us to fly up with him in a small private aircraft from La Guardia to Newport, Rhode Island to visit the Hall of Fame. Jim Cochrane and Margaret Mary came too. It was most interesting to see it, though the Museum part we felt did not compare at present with ours at Wimbledon. However, it was still growing and our two Museums are in regular close contact with each other.

At the Championships Connors beat Lendl and became the US Champion for the fourth time, having won on grass in 1974, on hard courts in 1976 and the cement in 1978 and 1982 – quite an achievement. Chris (Evert) Lloyd also regained her title of US Lady Champion for her sixth time beating Mandlikova in the Final, Navratilova having been beaten by Pam Shriver in the quarter-finals.

After getting back from America, we had a few days only at home before flying to Zurich in Switzerland for our Club match against the Lugano Lido Tennis Club. We were welcomed in Lugano on arrival by Chico Gusberti and taken to our hotel, the Splendide-Royal. Val and I had travelled separately from the rest of our own mixed team, which was captained by Humphrey Truman, as we were going on after the match to Ibiza. We met up with them later at the Lido Club where we were entertained to supper by the Lido team. The rest of the weekend was taken up by the friendly tennis matches and ended in an excellent dinner on the Sunday evening with Chico and his wife Elda. Chico had originally masterminded this match between the two clubs with Duncan Macaulay many years ago and I had great pleasure in presenting him, on behalf of the Club, with one of our Wimbledon Centenary Spode plates.

The next day Val and I caught the train to Zurich and flew to Barcelona where we had to change for our flight to Ibiza and ten days' summer holiday in the flat next to Joan and Johnny H-B. As usual we hired a car between us, so drove round to different lovely beaches every day for our picnic lunch and swim in the warm sea. Johnny's brother David had a small house on the island and lived there part of the year, so knew all the best uncrowded beaches and usually came with us.

After returning home I had a busy time at the Club with much business and many meetings, but I always managed to fit in my Tuesday game of tennis, tea and bridge. One day Val and I went to watch the semi-finals of the World Matchplay Toyota Golf Championships at Wentworth run by Mark McCormack and his IMG Organisation. Bimby and Daphne Holt came too and we had an excellent lunch with Mark and some of his other guests including his new wife, Betsy Nagelsen the American tennis player. Val and I got in quite a bit of golf at weekends and I also played in the Club match against the Royal Wimbledon Golf Club.

The Wightman Cup was then on again at the Albert Hall and we joined in the dinner for the players after watching. I can't remember the details now but I'm afraid the Americans were too good for us. There was also the LT Writers dinner dance at the Kensington Hilton which we were invited to and then at the weekend the IC of GB match v France followed by dinner at the Club.

At the end of November Val and I were invited by Philippe Chatrier to attend the final of the Davis Cup between France and the USA which was being held in Grenoble, so we flew down there and were put up with all the others at the Park Hotel. It was a very pleasant hotel but fairly small and with limited accommodation. Not surprisingly there were only two suites, which had been reserved for the French and American Tennis Presidents. However, when McEnroe arrived and asked for his suite he was told this but, in his arrogant way, insisted on taking the suite reserved for Marvin Richmond the USTA President, and moved in quickly before the latter arrived. Marvin, who frankly was quite pleased with himself anyway, was not exactly pleased when he heard about it, particularly as being rather short in stature he couldn't reach the hanging cupboards which were all rather high in the other rooms! This was the subject of considerable amusement amongst Randy Gregson and the rest of the Americans there. The tennis matches during the next three days on a slow hard court indoors, specially prepared for the occasion by the French, were all well fought but the Americans, with John McEnroe, were too strong for them. After the match was over, Philippe insisted on taking us all in a coach for a super dinner in a lovely restaurant a few miles outside Grenoble.

On the weekend after Val and I got home it was a very pleasant surprise to be invited to the LTA Awards dinner in London, when I was presented with the Carl Aarvold 1982 Men's Award for services to tennis while Virginia Wade received the Ladies' award. The next week Bruce and Chryssie brought Tom, our first grandchild, to stay at Heather Hill for a few days and it was good to have them again for several days after Christmas following Joan and Johnny H-B, Joan Bearder and Gus's stay.

In the meantime, Duncan Macaulay, the ex-Secretary of the Club who had done so much in getting Wimbledon going again in 1946 after World War II, had sadly died, and I went to his Memorial Service in London. At Wimbledon there always seemed to be an increasing amount of work to do, though I was still able to fit in my weekly game of tennis and bridge with Della-Porta's group in the covered courts throughout the winter.

1983

Soon after our now regular New Year's Eve dinner and bridge party for twelve with the Holders, Smiths, Murrays, Browns and Norrises, which it was our turn to host, we went to stay a weekend with Bob and Val, his latest girlfriend, at Waterton Stables Cottage, Ampney Crucis near Cirencester which he had recently bought. It had a swimming pool and Bob was in the process of putting in a hard tennis court which they made very good use of in later years.

Towards the end of January Val and I caught the night ferry from Portsmouth to Le Havre and drove down to France for our skiing holiday at Méribel. We spent the first night in Mottaret with the Balmes and skied with them all the next day before moving to La Gelinotte with the others in the Pertwee party, which now included Gerard and Ralphia and the Turners. After a wonderful two weeks skiing we drove home, catching the day-time ferry from Le Havre to Portsmouth, and we were then back to normal with me going to Wimbledon most days and Val to her painting, golf or bridge.

A few days later, I was invited as guest of honour by Ted Avory, the Prime Warden of the Worshipful Company of Dyers, to their dinner in Dyers Hall in London. Amongst other things, they were the official home of Swan-Uppers responsible for upping all the swans in the Thames every year. It was very interesting hearing all about it, but although we had an excellent dinner I was disappointed not to be dining off swans' eggs and roast cygnet!

After a month or so at home we set off for another ten days' skiing, first of all to Gstaad where we had been invited by Heinz and Marianne Grimm to stay with them in their lovely châlet. They were both very good skiers and we enjoyed tagging along behind them on the fairly easy slopes of Gstaad for the two days we were there. We then drove on to Verbier where we had a good afternoon's skiing with Bob and his Val, before being joined by Mike and Moyra Le Bas at Châlet Bergerie which Bob had taken for the season. Bob had to leave the next day, so we took over the châlet and the super châlet girl for the rest of the week which we had there with the Le Bas and Norman Pertwee who joined us for a few days later. David and Caroline Thompson were also staying in Verbier and we enjoyed skiing with them on several occasions. The snow was marvellous and we had some great skiing together. The Le Bas had their own car there and, after digging the cars out of the heavy snow in the car park opposite the châlet, we started on our way home the next weekend. We dropped Norman off at the railway station as he was going on to ski somewhere else. Val and I then had our usual night stop at Beaune to top up our wine stocks and the next day caught the night ferry from Le Havre to Portsmouth and home.

In March all the family gathered at Ampney Crucis in Gloucestershire where Bob and his Val had a big dinner party at their new house Waterton Stables to celebrate my seventieth birthday and it was great fun.

Bruce, Chryssie and Tom then came to Heather Hill for the long weekend over Easter, and I see from my diary that over the next three weeks Val and I had a number of dinners and bridge with some of our local friends – the Smiths, the Holders, the Surtees, the Browns and the Norrises – either with them or at home. There was also a lot going on at the Club, and I had several official lunches or dinners with the Baltic Exchange, the Wimbledon stewards, Art Watson of NBC Sports to discuss TV coverage and Mark McCormack regarding promotions. There was also the AELTC annual dinner at the Institute of Directors in London. Prize money was also much under discussion at this time, and the Committee finally agreed to a big increase to keep up with the other Grand Slams to make it up to nearly £1m for the first time, with the Women's remaining at 90 per cent of the Men's. Even so, this was still less than the prize money for the US Championships. Fortunately our profits from both the last two Wimbledon Championships, after all running expenses, had been over £1m – £1,067,860 in 1981 and

£1,623,230 in 1982 – all of which we passed on to the LTA for the benefit of British tennis.

At some stage around that time I had got the Club Committee to agree to put up a statue in the grounds of Fred Perry, our Singles Champion in 1934, '35 and '36, and to put up a plaque nominating the Somerset Road entrance gate the 'Fred Perry Gates'. We were lucky to get the well-known sculptor David Wynne to do the statue, and he conveniently lived and had his studio near Wimbledon on the south side of the Common. Fred had several sessions with him there for measurements and to discuss details of his racket grip and so on and I used to call in to see how he was getting on occasionally on my way to the Club. It was very interesting to see the exact detail and measurements to which he went, and we discussed where the statue would go at the south end of the main public lawn and not far from the Doherty entrance gates.

The Hard Court Junior Championships at Wimbledon were then starting and I watched the final, before going the next weekend with Val to the Bournemouth Hard Court Tournament. We stopped a night on the way with the Whitleys at Lymington before staying at the Royal Bath Hotel during the tennis. After returning home, we were into the start of the grass court season at Wimbledon again with Norman Pertwee coming to stay for the usual opening tournament and cocktail party. It was my favourite time for playing when the grass courts at the Club are immaculate in preparation for the Championships. At the end of the month Val and I went off to Paris for the second week of the French Championships, staying as usual at the Résidence du Bois and arriving in time for the World Champions dinner which Philippe had organized at the lovely Pavillon Gabriel. We had a very enjoyable week in Paris as usual and it was encouraging to see Jo Durie playing so well and reaching the semi-finals of the Ladies' Singles. During her semi-final match I was sitting next to Donald Budge who was very impressed by her play, although in the end she didn't manage to win. However, he said, 'Give her to me for a week or two and I will make her your Ladies' Champion.' The interesting thing also was that the same evening at one of Philippe's dinners Althea Gibson, the 1957 and 1958 Wimbledon Champion, said the same thing to me about Jo Durie. I passed this on to the LTA but I was told later that Jo didn't want to leave her English coach Alan Jones. Who knows? Perhaps her great loyalty to Alan was a mistake! Chris (Evert) Lloyd eventually beat Mimi Jausovec the 1977 Champion in the final and an interesting winner of the Men's was

Yannick Noah, the first Frenchman for thirty-seven years since Marcel Bernard in 1945.

On another occasion that year at a dinner party at Maxim's Philippe surprised me by presenting me with ten lovely champagne glasses each inscribed 'Stade Roland Garros' with the individual years 1974 to 1983 when I had, as he said, supported him at the French Championships. It was very kind of him and they marked the very friendly close association which we at Wimbledon had with Philippe and the French LTA.

On our return, the Queen's Club tournament was on and Val and I went to the semi-finals, before warmly welcoming my old 1938 girlfriend from Australia, Josephine (Hughes) Williams over the weekend at Heather Hill. Val and I had met her and her family fairly recently in 1970 in Sydney but it was good to see her again and we were glad to arrange for her daughter to come and see us the next year when she would be coming over to England for a visit.

The week before the Championships were due to start there was the usual Seeding Committee meeting and the draw which this year we had increased from 96 to 128 for the women, to give them the same number of matches as the men. It was also agreed to start play earlier at 12.30 p.m. on the outside courts in future. Otherwise, as the French say, '*Plus ça change, plus c'est la même chose*' as far as the programme and all the lunches, drinks parties and dinners went. In the tennis there were some surprising results with Kevin Curren from South Africa defeating last year's Champion Jimmy Connors in the last eight before losing 8-6 in the final set to Chris Lewis of New Zealand in the semis. Lewis was unseeded and had done very well to get through to the final but John McEnroe was merciless in regaining his title in three straight sets of 6-2. Martina Navratilova also retained her title for the fourth time in less than an hour against Andrea Jaeger. Both Champions also regained their Doubles titles with their respective partners Peter Fleming and Pam Shriver, but in the Mixed Doubles we had the rare pleasure of welcoming a British winner, John Lloyd, with his Australian partner Wendy Turnbull. Altogether, apart from the finals, it had been an exciting Wimbledon with many excellent matches, wonderful weather throughout and a number of new young faces with much promise for the future. It all ended in style with the dinner at the Savoy at which we were glad to have John McEnroe at last. As Champion again, he was now made an Honorary Member of the All England Club and I think he enjoyed the dinner. He was on his best behaviour and said to Val, who was sitting next to him, that the River Room at the Savoy was one of the loveliest he had ever seen. After taking a large helping of English mustard, thinking it was like the French, he gasped and said, 'Gee, that's hot! But I guess it's good for my sinus!' or words to that effect. It was also very good that evening for the first time to have all the year's Doubles Champions as well as the Singles runner-up at the final dinner. Financially too the Championships had been a great success with record attendances and our profits, including a big increase in royalities, were about £2.75 million compared with the £87,500 when I took over as Chairman. This, of course, all went to the LTA for British tennis but even more important the way was set for further very large increases in the future, to make more than £30 million a year.

On the Tuesday after the Championships were over, I had the Chairman's usual doubles on the Centre Court with some members of the Committee, including Bimby Holt, Ted Frith and Buzzer Hadingham and also some members of the hard working staff, Chris Gorringe, Richard Greer and Tony Hughes. After that my brother Douglas came to stay a few days with us at Heather Hill which was fun as we hadn't seen him for quite a while. He was accompanied by George, his stepson, and they were going on to Ballater, near Aberdeen in Scotland to visit Crathes Castle, the old home of some of the Burnett clan. Val and I then went for our usual few days with the Pertwees at Frinton during their tennis tournament. We always enjoyed watching the finals and meeting up with a number of friends there including Norman Lonsdale and Geofrey Atkins, and Gerard and Ralphia Noel from our Méribel skiing group.

After getting back from Frinton, we had various Club meetings to consider improvements for next year's Championships, and Val and I had a super invitation to drinks with the Duke and Duchess of Gloucester in Kensington Palace. We also went to the Lord's Test Match v New Zealand and a lunch party with Fred Perry and his wife at their home near Brighton.

At the Club we had a flood-lighting trial with the BBC for the Centre Court with Virginia Wade and John Feaver, I think, practising. As far as I remember there was no problem for the BBC but the matter went no further because of the likelihood of the court being too slippery on the grass in the evening conditions when the lighting might be wanted.

Earlier in 1983 I had informed the Wimbledon Committee that I had decided it was time for me to retire as Chairman in March next year. I

1983 champions John McEnroe and Martina Navratilova at the Champions Dinner

would have been on the Club and Championships Committee for twenty-three years, since 1961, and the Chairman for the last ten years which I felt was long enough for anyone. I was also seventy-one and I persuaded the Committee that seventy should be our normal retiring age, and not more than ten years as Chairman unless there were special circumstances. I had already started discussing with some of the Club members who should be my successor, and I wrote round to all members of the Committee asking whether they could spare the time for what was becoming more and more a full time job. In the end Buzzer Hadingham became the favourite to take over although he was already aged sixty-six, I think, and could normally only take over for four or five years. John Curry was the next favourite but he had not been on the Committee for long and he himself felt he should serve a bit longer on the Committee first. Everyone was happy with our decision. Buzzer was ideal in many ways; he was very popular with the members of the Club and through his connections with Slazengers was well known in the international tennis world and sporting media.

At the end of July, Val and I attended the finals of the RAF Championships and the Inter-Services Tennis at Wimbledon. As it was now known that I would be retiring as Chairman of the Club next year, the Inter-Services Tennis Association kindly presented me with a very nice desk 'calendar and pen set' to thank me for looking after them and ensuring they could play their Championships at Wimbledon. We also held a large farewell buffet lunch party at Heather Hill for all the Club Committee and one or two others. Luckily the weather was lovely and sunny so we could spread outside on to the patio and play boules on the lawn. At the end, on behalf of the Committee members, I was presented by Humphrey Truman with a very good large painting of the Centre Court to go above my bureau desk at the end of the sitting room.

Soon after that Val and I flew off again to New York to stay at the River Club for the US Championships at Flushing Meadow. For the Labour Day weekend Uppy and Ginny took us off to Rumson to stay with them again and have some golf and some tennis with Paul Lambert and Larry Krieger on the excellent grass courts at the Seabright Tennis Club. After getting back to New York and the tennis at Flushing Meadow, there were the normal USIC and USTA dinners in the evenings, and for me a new and interesting Wingfield Club meeting at Essex House at breakfast with full bacon and eggs being served. Rather a good custom, I thought. At the tennis Connors beat Lendl again in the final of the Men's and Martina Navratilova beat the previous six times

Champion Chris (Evert) Lloyd. In the doubles McEnroe and Fleming won the Men's for the third time and Martina and Pam Shriver the Women's for the first of many times.

After the Championships were over, we took the day flight back on the Monday which we far preferred to the more normal overnight flight to London. We were then at home for a couple of weeks before going off to Ibiza for our ten day summer holiday with Joan and Johnny H-B, when we were again able to rent the flat next door to them and join up with other friends from Lymington for our daily swim and picnic lunches at the many different lovely beaches. On return most evenings, after a quick shower, Johnny and I settled down to a game of chess on our joint balcony with a couple of large whiskies before taking Joan and Val out to dinner. With the lovely warm evenings, we enjoyed having dinner outside and watching the world go by in San Antonio, and sometimes we ended up having a game of bridge in our flat.

When we got home at the beginning of October we were back to normal with my tennis and bridge every Tuesday and meetings most days at the Club, and Val was busy with her golf and painting. We went one day to watch the Suntory World Match Play golf at Wentworth and have lunch with Mark McCormack there. We also had various weekends away including one with Digger and Molly Kyle near Sway in the New Forest, when we met up with our many friends in that area.

The first weekend in November we had the Annual IC Tennis match at the Club with the French IC followed by dinner in the Debenture Holders Lounge, and the following week Val and I were kindly invited to a farewell lunch with the Duke and Duchess of Kent at York House. The next excitement was the birth on 10 November of Bruce and Chryssie's second son, Ben, to give us our second grandchild, and Bob finally got married in Cirencester to his girlfriend Val.

The next week my Val and I were invited to the LT Writers dinner dance at the Kensington Hilton when I was presented with their 1983 annual award of a super whisky decanter for services to British Tennis. At Wimbledon we have always had a very close association with the media and have been fortunate to have such an enthusiastic bunch – or should I call them 'scribble' – of Lawn Tennis Writers, who are regarded as the best by nearly everyone in the tennis world. I always enjoyed the media sub-committee daily meetings with them during the Championships and I was pleased to take this opportunity of telling them that Philippe Chatrier, the President of the ITF in Paris, always read the

Bob and his Val at home in Ampney Crucis after their marriage in Cirencester

English papers first for the tennis news as he said they were so much better than the French. Quite a compliment!

It was by now well known that I would be retiring shortly as Chairman of the All England Club and the Wimbledon Championships Committee and at our annual dinner with the BBC the Managing Director, Alisdair Milne, kindly presented me with a beautiful decanter for gin suitably inscribed on the glass with a BBC television camera. These annual dinners, often following a short business meeting, were invaluable in helping both sides of our partnership to get to know each other better and appreciate each other's problems and points of view, both on BBC television and radio. This results, we think, in the best lawn tennis coverage in the world.

A few days later Val and I set off for the second week of the Australian Championships, flying overnight to Singapore where we stayed at the Raffles Hotel for the weekend, calling on various friends from our time stationed there, including Tan Chin Tuan who gave a large lunch party for us. From there we flew on to Sydney where we stayed a couple of days seeing Red and Sylvia Merson before going on to Melbourne. There we were booked in with many of the other overseas tennis officials to the

The four Grand Slam Chairmen with Brian Tobin (Australia), Philippe Chartrier (France) and Hunter Delatour (USA)

large hotel overlooking the Melbourne cricket ground and the nearby railway marshalling yards which the following year, I think, was taken over by the Australian LTA for their new Tennis Centre instead of Kooyong. Each day we were driven out for the tennis at Kooyong and were well looked after by many of our Australian tennis friends, including Brian and Carmen Tobin, Neale Fraser and the Sedgmans. One morning I attended a meeting of the Grand Slam Chairmen and one late afternoon, when we were invited out to the Sedgmans, I had a quick game of tennis on their private court with Frank, Hunter Delatour of the USA and Eiichi Kawatei of Japan. I picked the best partner and played with Frank, the three times Wimbledon Doubles winner!

We enjoyed watching the tennis on the excellent Kooyong grass courts. I was sorry their LTA had decided to move from Kooyong with its Club House and 'cosy' atmosphere not unlike the All England Club at Wimbledon, but they had problems there, not least with room for car parking as the Americans had had at Forest Hills. On the whole though it made sense for them to move to where they could expand and build a new stadium, with an adjustable sliding roof so that it could be used for other functions in winter, and where they could share the cricket ground's car parking facilities, but unfortunately it meant abandoning grass for their Australian Tennis Championships.

One evening there was an excellent dinner of the Australian ILTC of which I had previously been made an Honorary member, and towards the end of their Championships the Australian LTA had a dinner for all the overseas officials, and to mark the occasion of Val's and my probable last visit I was presented by Brian Tobin with a lovely silver model of a duck-billed platypus, a creature unique, I think, to Australia. This was the conclusion of our most enjoyable visit to the Australian Championships.

The next day we flew back after lunch and overnight to London in time for the Wimbledon staff Christmas lunch when Chris Gorringe, on behalf of all the staff, kindly presented me with a dozen lovely Caithness wine glasses with tennis rackets engraved on them. They are greatly admired by friends when they come to dinner and are a very happy reminder to us of all our friends on the Club staff.

On 21 December I had my last Club AGM as Chairman. It was held at the Café Royal in London and at the end Russell Young, our senior Club Trustee, presented Val and me on behalf of all the members with a beautiful claret jug suitably engraved, together with an enormous cheque with which to buy a further parting present. Val and I were very touched not only by the size of the cheque but by the very large number of members, including many from overseas, who had so generously contributed towards it. When the AGM was finally over, there was a brief press conference for me to introduce Buzzer Hadingham as my successor and then a very pleasant dinner with all the Club Committee.

In due course, Val and I enjoyed looking round the antique shops in Surrey and bought a super antique mahogany bureau for my sitting room. I keep all my papers in it, and it is in constant use and a happy reminder of my tennis friends and my days as Chairman of the All England Club.

After that it was home for Christmas with our usual party of Joan Bearder, Gus Holden and Joan and Johnny H-B. For New Year's Eve we went to join Bruce, Chryssie and Tom to meet Ben for the first time.

1984

On 11 January I had one more meeting of the Wimbledon Ground Company, which was responsible for all the buildings and works services at the Club, when I handed over that Chairmanship also to Buzzer. Finally, after we had had our annual skiing holiday at Méribel, I was dined out on 1 March 1984 by the Wimbledon Championships Committee of Management when Val and I were given a superb twelve-piece dinner service of Wedgwood Florentine china. It was a perfect parting present and reminder of many happy memories of my ten years as Chairman of the Championships Committee. We had come a long way together – Wimbledon and the LTA – and helped to maintain the Championships in the eyes of both the public and the players as the best in the tennis world. I had a letter at that time from Arthur Ashe, the well known American champion and Wimbledon winner in 1975, saying, 'Wimbledon has been, and remains, an example to all other tournaments in the world, and the one by which all others are measured.' It was certainly a pleasure to hear that from him as one of the leading players and administrators in the game in recent years. I am glad to say that under the successive Chairmen, Buzzer, John Curry and Tim Philips, this continues to be the case.

My only unfinished business then at Wimbledon was, I felt, the completion of the Fred Perry statue. It was finally ready for transfer to the Club where I saw it unveiled on 20 May by the Duke of Kent, with Buzzer, in the presence of David Wynne and Fred who was delighted and expressed his happy approval of it. The same afternoon the Duke unveiled a plaque at the Somerset Road entrance to the Club nominating the gates the 'Fred Perry Gates' opposite the Doherty Gates at the main entrance to the Club in Church Road.

I was now retired for the second time, but life goes on and Val and I carried on living our full and active lives together for many more happy years, but I finally gave up skiing at eighty, golf at eighty-eight and tennis at ninety-four. I still enjoy an occasional game of chess and bridge twice a week.

I have been extremely lucky in so many ways and altogether have had a most interesting, exciting and wonderful life so far!

INDEX OF NAMES